MW00817790

Praise for *The Slain God*

'Readers interested in continuing debates over faith, science, and secularism will find much of value in this very important book. The further you get into the book, the more astonished you are that no predecessor has written such a full-length study of this critically important topic.'

Philip Jenkins, Distinguished Professor of History,
Baylor University

'Larsen's book is beautifully written and based on the most patient scrutiny of every scrap of evidence. It provides an authoritative account of some of anthropology's most influential practitioners.'

David Martin, Professor of Sociology Emeritus,
London School of Economics

'This book will be greeted as something of a bombshell amongst anthropologists of religion... a highly original book that should be with us for a long time to come.'

Joel Robbins, Sigrid Rausing Professor of Social Anthropology,
University of Cambridge

'As in his earlier work, Larsen disrupts a teleological vision of religion condemned to disappear before the forces of progress and modernity. He is to be congratulated for challenging this narrative head-on and confronting what amounts to anti-religious bias in the human sciences.'

Journal of Theological Studies

'This well-documented and well-written book is an interesting account of the lives and works of some of the most influential anthropologists and their own Christian faith, or lack thereof... This book is relevant to researchers and students alike, who have a general interest in anthropology, and a particular interest in the study of Christianity from an anthropological perspective.'

Journal of the Royal Anthropological Institute

THE SLAIN GOD

Throughout its entire history, the discipline of anthropology has been perceived as undermining, or even discrediting, Christian faith. Many of its most prominent theorists have been agnostics who assumed that ethnographic findings and theories had exposed religious beliefs to be untenable. E. B. Tylor, the founder of the discipline in Britain, lost his faith through studying anthropology. James Frazer saw the material that he presented in his highly influential work, *The Golden Bough*, as demonstrating that Christian thought was based on the erroneous thought patterns of 'savages.' On the other hand, some of the most eminent anthropologists have been Christians, including E. E. Evans-Pritchard, Mary Douglas, Victor Turner, and Edith Turner. Moreover, they openly presented articulate reasons for how their religious convictions cohered with their professional work.

Despite being a major site of friction between faith and modern thought, the relationship between anthropology and Christianity has never before been the subject of a book-length study. In this groundbreaking work, Timothy Larsen examines the point where doubt and faith collide with anthropological theory and evidence.

Timothy Larsen is McManis Professor of Christian Thought, Wheaton College, Illinois, and an Honorary Research Fellow, the University of Wales Trinity Saint David. He is a Fellow of both the Royal Historical Society and the Royal Anthropological Institute. He has been a Visiting Fellow in History, Trinity College, Cambridge, and some of the research for this volume was undertaken while a Visiting Fellow, All Souls College, Oxford. His publications include *A People of One Book: The Bible and the Victorians* (2011) and *Crisis of Doubt: Honest Faith in Nineteenth-Century England* (OUP, 2006), which was *Books and Culture*'s Book of the Year 2006.

The Slain God

Anthropologists and the Christian Faith

TIMOTHY LARSEN

OXFORD
UNIVERSITY PRESS

OXFORD

UNIVERSITY PRESS

Great Clarendon Street, Oxford, OX2 6DP,
United Kingdom

Oxford University Press is a department of the University of Oxford.
It furthers the University's objective of excellence in research, scholarship,
and education by publishing worldwide. Oxford is a registered trade mark of
Oxford University Press in the UK and in certain other countries

First published 2014
First published in paperback 2016

Published in the United States of America by Oxford University Press
198 Madison Avenue, New York, NY 10016, United States of America

British Library Cataloguing in Publication Data
Data available

Library of Congress Cataloging in Publication Data
Data available

ISBN 978-0-19-965787-2 (Hbk.)
ISBN 978-0-19-875742-9 (Pbk.)

For the Warden and Fellows of All Souls College, Oxford

Contents

Introduction: Anthropology, History, and Doubt

The theme of this volume is how findings and theories in the discipline of anthropology have been interpreted as undermining or even discrediting the claims of Christianity, as well as, conversely, how anthropological insights have been perceived to be compatible with or even to reinforce Christian faith.

People have often asked me how I became interested in the history of the relationship between anthropologists and the Christian faith. For most of the years of research for this project, my honest answer was that I could not remember. However, I think I have now reconstructed it. A decade ago I was working on what became my monograph *Crisis of Doubt: Honest Faith in Nineteenth-Century England.*[1] My basic theme in that study was the intellectual prompts and contours of the loss of faith and, alternatively, the intellectual reasons for the regaining of faith—for the deconversions of erstwhile believers and the Christian conversions of erstwhile sceptics. As part of my effort to understand the wider context, I read James Turner's valuable study, *Without God, Without Creed: The Origins of Unbelief in America.*[2] My own research had made me well aware of many of the standard intellectual triggers for the loss of faith during the Victorian age, notably biblical criticism, Darwinism, philosophical critiques of beliefs such as miracles, ethical objections to doctrines such as substitutionary atonement and, more generally, the problem of evil. The

[1] Timothy Larsen, *Crisis of Doubt: Honest Faith in Nineteenth-Century England* (Oxford: Oxford University Press, 2006).

[2] James Turner, *Without God, Without Creed: The Origins of Unbelief in America* (Baltimore: John Hopkins University Press, 1985).

discipline of anthropology, however, was an intriguing addition to this list which kept reappearing in Turner's captivating narrative. In particular, I was thunderstruck by one sentence: 'George Frederick Holmes's battle-tested orthodoxy, which absorbed Strauss without crumbling, eventually collapsed under the strain of Lubbock and Tylor'.[3] This little vignette particularly caught my eye as a key figure in *Crisis of Doubt* was the Chartist Thomas Cooper (1805–92), who had shed his religious convictions precisely because of his encounter with the work of the biblical critic D. F. Strauss (1808–74). What faith-destroying powers did these anthropologists have that could lay low even someone who had proven himself immune to radical German biblical criticism? Turner's work, of course, was about America, while I am a historian of modern Britain, but the transatlantic commonalities are often strong: Holmes had studied in England at the University of Durham and both John Lubbock (1834–1913) and E. B. Tylor (1832–1917) were Englishmen.

What had anthropology discovered that made Christianity appear no longer tenable? I wondered. I started keeping my eye on this little guild of academics, reading up and asking around as occasions arose. Soon people were telling me that some of the most respected anthropologists of the twentieth century had been Christians. Why did George Frederick Holmes's hound not bark for them, I mused. How had Francis Thompson's Hound of Heaven relentlessly tracked them down even in the field in Africa?

I soon discovered that most of the scholars who kept reappearing as central characters in this discussion were British social anthropologists. I therefore decided to confine my inquiries to this tradition. Not only would this be in line with my own area of expertise as a historian, but it would also give this story added coherence as all taking place on the same stage. In fact, the lineage is often direct: Frazer first became interested in anthropology by reading Tylor; Evans-Pritchard by reading both Tylor and Frazer; and so on. On the other hand, the international influence and reputations of these world-renowned anthropologists would spare this study from becoming a parochial one.

The eminent anthropologists whose lives and thoughts had most to offer on this question emerged as E. B. Tylor, James Frazer

---

[3] Turner, *Without God*, p. 152.

(1854–1941), E. E. Evans-Pritchard (1902–73), Mary Douglas (1921–2007), and Victor Turner (1920–83) and Edith Turner (1921–). My confidence that these were the right ones to choose has been reinforced by the fact that I have discussed this project with numerous anthropologists and historians and no one has ever argued that any of these figures should be replaced by someone else whom they deemed a more worthy or revealing case study (nor did the anonymous readers when the proposal for this book went out for evaluation). People have sometimes made suggestions for figures that could be added if the list were to be expanded. Oxford anthropologists, in particular, have a soft spot for Godfrey Lienhardt (1921–93), not least because his *Divinity and Experience: The Religion of the Dinka* is judged to be a landmark account of a traditional African religion.[4] No one wanted him included at the expense of any of the others, however, and Evans-Pritchard is located so closely to Lienhardt in so many ways that adding him would have had diminishing returns (moreover, he was also an exact contemporary of Mary Douglas and Edith Turner). Other anthropologists appear or reappear like seasoned character actors in this volume and several would have made splendid additional chapters. Knowing what I know now, if I were asked to select one more for inclusion it would be Edmund Leach (1910–89) as he would provide an articulate religious sceptic further downstream chronologically.[5] Leach was raised in a devout Christian home, but was so committed to an explicitly non-religious perspective as an adult that he eventually became president of the British Humanist Association. Another advantage of adding Leach is that one would thereby include another Cambridge anthropologist after Frazer.

Moreover, to carry on this fantasy, if asked to name yet another after Leach it would be Andrew Lang (1844–1912), who would provide an example of someone who came to take faith claims more seriously during the earlier decades covered in this study. William Robertson Smith (1846–94) is another obvious choice, but I had an aversion to taking him on for personal reasons: he was a major biblical critic and, as my last monograph was on the Bible and the Victorians, I had become interested in the history of the discipline

---

[4] Godfrey Lienhardt, *Divinity and Experience: The Religion of the Dinka* (Oxford: Clarendon Press, 1961).

[5] For Leach, see Stanley J. Tambiah, *Edmund Leach: An Anthropological Life* (Cambridge: Cambridge University Press, 2002).

of anthropology precisely in order to think about something different for a change![6] Another possibility is the Revd Edwin William
Smith (1876–1957), a Primitive Methodist missionary whose ethnological contributions were so well respected that he served as president of the Royal Anthropological Institute in 1933–35.[7] Adding
Edwin W. Smith would have the additional advantage of including a mid-twentieth-century Christian anthropologist who was a
Protestant. On the other hand, no one considers him as influential
in the discipline as the figures covered in this book. I hope that the
anthropologists about whom I offer chapter-length cases studies will
serve to generate a conversation that can then be continued in the
future with further studies of additional figures—whether written by
myself or (even better) by other scholars.

One of the conceits of the figures that have been chosen is that
the entire history of social anthropology as an academic discipline
is thereby encompassed. Tylor is often referred to as 'the father of
anthropology'. While such a judgement can be contested, what is
indisputable is that he is the first person to hold a faculty position
in the discipline at a British university, being appointed a Reader in
Anthropology at Oxford in 1884. At the other end of the chronological spectrum, at the time this introduction is being written, Edith
Turner is aged 92 and still teaching anthropology at the University of
Virginia, as well as actively pursuing research and writing projects in
the discipline. I think I can therefore claim legitimately that this book
has a chronological span that goes from the founding of the academic
study of anthropology all the way to the present.

It might be worth orientating the reader entering this subject
area for the first time to the basic contours of the history of British
social anthropology, particularly as it intersects with the case studies.
Ethnology and anthropology existed before Tylor's work and therefore many have looked for the roots of the discipline earlier in the
nineteenth century or even in the eighteenth century. In a British
context, for example, the work of the evangelical ethnologist James
C. Prichard (1786–1848) is an influential precursor.[8] E. B. Tylor's way

---

[6] Timothy Larsen, *A People of One Book: The Bible and the Victorians*
(Oxford: Oxford University Press, 2011).

[7] For Smith, see W. John Young, *The Quiet Wise Spirit: Edwin W. Smith 1876–1957
and Africa* (Peterborough: Epworth Press, 2002).

[8] The classic study of this prehistory, as well as the age of Tylor, is George W.
Stocking, Jr., *Victorian Anthropology* (New York: The Free Press, 1987).

of thinking about anthropology was as a social evolutionist. He envisioned the human story as one of progress, and saw these advances as occurring in three basic stages: the savage, the barbaric, and the civilized. Victorian Britain, of course, was civilized, but Europeans had inevitably passed through the first two stages—states which some other peoples around the world still inhabited. Moreover, everyone at the same stage shares a common mentality. This meant that one could study contemporary 'savages' such as aborigines in Australia in order to understand what Britons were once like. Tylor also believed that erroneous ways of thinking from the primitive past, although now discredited by the light of the more advanced stage which had been arrived at, were sometimes still passed down and maintained. He called these 'survivals'. One fruit of this way of thinking was that religion could be identified as a savage falsehood that had survived into civilized contexts—not on its merits—but by sheer, misguided conservatism. The Cambridge scholar James Frazer continued this social evolutionist, Tylorian anthropology well into the first half of the twentieth century. His refinement was to identify the three stages of progress as the magical, the religious, and the scientific. Frazer inherited from Tylor the comparative method in which what one learned from people at one level of development could be used to understand others in a different time or place deemed to be at the same level: in short, savages are savages the world over. He too thought that he was discovering the origins of religion in the untenable mentality of a now superseded stage. To state it more generally, the social evolutionists were interested in uncovering the origins of certain current practices and beliefs in the primitive past and exposing them as fallacious by the truthful standards of modern, scientific civilization.

The next great twist in British social anthropology is usually most associated with Bronislaw Malinowski (1884–1942), who became a lecturer in social anthropology at the London School of Economics in 1923. The most important new development was an emphasis on good ethnography arising from first-hand, intensive, long-term, participant observer fieldwork. Tylor and Frazer were from the age of armchair anthropology, sitting in their studies reading the reports of missionaries, colonial officers, traders, travellers, and adventurers. Frazer had never even been on holiday anywhere outside Europe, while Malinowski spent the best part of two years in Mailu and among the Trobriand Islanders. Malinowski also swept aside the social evolutionist viewpoint and replaced it with functionalism.[9] Functionalists rejected the entire quest to reconstruct the past, insisting that every existing belief and practice had a contemporary use and it was this present function that was the task of an anthropologist to grasp. Such a function, in a utilitarian manner, would be rooted in the biological needs of the individual—or in derivative needs of a more psychological variety. Functionalists also stressed that one could not analyse a particular rite, belief, practice, or custom in isolation: its purpose was revealed in its relationship to the whole, just as one understands the workings of a particular internal organ by grasping how the entire body functions.[10]

Functionalism was added to—and, to a certain extent, corrected by—structuralism. The Oxford anthropologist A. R. Radcliffe-Brown (1881–1955) is most often credited as being the founder of the structural-functionalist school. Structuralism turned away from the interest in individualistic motivations and instead focused on enduring categories of relationships. The goal was to not be distracted by the particular and contingent, but rather to see what was happening at a higher level of abstraction. The result was a flourishing of kinship studies. For at least the first half of his career, Evans-Pritchard was seen as a major exemplar of structural-functionalism, and both Mary Douglas and Victor Turner were trained in this tradition. When Evans-Pritchard witnessed the outbreak of a feud among the Nuer, for example, he did not attend to this incident in terms of the immediate personalities and grievances. Rather, he analysed such occurrences as

[9] For a study of functionalism, see George W. Stocking, Jr. (ed.), *Functionalism Historicized: Essays on British Social Anthropology* (Madison: University of Wisconsin Press, 1984).

[10] For histories of British social anthropology which cover at least part of the twentieth century, see Adam Kuper, *Anthropology and Anthropologists: The Modern British School* (London: Routledge & Kegan Paul, 1983); George W. Stocking, Jr., *After Tylor: British Social Anthropology, 1888–1951* (Madison: University of Wisconsin Press, 1995); Henrika Kuklick (ed.), *A New History of Anthropology* (Oxford: Blackwell, 2009); Henrika Kuklick, *The Savage Within: The Social History of British Anthropology, 1885–1945* (Cambridge: Cambridge University Press, 1991); David Mills, *Difficult Folk? A Political History of Social Anthropology* (Oxford: Berghahn Books, 2008); Adam Kuper, *The Reinvention of Primitive Society: Transformations of a Myth* (London: Routledge, 2005); Fredrick Barth, 'Britain and the Commonwealth', in Fredrik Barth et al., *One Discipline, Four Ways: British, German, French, and American Anthropology* (Chicago: University of Chicago Press, 2005), pp. 3–57. Although the title might misdirect the reader, the following study is also primarily about the first half of the twentieth century: James Urry, *Before Social Anthropology: Essays on the History of British Anthropology* (London: Routledge, 1993).

an outworking of the perennial relationships between segmentary lineages at the structural level. Later in his career Evans-Pritchard himself became dissatisfied with the pretension that structural-functionalism was discovering the laws of society. He came to see anthropology as more of a humanistic discipline such as history rather than a scientific one. He also began to value what informants in the field themselves believed about their own rites and practices, rather than assuming that the ethnographer's task was simply to discern an explanation of which they were unaware. These were portents of things to come.

Another criticism of structural-functionalism was that it imagined societies were existing in a state of static equilibrium: everything existed for a reason, which together made a smoothly functioning whole that endured from generation to generation. This was always a fiction, and it was kept alive by ignoring as much as possible the changes that were happening, for example, as a result of colonialism and other Western influences. Max Gluckman (1911–75) was trained in Oxford structural-functionalism but once he established the Department of Anthropology at the University of Manchester he became committed to offering a corrective to this static bias by a new focus on process. His student Victor Turner would be an exemplar of this new tendency. Turner's other contributions to changes in the discipline include a turn towards symbolism. Mary Douglas was also trained in Oxford structural-functionalism, but her appreciation for Durkheimian anthropology would take her in new directions, notably an emphasis on what was perceived as ambiguous in schemes of categorization. Douglas and Victor and Edith Turner also participated in a move towards applying anthropological analysis to modern industrial societies rather than just 'primitive' peoples: to turning the ethnographic gaze directly onto 'us'. The later Evans-Pritchard, Douglas, and the Turners all reflected a new interest in meaning and indigenous exegesis, but Edith Turner has taken deferring to the beliefs of informants to new heights in the twenty-first century. Finally, Douglas and the Turners took positions in the United States and thus helped to blur the lines between British social anthropology and American cultural anthropology.

As this volume moves chronologically from the nineteenth century into the twenty-first century, I have used the terminology of the time period under discussion in order that readers may better grasp the mentality and context of the anthropologists being studied. I have deemed that it would be cumbersome to be continually putting words in quotation marks, even though they are offensive, discredited, or outdated ('savage' and 'primitive', for example). The reader should keep in mind that these are used to reflect the views and usage of the figures being studied rather than my own. Moreover, as the chronology moves along, terms will change and sometimes an anthropologist will even explicitly recant their own earlier usage.

The preceding account is my attempt to give a rough guide to the history of British social anthropology for the uninitiated, but it must be borne in mind that anthropologists have had a strong desire to distinguish their work—even at the level of theory—from that of their predecessors and contemporaries and therefore there is sometimes a tendency to exaggerate differences. As Cambridge anthropologist Jack Goody has conceded: 'The history of anthropological theory does not offer much firm ground to tread upon. On the more general level, it is often characterized by a series of paradigm reversals at the higher level which resemble changes in clothing fashions more than paradigm shifts of the Kuhnian kind'.[11] This is not only true on the functionalist level, as it were, of individual rivalries, but also at the level of structural oppositions. Notably, the leading departments of anthropology have sought to distinguish their work from that of their competitors, and to narrate the history of the discipline so as to exalt the role of their departmental forebears over anthropologists elsewhere. Oxford looms large in this study as the university where Tylor and Evans-Pritchard taught and where Douglas was trained.[12] Although Frazer's primary identity was always as a Fellow of Trinity College, Cambridge, the other place is not given its full due here.[13] The London School of Economics, alas, only appears as the place of Evans-Pritchard's training (which he made largely into a foil).[14]

---

[11] Jacky Goody, *The Expansive Movement: Anthropology in Britain and Africa, 1918–1970* (Cambridge: Cambridge University Press, 1995), p. 80.

[12] For an account, see Peter Riviére (ed.), *A History of Oxford Anthropology* (Oxford: Berghahn Books, 2007).

[13] For Frazer's influence there, see Robert Ackerman, *The Myth and Ritual School: J. G. Frazer and the Cambridge Ritualists* (New York: Garland, 1991). For Rivers and his influence, see Ian Langham, *The Building of British Social Anthropology: W. H. R. Rivers and his Cambridge Disciples in the Development of Kinship Studies, 1898–1931* (Dordrecht: D. Reidel, 1981). For an account that seeks to put Cambridge at the centre of the story, see Anna Grimshaw and Keith Hart, *Anthropology and the Crisis of the Intellectuals* (Cambridge: Prickly Pear Press, 1993).

[14] For a comparison and contrast of Oxford and the LSE, see Mill, *Difficult Folk?*, pp. 29–48.

University College London is where Douglas spent her career (except for her sojourn in America), and where Victor Turner first studied anthropology. Turner then went on to earn his PhD at Manchester and to join the faculty there, becoming a leading anthropologist of the Manchester School.[15] It should also be observed that all the anthropologists in this volume after Tylor and Frazer (whose work was done before the move to participant observation) did their fieldwork in Africa.[16] Several figures in this volume have also been studied through the related lens of the history of the discipline of religious studies.[17]

Throughout its entire history there has been a perception that the discipline of anthropology has an anti-faith bias. I am making no claim about whether this is actually true, but only that the conventional wisdom is that it is true. I am not even sure how one would go about persuasively proving or disproving the veracity of such an assumption. The perception, however, certainly provides the background colouring, if nothing else, for this study. The historian Henrika Kuklick's summative judgement on anthropologists when the social evolutionists reigned in the late Victorian period and the early twentieth century was: 'In the aggregate, however, their attitude to religion was hostile.'[18] Likewise Edmund Leach generalizes about the founding fathers of British social anthropology: 'They were mostly men of agnostic rationalist persuasion.'[19] Malinowski rejected the methods and preoccupations of the social evolutionists, but he nevertheless was also someone who had shed the Catholicism of his childhood and come to believe that religion was 'a kind of noble lie.'[20] Evans-Pritchard looked into this matter rather systematically, and was

[15] T. M. S. Evens and Don Handelman (eds.), *The Manchester School: Practice and Ethnographic Praxis in Anthropology* (Oxford: Berghahn Books, 2008); Richard P. Werbner, 'The Manchester School in South-Central Africa', *Annual Review of Anthropology*, 13 (1984), pp. 157–85.

[16] Goody, *Expansive Moment*; Lyn Schumaker, *Africanizing Anthropology: Fieldwork, Networks, and the Making of Cultural Knowledge in Central Africa* (Durham: Duke University Press, 2001).

[17] Marjorie Wheeler-Barclay, *The Science of Religion in Britain, 1860–1915* (Charlottesville: University of Virginia Press, 2010); Daniel L. Pals, *Seven Theories of Religion* (New York: Oxford University Press, 1996).

[18] Kuklick, *Savage Within*, p. 79.

[19] Edmund Leach, 'Anthropology of Religion: British and French Schools', in Ninian Smart, John Clayton, Steven Katz, and Patrick Sherry (eds.), *Nineteenth Century Religious Thought in the West* (Cambridge: Cambridge University Press, 1985), vol. III, p. 217.

[20] Ivan Stenski, 'The Spiritual Dimension', in Kuklick, *New History*, p. 124.

quite willing to declare publicly in 1959 that twentieth-century British social anthropology's collective ethos was one that treated Christian faith, like all religious belief, as erroneous and untenable:

> All the leading sociologists and anthropologists contemporaneous with, or since, Frazer were agnostics and positivists—Westermarck, Hobhouse, Haddon, Rivers, Seligman, Radcliffe-Brown and Malinowski; and if they discussed religion they treated it as superstition for which some scientific explanation was required and could be supplied. Almost all the leading anthropologists of my own generation would, I believe, hold that religious faith is total illusion, a curious phenomenon soon to become extinct and to be explained in such terms as 'compensation' and 'projection' or by some sociologistic interpretation on the lines of main-tenance of social solidarity...Religion is superstition to be explained by anthropologists, not something an anthropologist, or indeed any rational person, could himself believe in.[21]

When Douglas first met anthropologists during the Second World War, they informed her: 'No anthropologist can be a sincere Catholic'.[22] When Victor Turner became a Catholic in 1958 he was told that he had betrayed his Manchester School colleagues. This study sits on the fault line where doubt and faith collide with anthropological theory and evidence.

* * *

This book is dedicated with heartfelt gratitude to the Warden and Fellows of All Souls College, Oxford, where I was a Visiting Fellow in History, Trinity term 2012. All Souls is an astonishingly friendly place where the Fellows freely, instinctively, and habitually go the extra mile to welcome Visiting Fellows into their community. Disregarding all worries about clichés and sentimentality, I cannot resist declaring that they became a kind of family to me; that I often find myself sud-denly thinking about them with great fondness; and that I miss them and look forward to seeing them again soon. I have gone through the directory of the Fellows of All Souls again in order to write this, but there are so many of whom I have specific, warm memories that

---

[21] E. E. Evans-Pritchard, *Social Anthropology and Other Essays* (New York: The Free Press, 1962), p. 162. (This is from his 1959 Aquinas lecture, 'Religion and the Anthropologists'.)

[22] Mary Douglas, 'A Feeling for Hierarchy', in James L. Heft SM (ed.), *Believing Scholars: Ten Catholic Intellectuals* (New York: Fordham University Press, 2005), p. 105.

I dare not start naming individuals. Thank you each and every one for your kindness to me. I must make an exception, however, for the two Fellows who I suspect were instrumental in my appointment. Simon Green certainly smoothed the way for my election as a Visiting Fellow, and I am deeply grateful for his confidence in me and for his remarkable generosity before, during, and after my time there. On similar grounds, I am also grateful to Scott Mandelbrote who was able to speak to my work first-hand when my application was considered, and who has also attended to me and my work more than I could possibly expect. Given the contents of this book, it was particularly magical to be able to attend the Evans-Pritchard lectures which were delivered in college during the Trinity term. While I was at All Souls, numerous Fellows at other Oxford colleges hosted me delightfully, including Sarah Foot, Michael Ward, Simon Skinner, Matthew Grimley, Anthony Cross, Peter Nockles, Alison Salvesen, and Jane Garnett—as well as one college president, Richard Carwardine. If I knew that the result would be suffering from gout for the rest of my days, I would still long to live it all over again. My editor at Oxford University Press, Tom Perridge, was also a hospitable host and while I was in Oxford we hatched plans for new, exciting projects. I want to underscore once again that working with Tom has been a tremendous pleasure and boon for my scholarly life.

I gratefully acknowledge the *British Journal for the History of Science* where an earlier version of chapter one was published as Timothy Larsen, 'E. B. Tylor, religion and anthropology', *British Journal for the History of Science*, 46, 3 (September 2013), pp. 467–85. Many British social anthropologists have kindly read a chapter in draft or answered my queries, including Richard Fardon, Wendy James, David Gellner, and David Parkin. I was also thrilled to be in Oxford to hear Adam Kuper deliver the Marett Lecture (and on such an apposite theme for my research as 'Anthropologists and the Bible'). Christopher Morton at the Pitt Rivers Museum was also wonderfully helpful. Bob Ackerman is another scholar who has given of his time sacrificially. I owe a particular debt to Evans-Pritchard's friend Bruce Ross-Smith, not only for providing access to primary sources in private hands and sharing his own recollections, but also for befriending me, entertaining me in his home, charming the current owners into giving me a tour of the house where E-P lived for many years, and even commenting insightfully on other parts of the project. Indeed, I appreciate all of the numerous relatives, former students, colleagues, and friends of some of these anthropologists that I interviewed for this project, although I have deliberately kept most of their names out of this book so that I alone would be responsible for the general judgements I have made about my subjects. A special case is Edith Turner. I have never met her and I have only ever had one conversation with her (by phone), but I have swapped a dozen or so emails with her. Although I tried to interact with her sparingly so as not to let her current vantage point overwhelm a more historical perspective, I was always astounded by her cheerful helpfulness. John Wilson, Michael Graves, Dean Arnold, and Brian Howell all provided valuable comments on draft chapters, as well as general encouragement. Alan Jacobs has been a guide and inspiration for my academic life in recent years, as have Dan Treier, Brett Foster, Rick Gibson, and everyone in Café Padre. Postgraduate research assistants of mine who have done many tedious things to make my work on this book easier include Eric Brandt, Jonathan De la O, Katherine Graber, David Reagles, and Grant Kelley. I am utterly, indescribably grateful to my dear wife Jane and our children, Lucia, Theo, and Amelia, for being so supportive of my life and work in so many ways—even to the point of letting me skive off to Oxford for an entire term!

1

Edward Burnett Tylor

Certainly in a British context and arguably more widely, Edward Burnett Tylor (1832–1917) is generally acknowledged to be 'the father of anthropology'.[1] In an oft-repeated phrase, Friedrich Max Müller (1823–1900), professor of comparative philology at the University of Oxford, even referred to the new discipline as 'Mr. Tylor's science'.[2] While appreciations in festschrifts are apt to be over-generous, they also tend to be careful about claims that might slight other eminent scholars. Even though the very contributors to the volume in Tylor's honour were distinguished figures such as Andrew Lang, J. G. Frazer, and W. H. R. Rivers, nevertheless the preface declared unequivocally that Tylor was 'the greatest of English anthropologists', and the first chapter gave him pride of place as 'the founder of this science'.[3] Obituaries reaffirmed these generative claims, as have scholars ever since.[4] Tylor has also been widely credited with providing the first definition of 'culture' in its modern anthropological sense.[5] He also gave the English-speaking world its first proper anthropological

---

[1] George W. Stocking, Jr., *Victorian Anthropology* (New York: Free Press, 1987), p. 300. An earlier version of this chapter was first published as Timothy Larsen, 'E. B. Tylor, religion and anthropology', *British Journal for the History of Science*, 46, 3 (September 2013), pp. 467–85. W. John Young astutely caught a few errors in a late draft.

[2] Peter Melville Logan, *Victorian Fetishism: Intellectuals and Primitives* (Albany: State University of New York Press, 2009), pp. 89–114.

[3] [Northcote W. Thomas (ed.)], *Anthropological Essays presented to Edward Burnett Tylor in honour of his 75th birthday Oct. 2 1907* (Oxford: Clarendon Press, 1907), pp. [i], 6.

[4] 'Late Sir Edward B. Tylor', *Wellington Weekly News* 10 January 1917, p. 8.

[5] Joan Leopold, *Culture in Comparative and Evolutionary Perspective: E. B. Tylor and the Making of 'Primitive Culture'* (Berlin: Dietrich Reimer Verlag, 1980), p. 67.

textbook.[6] Even more clear cut is the unique position Tylor occupied as the first holder of a professorship in anthropology in Britain (at the University of Oxford). Chris Holdsworth has also observed, 'Tylor was the only nineteenth-century anthropologist who devoted his entire time to anthropology'.[7]

Given this level of significance, it is stunning to realize that there has never been a biography. In the festschrift chapter entitled 'Edward Burnett Tylor', the historian is disappointed to read: 'It has been no part of my conception of my task to enter into the details of Mr. Tylor's biography'.[8] This pattern of commenting on the work rather than the life has been followed ever since.[9] In contrast with many Victorians of his eminence, he was not the subject of a 'Life and Letters' volume: one suspects this was because he had made the mistake of living too long; by the time of his death the younger generations of anthropologists did not wish to dishonour their founder by documenting how his theories had largely gone out of fashion. This chapter is also mainly about Tylor's work, albeit in relation to his personal life and beliefs. Still, several major and illuminating biographical details which are not in the existing scholarship have been discovered in the process of researching it.

The one biographical point which everyone highlights is that Tylor had been raised a Quaker, nevertheless, scholars have failed to discern the most significant ways in which this influenced his work. Indeed, the most important alleged implication of Tylor's Quaker formation usually given is simply wrong. To take a recent example, his entry in the *Oxford Dictionary of National Biography* states: 'A Quaker by birth, Tylor was educated at Grove House, Tottenham, a school belonging to the Society of Friends. His faith, which he abandoned later in life, precluded a university education'.[10] In fact, there was no required oath to prevent Tylor from gaining a full Cambridge education (albeit without obtaining the actual degree), or a Scottish higher

---

[6] Edward B. Tylor, *Anthropology: An Introduction to the Study of Man and Civilization* (London: Macmillan and Co., 1881).

[7] Chris Holdsworth, 'Sir Edward Burnett Tylor (1832–1917)', in *Oxford Dictionary of National Biography*, eds. H. C. G. Matthew and Brian Harrison (Oxford: Oxford University Press, 2004), vol. 55, pp. 773–75; Stocking, *Victorian*, p. 263.

[8] Andrew Lang, 'Edward Burnett Tylor', in Thomas, *Anthropological*, p. 14.

[9] R. R. Marett, *Tylor* (London: Chapman and Hall, 1936).

[10] Holdsworth, 'Tylor', p. 773; Frédéric Regard, 'Catholicism, Spiritual Progress, and Ethnology: E. B. Tylor's Secret War of Culture', *REAL* (2004), 20, p. 223.

education, diploma and all. (Edinburgh was a popular destination for English Quakers seeking a medical degree.) The most obvious option, however, was London, which, as part of its raison d'être, providing non-Anglicans of any stripe an opportunity to obtain a university degree. To take just one example to hand, the historian and lifelong Friend Thomas Hodgkin (nephew of his namesake who was a founder of the Ethnological Society of London) was a year older than Tylor and as they had both attended the same Quaker school it could hardly have escaped Tylor's notice that Hodgkin had gone on to University College London.[11] In short, there was nothing in the letter or spirit of the rules and ways of either University College London or of the Society of Friends to have prevented Tylor from gaining a university degree in his home country.

Tylor was born at Camberwell, Surrey, into a Quaker family. His father was the prosperous owner of a brass foundry. One of his older brothers, Alfred, would become a noted geologist while also having a flair for generating wealth in the family business. Edward was sent to the Quaker school at Tottenham, and then came to work at the brass foundry at the age of sixteen. His health was fragile, however, and in that wonderfully Victorian way for financially comfortable families this led to a life of pleasant trips abroad. Tylor's wife, Anna, compiled a diary of their life together which primarily consists of chronicling health concerns and travels. An early entry reads: 'Were [*sic*] engaged—He came to Linden—Chest delicate, & he spent the winter at Nice'.[12] The first significant such trip was a wander through parts of the New World which began in 1855. He spent 'the best part of a year' touring the United States, but the turning point of his professional life came on an omnibus in Havana, Cuba, in the spring of 1856, [13] where he happened to meet the ethnologist Henry Christy (1810–65). Christy was planning a Mexican expedition to collect artefacts and Tylor agreed to accompany him, thereby learning to focus his intellectual curiosity on the study of primitive culture.[14]

[11] G. H. Martin, 'Thomas Hodgkin (1831–1913)', *Oxford DNB*, vol. 27, pp. 476–77.
[12] Natural History Museum, London, Tylor Papers, Mss TYL 1, Anna Tylor, 'Notebook, chronicling the life of her husband Sir E. B. Tylor', [1917].
[13] Edward Burnett Tylor, *Anahuac, Or Mexico and the Mexicans, Ancient and Modern*, 1861 (Boston: IndyPublish, 2007), p. 1.
[14] I have judged that it would be tedious to be continually putting words in quotation marks, but the reader should understand that terms such as 'primitive' and 'savage' and so on are used to aid a historical understanding of Tylor's mind, vocabulary, and milieu.

This initiation itself reflects a deeply Quaker lineage. At the time of their Mexican journey, both Christy and Tylor were devout Friends, and Christy would remain so.[15] Tylor himself reflected in 1884 (by which time he was a religious sceptic of long standing) on how Christy had become interested in ethnology:

> He was led into this subject by his connection with Dr. Hodgkin; the two being at first interested, from the philanthropist's point of view, in the preservation of the less favoured races of man, and taking part in a society for this purpose, known as the Aborigines' protection society.[16]

Thomas Hodgkin (1798–1866) was a deeply devout Quaker. He founded the Ethnological Society of London, which would become the intellectual centre of the emerging discipline of anthropology. When T. H. Huxley (1825–95) served as president in 1871 he brought about a merger with an upstart rival that led to its becoming what is now entitled the Royal Anthropological Institute. The Quaker component in this story of the development of anthropological institutions was, of course, only one current and by no means the whole, but it is the germane one to highlight here because Tylor came into this field on that particular current. In short, Quaker spirituality resulted in Friends being leading humanitarian activists.[17] Quaker abolitionism is well known. Another such cause was the interests of indigenous peoples who were being mistreated in colonial encounters. This religiously motivated concern, in turn, led on to a scholarly interest in 'savages'.

R. R. Marett observed that 'Tylor's anthropological apprenticeship was served in Mexico'.[18] Tylor decided that his travels with Christy could be the subject of a book. He had married Anna in 1858 and her diary entry for 27 June 1859 was: 'E. going on with "Anahuac"'.[19] *Anahuac, Or Mexico and the Mexicans, Ancient and Modern* (1861) was Tylor's first publication. This book has justly been ignored as not an important contribution to anthropology. It is not even clear that Tylor had a working definition of 'Mexican'.[20] Nevertheless, one can

---

[15] Christy died a Friend in good standing: *The Annual Monitor for 1866* (London: A. W. Bennett, 1865).

[16] E. B. Tylor, 'How the Problems of American Anthropology Present Themselves to the English Mind', *Science* IV, 98 (19 December 1884), p. 549.

[17] For Friends during this period, see Elizabeth Isichei, *Victorian Quakers* (Oxford: Oxford University Press, 1970).

[18] Marett, *Tylor*, p. 29.   [19] Tylor, 'Notebook'.

[20] Tylor, *Anahuac*, pp. 26–27, 107.

see already present several subjects that would interest Tylor throughout his career (such as tracing decimal numeration to counting on fingers).[21]

The main scholarly examinations of *Anahuac*, a couple of articles by Frédéric Regard, aptly focus on its marked anti-Catholicism.[22] Nevertheless, these and all other studies are hampered by ignorance of the chronology of Tylor's spiritual autobiography. Regard elides this by merely saying that Tylor was the son of a Quaker.[23] In fact, Tylor was himself still a devout Friend when he wrote *Anahuac*. At one point his faith is on display in a reference to 'our Saviour'.[24] There are numerous opinioned passages in *Anahuac* that reflect Quaker values, such as denunciations of gambling and showy clothing. He even praised the 'good sense' that founder of the Society of Friends George Fox (1624–91) had shown in his practical wardrobe.[25] More importantly, Tylor's Quaker anti-militarism is readily apparent.[26]

In other words, Tylor was offering a Quaker critique of Catholicism. Friends practiced one of the least elaborate versions of Christianity that existed in the nineteenth century. It was therefore easy for Tylor to condemn Catholic ways in the certainty that his own spiritual house was in order. He could attack Catholicism as priest-ridden, safe in the knowledge that there were no Quaker priests; decry their greedy schemes, confident that Quaker ministers did not receive any payments; object to the idolatrous treatment of statues, knowing that Friends did not even allow religious images, and so on. The polemical pay-off was the assertion that Catholicism was little better than the pagan religion of the Aztecs:

> Practically, there is not much difference between the old heathenism and the new Christianity...They had gods, to whom they built temples, and in whose honour they gave offerings, maintained priests, danced and walked in processions—much as they do now...[27]

[21] Tylor, *Anahuac*, pp. 67–68. For this interest of Tylor's, see H. H. Godwin-Austen et al. (eds.), *Hints to Travellers: Scientific and General* (London: Royal Geographical Society, 1883), p. 227.

[22] Regard, 'Catholicism'; Frédéric Regard, 'The Catholic Mule: E. B. Tylor's Chimeric Perception of Otherness', *Journal of Victorian Culture* 12, 2 (2007), pp. 225–37.

[23] Regard, 'Catholic', 226.   [24] Tylor, *Anahuac*, 33.

[25] Tylor, *Anahuac*, 106.   [26] Tylor, *Anahuac*, 72.

[27] Tylor, *Anahuac*, 185. The wider context and resonance of such critiques during this period was the rise of Anglo-Catholicism and the ritualistic controversy in the Church of England.

The message of *Anahuac* was simple: Catholicism is like paganism and paganism is like Catholicism.

Tylor's anti-Catholicism was lifelong. Another way of saying that Catholics were pagans was to say that they were savages. Tylor's greatest work, *Primitive Culture*, is particularly thick with anti-Catholic gibes. For instance:

> That the guilt of thus bringing down Europe intellectually and morally to the level of negro Africa lies in the main upon the Roman Church, the bulls of Gregory IX. and Innocent VIII., and the records of the Holy Inquisition, are conclusive evidence to prove.[28]

Again and again, such parallels are made: the Catholic attitude to saints on high is no different from ancestor worship—or polytheism—or idolatry.[29] The man of science and Jesuit Alfred Weld unsurprisingly spoke of Tylor's 'hatred' of the Catholic Church.[30]

Tylor's breakthrough book was *Researches into the Early History of Mankind and the Development of Civilization* (1878 [1865]).[31] A. C. Haddon identified *Researches* as a 'masterly work' which 'at once brought Tylor to the forefront as an ethnologist'.[32] It has been observed that this volume never explored religion, and this omission is intriguing in the light of his next book, *Primitive Culture*, where examining religion literally fills half the book and intellectually engulfs the project.[33] Marett remarked that in *Researches* Tylor 'reserved the subject of religion as not yet ripe for treatment'.[34] As will be shown, the reason for this is that Tylor lost his faith while working on *Researches*. It was simply too soon: he was not yet willing or able to tackle religion directly from a sceptical perspective. Nevertheless, there are incidental clues. The most positive portrayal of Christianity in the book is a poignant account of a Lutheran worship service at the Berlin Deaf and Dumb Institute.[35] Tylor had experienced this when

---

[28] Edward B. Tylor, *Primitive Culture: Researches into the development of mythology, philosophy, religion, language, art and custom*, 2 vols. (New York: Henry Holt and Company, 1874), vol. I, p. 139.

[29] Tylor, *Primitive*, vol. II, pp. 120, 168–69, 331.

[30] A. Weld, 'Our Ancestors', *The Month* (1872), XVII, pp. 78–106.

[31] Edward B. Tylor, *Researches into the Early History of Mankind and the Development of Civilization*, 3rd ed. (London: John Murray, 1878).

[32] A. C. Haddon, 'Sir E. B. Tylor, F.R.S.', *Nature* 98, 2463 (11 January 1917), pp. 373–74.

[33] Stocking, *Victorian*, p. 161.

[34] Marett, *Tylor*, pp. 63, 102; Leopold, *Tylor*, p. 17.

[35] Tylor, *Researches*, p. 33.

still a believer.[36] Elsewhere, scepticism can be seen encroaching. Tylor suggests that 'the idea of a future life' had occurred to savages through an unsound procession of reasoning.[37] He complains that Victorian society was too trusting of ancient authors. That this was a jab at the authority of the Bible is reinforced by other passages such as the seemingly irreverent glibness of comparing the story of Jonah with those of Tom Thumb and Little Red Riding-Hood and a reference to 'the Jewish superstition that a man's destiny may be changed by changing his name' which sets a whole series of biblical narratives in a dismissive light.[38] Tylor complained that Archbishop Whately (1787–1863) had brought the notion of supernatural revelation into his account of human cultural development despite such a theory lacking 'any real evidence.'[39]

Before carrying on with his anthropological writings, it is necessary now to circle back chronologically in order to trace more of Tylor's biography. The commonest reason why members left the Society of Friends during this period was because of marrying out: the Society required all members only to wed a Friend, and to marry an outsider inevitably meant expulsion. It is a mark of his devout Quaker identity that Tylor conformed to this expectation. Anna Fox was from a Quaker family whose business was the Tonedale Mills, Wellington, Somerset.[40] More than merely marrying a Friend, Tylor actually met Anna at a religious meeting. Anna's diary is devoid of comments on their inner lives, but like a real estate agent she assumed that it is all about location. She recorded how their relationship started in 1857: 'We met at Stoke Newington at Yearly Meeting time.'[41] Yearly Meeting was the high point of the Quaker annual spiritual calendar— a time when Friends gathered from across the country for worship, fellowship, and to conduct the business of the Society. Tylor was living in the family home at Stoke Newington and the Stoke Newington Friends Meeting House would become his and Anna's congregation as a married couple. The Yearly Meeting was generally recognized as an apt time for Friends to find a spouse, and Tylor conformed to this established custom. Edward and Anna were married on 16 June 1858.

---

[36] Tylor, 'Notebook': an entry for 1862.   [37] Tylor, *Researches*, p. 5.

[38] Tylor, *Researches*, pp. 325–29, 346, 125.

[39] Tylor, *Researches*, pp. 161–63.

[40] 'Death of Lady Tylor', *Wellington Weekly News* (1 June 1921), p. 8.

[41] Tylor, 'Notebook', an entry for 1857.

It was also a custom among Friends at that time to have the wedding ceremony in the bride's home and it would seem they followed this tradition as well: their marriage was recorded by the West Somerset Monthly Meeting.[42]

Edward and Anna then settled down to six years of married life as faithful Friends. Tylor's move away from religion can be formally dated as he and Anna resigned their Quaker membership on 17 July 1864.[43] This fact has never before been uncovered, and indeed the Tylors themselves were prone to obscure it, perhaps because it was socially awkward given that close family members, including Tylor's geologist brother, kept the faith unto death. Anna did not mention it in the diary that she painstakingly prepared after Tylor's death, although it is packed with much more trivial events (the most notable occurrence in 1864 is therefore not the severing of their Christian ties but rather a holiday at Teignmouth, Devon).[44] Likewise, Tylor would merely say that he had been 'brought up among the Quakers', thus eliding that he was himself a faithful Friend until the age of 32.[45] Their resignation was a solemn act and a much more decisive one than simply allowing one's Quaker identity to wither through neglect. Given Tylor's known religious scepticism thereafter, it is safe to assume that the resignation was prompted by a loss of faith. Moreover, the timing is significant: his *Researches* would appear one year later. By his own account, studying anthropology was his life's work from 1861.[46] It is therefore also reasonable to infer that Tylor's loss of faith was triggered by his concerted grappling with anthropological evidence and theories: he could not find a way to think anthropologically and as a Christian at the same time.

* * *

Tylor's *Primitive Culture: Researches into the development of mythology, philosophy, religion, language, art and custom* was published in 1871. It went through multiple editions and was also translated into French, German, Russian, and Polish.[47] In his festschrift it was referred to as his 'masterpiece', and at Tylor's death Haddon declared

---

[42] Friends House, London, Digest of Marriages of the Society of Friends. I am grateful to Joanna Clark, Assistant Librarian.

[43] Friends House Library, London, Devonshire House Monthly Meeting records, ref. 11 b c.

[44] Tylor, 'Notebook', entries for 1864.

[45] Tylor, 'How the Problems', p. 546.   [46] Tylor, *Primitive*, vol. I, p. vi.

[47] Thomas, *Anthropological*, p. 379.

that *Primitive Culture* 'speedily became a "classic", and such will always remain.'[48] *Anthropology: An Introduction to the Study of Man and Civilization* appeared in 1881. Rather than weary the reader by presenting the contents of these volumes *in seriatim*, it seems more profitable to draw upon them (and other works where desirable) to present Tylor's major anthropological ideas, particularly those that have a strong bearing on his view of religion.

Tylor's anthropological thought was stadial, developmental, and progressive, based in an evolutionary model of human culture. He was deeply indebted to the work of French philosopher Auguste Comte (1798–1857). Comte believed he had found a Casaubon-like key to all human progress, a law of a three stages: 'the Theological, or fictitious; the Metaphysical, or abstract; and the Scientific, or positive.'[49] Such a scheme was overtly antithetical to Christianity: it placed theology in the earliest stage of development and marked it off as something that had to be dispensed with in the name of progress. Tylor sometimes used Comte's categories.[50] His standard scheme, however, deployed pre-Comtean terminology: 'Human life may be roughly classed into three great stages, Savage, Barbaric, Civilized.'[51] (To play with Tylorian language, it seems a curious survival of theological modes of thought that the stages in such schemes always needed to be three in number—one thinks of Joachim of Fiore's Trinitarian scheme of human history. As will be explored in the next chapter, J. G. Frazer would continue this convention, deciding upon magical, religious, and scientific as his triad.) Tylor's example of a savage was 'the wild Australian', while, although it was surely superfluous to say it for his readers, 'the Englishman', of course, was the very model of modern, civilized *homo sapiens*.[52] The South Sea islanders he discerned to be 'intelligent barbarians'.[53] Every human culture could be identified as occupying one of these three standard stages which Tylor had inherited.

Moreover, the arrow of history pointed in the direction of progress.[54] Tylor was influenced by the Pitt Rivers collection and he was one of the main anthropologists associated with it. Augustus Pitt-Rivers (1827–1900) himself had arranged his artefacts as a 'museum of

---

[48] Thomas, *Anthropological*, p. 1; Haddon, 'Tylor', p. 373.
[49] Harriet Martineau (trans. and ed.), *The Positive Philosophy of Auguste Comte*, 3 vols (London: George Bell & Sons, 1896), vol. I, pp. 1–2.
[50] Tylor, *Primitive*, II, p. 109.   [51] Tylor, *Anthropology*, pp. 23–24.
[52] Tylor, *Primitive*, I, p. 28.   [53] Tylor, *Anthropology*, p. 374.
[54] Tylor, *Researches*, p. 191.

development' from the primitive to the most advanced. Tylor came to see this as revealing a general truth about all aspects of culture: 'The principle that thus became visible to him in weapon-development is not less true through the whole range of civilization'.[55] For Tylor, cumulative progress was true not only in technology, but in all areas, including mental culture and morality.

Tylor's stadial consciousness led on to his particular use of the comparative method. He believed that everyone at the same stage had the same patterns of thought. Therefore one could apply what one learned from one group of savages to another. Moreover, thinking of savages as 'grown-up children' was 'in the main a sound' comparison.[56] Have you ever noticed that they both are fond of rattles and drums?[57] The main pay-off of the comparative method was that the early history of 'the white race' could be recovered by studying contemporary savages.

Next is Tylor's notion of survivals. In his lexicon, a 'survival' was something in a culture that did not make sense there in the present context but rather bore witness to an earlier stage. It existed not by inherent logic but 'had lasted on by mere conservatism into a new civilization, to which it is unsuited'.[58] Survivals were obsolete stock that had failed to be thrown out when their sell-by date had passed. Tylor would illustrate this from clothing fashions and would incidentally apply it to a range of practices such as vendettas.[59] Nevertheless, Tylor's mind was not really preoccupied with such matters but rather with what he acknowledged was a close synonym:

> Such a proceeding as this would be usually, and not improperly, described as a superstition; and, indeed, this name would be given to a large proportion of survivals generally. The very word 'superstition', in what is perhaps its original sense of a 'standing over' from old times, itself expresses the notion of a survival.[60]

Tylor's deployment of the doctrine of survivals was overwhelmingly in order to elucidate religion, and scholars have observed that the concept was developed in order to help him find a way to think about spiritual matters.[61]

---

[55] Tylor, 'How the Problems', p. 549.   [56] Tylor, *Researches*, p. 106.
[57] Tylor, *Researches*, pp. 138–39.   [58] Tylor, 'How the Problems', p. 550.
[59] Godwin-Austen, *Hints*, p. 238.   [60] Tylor, *Primitive*, I, pp. 71–72.
[61] George W. Stocking, Jr., 'Animism in Theory and Practice: E. B. Tylor's Unpublished "Notes On *Spiritualism*"', *Man*, n.s. 6, 1 (March 1971), p. 91; Leopold, *Tylor*, pp. 51, 118.

Tylor's anthropological approach to religion can now be explored. In *Primitive Culture*, he set out as a condition that 'as to the religious doctrines and practices examined, these are treated as belonging to theological systems devised by human reason, without supernatural aid or revelation'.[62] In actuality, this methodology was undergirded by a much stronger, unstated conviction, namely, that there were no souls or spiritual beings. Without ever addressing the matter, Tylor tacitly ruled out the possibility that people might believe in these things because they actually exist. Given that starting point, Tylor saw it as his task to account for how people had come to adopt these erroneous beliefs.[63]

Tylor appropriated the term 'animism' for belief in spiritual beings and thus as a synonym for the indispensable essence of religion. His view of the origin of religion has been called the 'dream theory'.[64] The argument ran thus: when we dream it appears that a part of us leaves our body. Our body is sleeping at home, but we swim in a lake. Savages assume this literally happens and therefore infer that they have a part of themselves separable from their body—this is how the notion of a 'soul' developed (as well as the supposition of an afterlife as the 'soul' can apparently exist without the body—a theory undergirded by the fact that dead people still come to us in our dreams, which savages interpret as an actual visit). The notion of a soul, in turn, leads on to spirits. Tylor viewed ghosts and demons as the fundamental spiritual beings in the early stages of religion. (One is delighted to learn that the traditional way to describe a ghost's voice is as a 'twitter'.)[65] Darwin's *The Descent of Man* affirmed: 'It is also probable, as Mr. Tylor has shewn, that dreams may have first given rise to the notion of spirits'.[66] Spirits, in turn, are ranked, leading to gods, and this eventually gives rise to thinking about a supreme god, the road to monotheism. Tylor summarized his own view as the 'theory that the conception of the human soul is the very "*fons et origo*" of the conceptions of spirit and deity in general'.[67]

If some of this seems improbable to us, Tylor avers, that is precisely because we have advanced and therefore have a higher mental culture. The primitive mind is incapable of distinguishing between

---

[62] Tylor, *Primitive*, I, p. 417.   [63] Tylor, *Primitive*, I, p. 425.
[64] Marett, *Tylor*, pp. 112–13.   [65] Tylor, *Primitive*, I, p. 453.
[66] Charles Darwin, *The Descent of Man* (London: John Murray [1871] 1901), p. 144.
[67] Tylor, *Primitive*, II, p. 247.

objective and subjective. We consider dreams 'subjective processes of the mind'.[68] That they could not think this way helps to account for how claims to divine revelation arose. Savages, as it were, did not have the imagination to realize that they were simply imagining something and therefore objectified it as the voice of a god. In the mystical tradition, typically this is physically induced by fasting which generates hallucinations mistaken for interactions with spiritual beings.[69] Tylor also thought of modern spiritualism as primitive religion redux. Armchair anthropologist though he was, Tylor attended some séances as a sort of fieldwork and recorded his observations. For one session his verdict was simply 'subjectivity', by which he meant that these people could not distinguish their own fancies from reality.[70] Tylor never tired of insisting that the primitive mind could not rise to the notion of a metaphor. He always latched on to examples of literalistic thinking as indicative of the whole. He was delighted with St Patrick's Purgatory at Lough Derg, as expressing the uncivilized assumption that purgatory must be a physical place to which one could walk.[71] Literal also meant material. Tylor hoped that the American anthropologist Franz Boas (1858–1942) would provide an artefact for the museum: 'I should much like to possess one or two genuine "soul-catchers". They are of the greatest value to enable the public to realise what the barbaric doctrine of souls really is'.[72] Perhaps it will not be amiss to give an example of Tylor overreaching in this way as illuminating the groove in which his mind ran. In both *Primitive Culture* and *Anthropology* Tylor avers that the supreme god was originally literally the sky: 'Who, we may ask, is this divinity, calm and indifferent save when his wrath bursts forth in storm, but the Heaven himself?'[73] This Heaven-Father later evolves into our Father in Heaven. Tylor insisted that a survival of this can be found in language: 'Among all the relics of barbaric religion which surround us, few are more striking than the phrases which still recognise as a deity the living sky, as "Heaven forgive me!"'[74] The actual origin of such phrases is much more likely to be a reverent reluctance to say

---

[68] Tylor, *Researches*, p. 6.   [69] Tylor, *Primitive*, II, p. 415.

[70] Stocking, 'Animism', p. 95.

[71] Tylor, *Anthropology*, p. 349; Tylor, *Primitive*, II, p. 93.

[72] Alison Brown, Jeremy Coote, and Chris Gosden, 'Tylor's Tongue: Material Culture, Evidence, and Social Networks', *Journal of the Anthropological Society of Oxford* (2000), 31, 3, p. 268.

[73] Tylor, *Primitive*, II, p. 249.   [74] Tylor, *Anthropology*, p. 359.

the divine name, which caused 'heaven' to be used as a euphemistic substitute, but Tylor instinctively assumed literalism.

For Tylor, animism was the scientific thought of savages. Magic was merely 'a sort of early and unsuccessful attempt at science', and the same can be said for religion.[75] In developing what we would term religious ideas, 'their purpose is to explain nature'.[76] When thinking about religion, civilized people tend to dwell on doctrines that developed quite late rather than the true basis of spirituality in 'the primitive spiritualistic science which interpreted nature to the lower races'.[77] Animist beliefs were a rational effort by a limited mental culture.[78] Thinking has made progress, however, and therefore we know better.

By its subsequent critics, this view has been labelled the 'intellectualist' tradition in British anthropology—one that assumes that religion was the result of savage philosophers contemplating the natural world. For the purpose at hand, what needs to be highlighted is the way that Tylor's theory fuelled the warfare model of the relationship between religion and science.[79] This model was propounded by polemical secularists. It asserted that religion and science were locked in a zero-sum struggle over the same turf: whenever religion was accepted, it hampered scientific thinking, and whenever scientific thinking was accepted it dispensed with religion.[80] Sprinkled throughout Tylor's works are comments on how theology or priests thwarted scientific advances.[81] Indeed, it would seem that he himself thought that he sometimes expressed this view too intemperately. In the proof sheets for his last, unpublished book was this sentence: 'It is often and not untruly complained that theological teaching was a

[75] Godwin-Austen, *Hints*, p. 234.   [76] Tylor, *Primitive*, II, p. 183.

[77] Pitt Rivers Museum, Oxford, Tylor Papers, Manuscript Collections, Box 15, Notes and Proof Sheets for 'The Natural History of Religion', section on 'Christian Animism', p. 24 (handwritten note).

[78] Tylor, *Anthropology*, p. 353.

[79] George W. Stocking, Jr., 'Edward Burnett Tylor and the Mission of Primitive Man', in *The Collected Works of Edward Burnett Tylor*, ed. George W. Stocking, Jr. (London: Routledge, 1994), I, p. xviii.

[80] James R. Moore, *The Post-Darwinian Controversies: A study of the Protestant struggle to come to terms with Darwin in Great Britain and America, 1800–1900* (Cambridge: Cambridge University Press, 1979), pp. 19–100. For a critique in the context of Tylor's thought, see Dewi Zephaniah Phillips, *Religion and the Hermeneutics of Contemplation* (Cambridge: Cambridge University Press, 2001), pp. 152, 160.

[81] Tylor, *Anthropology*, p. 324.

great obstacle to the rise of geology'. Apparently deciding he had gone too far, Tylor deleted 'great'.[82]

Another anthropological theory of Tylor's that needs to be set in the light of wider debates in the nineteenth century is his view on morality in early history. Tylor was concerned to keep morality and religion as discrete, unconnected categories: 'savage animism is almost devoid of that ethical element which to the educated modern mind is the very mainspring of practical religion'.[83] A section heading for a Gifford lecture he gave put it succinctly: 'Primitive Morality independent of Religion'.[84] Tylor also insisted, however, that savages were highly moral.[85] Many Victorians believed that religion was essential for maintaining morality. A major criticism of free thought was that it would undercut people's motivation for being moral.[86] It seems that Tylor was covertly attempting to reassure people that they could abandon religion without fearing for morality: the future could be like the past in which people were moral without being religious.

There is more warrant to assume that he was tacitly furthering wider contemporary causes in his scholarship than there is for some others because Tylor himself commended his work for serving this purpose. The famous last words of *Primitive Culture* were that 'the science of culture is essentially a reformer's science'.[87] Tylor's task was 'to expose the remains of crude old culture which has passed into harmful superstition, and to mark these out for destruction'.[88] *Anthropology* ends in the same sermonic way, with Tylor revealing 'the practical moral' of what his readers had learned, namely that they must apply these anthropological insights to 'the practical business of life' and therefore create a better world.[89] Tylor reminisced to an American audience about discovering this:

> By and by it did become visible, that to show that a custom or institution which belonged to an early state of civilization had lasted on by mere conservatism into a newer civilization, to which it is unsuited, would somehow affect the public mind as to the question whether this custom or institution should be kept up, or done away with. Nothing

---

[82] Tylor, 'Natural', unnumbered chapter, 'Deluge-Legends', p. 40.
[83] Tylor, *Primitive*, II, p. 360.   [84] Thomas, *Anthropological*, p. 399.
[85] Tylor, *Anthropology*, pp. 406–409.
[86] This theme is explored in Timothy Larsen, *Crisis of Doubt: Honest Faith in Nineteenth-Century England* (Oxford: Oxford University Press, 2006).
[87] Tylor, *Primitive*, II, p. 453.   [88] Tylor, *Primitive*, II, p. 453.
[89] Tylor, *Anthropology*, pp. 439–40.

has for months past given me more unfeigned delight than when I saw in the *Times* newspaper the corporation of the City of London spoken of as a 'survival'. You have institutions even here which have outlived their original place and purpose...[90]

The corporation of the City of London is a mere illustrative red herring. An American audience would presumably have found the monarchy and the House of Lords survivals, but Tylor never declared that politics needed to be reformed. Indeed, his calls in earnest for reform were all exclusively confined to religion. Even in this area he much preferred to leave it to others to connect the dots, but he could not resist repeatedly declaring that his theories would necessitate some hard rethinking by theologians specifically, while he never commended these for the particular domains of politicians or lawyers or heads of Oxbridge colleges. For example, Tylor argued that the eastward orientation of the priest (which had been reinstated by Tractarians) should not be discussed as a point of liturgical correctness, but rather as a survival of sun worship:

> How many years must pass before it shall be expected of every theologian that he shall have studied the development of religious ideas in the world before he reasons about them? Such a time will come, and with it the time when a theologian's education will necessarily include an elementary knowledge of the laws of nature. On these two steps will follow the second Reformation in England, and it will be greater than the first.[91]

The final prophetic pronouncement identifies Tylor with Huxley's Christianity-puncturing, agnostic crusade which he was pursuing under the banner of the 'New Reformation'.[92]

* * *

The first person to hold a post as an anthropologist in Britain, E. B. Tylor was appointed a reader in anthropology at the University of Oxford in 1884 and elevated to a professorship in 1895.[93] Tylor was also one of the first to give Gifford lectures, an endowed series

---

[90] Tylor, 'How the Problems', p. 550.

[91] E. B. Tylor, letter to *The Times*, 15 July 1875.

[92] Bernard Lightman, 'Interpreting Agnosticism as a Nonconformist Sect: T. H. Huxley's "New Reformation"', in *Science and Dissent in England, 1688–1945*, ed. Paul Wood (Aldershot: Ashgate, 2004), pp. 197–214. Tylor, *Primitive*, II, pp. 449.

[93] Peter Riviére (ed.), *A History of Oxford Anthropology* (Oxford: Berghahn Books, 2007), pp. 26, 28.

on natural theology. Tylor gave these lectures at the University of Aberdeen beginning in December 1889. Although, in the end, they never would be published, he intended to turn them into a book entitled *The Natural History of Religion* (echoing the philosopher David Hume (1711–76) who is a foil in the piece.) Working with Oxford University Press, Tylor proceeded so far as to have portions of it turned into proof sheets. The press date-stamped these sheets, revealing that this flurry of activity happened in 1899 and 1900. Tylor hand-corrected a reference to reflect the new sovereign, demonstrating that he was still at it in 1901, but he must have given up on working on it in earnest thereafter.

The proof sheets for *The Natural History of Religion* reveal Tylor deploying his established anthropological theories to reform society by challenging its religious beliefs. Chapter 1 entitled 'History of the Doctrine of Natural Religion', was primarily an attack on the views of the eighteenth-century deists, who had identified natural religion as a simple, moral monotheism.[94] Even for the deists this was primarily a statement of what people *ought* to have discovered rather than what they did, but Tylor took it to be a theory about the actual beliefs and practices of early humans. He then pretended that this supposed theory of primitive culture is what orthodox Christians meant by natural theology. (Quite to the contrary, orthodox theologians standardly claimed that human beings were natural idolaters.)

The main argument of *The Natural History of Religion* was an attempt to show that all religions, however advanced and sophisticated, were based in the crude animistic theories of savages.[95] This is done through charts that endeavour to reveal the common elements in the religions of primitive societies such as 'Tasmanian Animism' and 'Algonquin Animism' through to 'Christian Animism'. Although he must have found this very telling, all he really seems to be demonstrating is his definition of religion, a general category which therefore necessitates that the items in the set have features in common. This method of exposé by classification is further compromised by the fact that Tylor had considerable liberty in deciding which features warranted inclusion.[96] He makes the links between primitive religions and

---

[94] Tylor, 'Natural', ch. 1, p. 5.   [95] Tylor, 'Natural', ch. 2, p. 25.
[96] George W. Stocking, Jr., 'Charting the Progress of Animism: E. B. Tylor on "The Common Religion of Mankind"', *History of Anthropology Newsletter* (1992), 19, pp. 3–10.

Christianity stronger both by anachronistically importing elements back to earlier stages and by keeping explicitly rejected elements in later ones. As to the former, Aztec animism includes 'Ecclesiastical Influence on Society'. (The use of the Christian term 'ecclesiastical' seems to be an attempt to show how the religions of the Aztecs and of Catholics are similar, thus bringing Tylor in his last attempt at a book back full circle to the argument of his first one, *Anahuac*.) At the other end of the scale, the 'Christian Animism' chart has 'Nature-Spirits and Polytheistic Deities' as one of eight basic categories. This is apologetically accounted for with the parenthetical explanation, 'retained in folklore'. As Christian teaching explicitly repudiates these things they cannot have a place in a chart of the Christian religion *qua* Christian. Tylor also insisted throughout that 'demons' were the most basic category of religious belief, second only to the soul. 'Guardian angels' were just a subset of demons. While this categorization makes sense for 'Greco-Roman Animism', in Jewish and Christian thought this is reversed: angels are the basic category (though much more marginal to these faiths than second after the soul), and 'demons' are only a subset—'fallen angels'. It is possible that Tylor himself began to feel the force of some of these critiques and that is why he abandoned the project. An additional factor might have been that another anthropologist, Andrew Lang, a friend and one-time disciple, had come out with a book which argued that monotheism was part of primitive culture.[97] Tylor's unease about this conflict with Lang is demonstrated by his multiple attempts to describe it in the right tone, with crossed-out, handwritten efforts piled on top of each other.[98]

The proof sheets also contained a chapter that was unnumbered and it is tempting to see this as a reflection of the fact that there was no obvious place to put it, as it is not clear how this material would have contributed to any formal, overarching argument being pursued in the book. It was entitled 'Deluge-Legends'. Tylor was well aware that Christian apologists averred that the existence of stories of a great deluge in so many different scattered cultures was evidence for the historical veracity of the biblical narrative. In his earlier work, Tylor had tended to counter this with the claim that missionaries had probably infected these cultures with these stories rather than found them there. As more evidence emerged, however, this suspicion did not

---

[97] Andrew Lang, *The Making of Religion* (London: Longmans, Green, 1898).
[98] Tylor, 'Natural', ch. 3, p. 27.

hold up, so a new theory was needed. The argument of this chapter was that the story of the flood had indeed disseminated from a single source across the globe but this was not because of a historical event or from the Jewish account but rather the Babylonian one (which Tylor asserted is plagiarized in the Hebrew Bible). As this watery excursus does not connect to the unfolding argument of the rest of the book it seems to have been included simply as additional material that undermines Christianity. This suspicion is supported by a section on how higher critics have discerned that biblical books are compilations from multiple authors. This theory unsettled some conservative Christians—which again seems to be why it interested Tylor—but it was not relevant to the chapter's thesis. Tylor himself half realized this from the start, writing by way of apology in the typeset version, 'Although this division has not such importance in the present inquiry as it has theologically'.[99] He nonetheless traced the seams in the Pentateuch with relish. Reading it over again, Tylor apparently realized that this material was not germane to the ostensible theme of the chapter and therefore decided it had to be excised.

Tylor's anti-Christian stance has been generally acknowledged by scholars. Holdsworth noted, 'Tylor was openly hostile to organized religion'.[100] Henrika Kuklick has observed that it was typical of that generation of anthropologists. She quotes an observation made in a memorial tribute to A. C. Haddon: 'In their day, to be an anthropologist was generally considered equivalent to being an agnostic and freethinker'.[101] George W. Stocking Jr. emphasized the way that Tylor's animus against Christianity was expressed in some verses of poetry he wrote which were published anonymously, the key lines being: 'Theologians all to expose,—/'Tis the *mission* of Primitive Man'.[102] In other words, Tylor avowed that anthropology discredited Christian doctrine. While in *Anahuac* Tylor laboured to demonstrate that Catholicism was essentially paganism, from *Primitive Culture* onwards this approach was broadened to the claim that Christianity in generally is fundamentally pagan. Throughout his writings Tylor worked to lead the reader to this conclusion, both by describing savage

[99] Tylor, 'Natural', unnumbered chapter, 'Deluge-Legends', p. 46.

[100] Holdsworth, 'Tylor', p. 775.

[101] Henrika Kuklick, *The Savage Within: The Social History of British Anthropology, 1885–1945* (Cambridge: Cambridge University Press, 1991), p. 79.

[102] Andrew Lang, *XXXII Ballades in Blue China* (London: Kegan Paul, Trench, & Co., 1888), p. 46; Stocking, 'Mission'.

religion with words familiar from Christian contexts (for example, referring to a Maori rite as baptism and to Sioux theologians) and by insisting that Christian beliefs were no different from savage ones. For instance, here is how one ought to think about the doctrine of the virgin birth:

> in the Samoan Islands such intercourse of mischievous inferior gods caused 'many supernatural conceptions'; and in Lapland, where details of this last extreme class have also been placed on record. From these lower grades of culture we may follow the idea onward.[103]

This is not the place for a systematic evaluation of Tylor's anthropological thought, but in exploring its relationship to religion, it is worth noticing a few critiques. Even when at the height of his career not everyone was enamoured with Tylor's thought. Weld satirized Tylor's unexplained assumption that the spiritual realm did not exist, comparing it to 'if a historian were to discuss the origin of the widespread belief in the exploits of Alexander of Macedon, without touching on the hypothesis that such a conqueror perhaps really did exist'.[104] Alfred Russel Wallace (1823-1913), the co-discoverer of what came to be called Darwinism, made the same argument. On another point, he argued that it was wrong to assume that humanity was making general progress. Finally, in a critique that is even more apt when applied to the unpublished *Natural History of Religion*, Wallace observed:

> We are constantly told that each such belief or idea 'finds its place', with the implication that it is thus sufficiently accounted for...Any great mass of facts or phenomena whatever can be classified, but the classification does not necessarily add anything to our knowledge of the causes which produced the facts or phenomena...Although the details given on these subjects are so numerous...they are yet altogether one-sided. They have been amassed with one object and selected, no doubt unconsciously, so as to harmonize with the *à priori* convictions of the writer.[105]

Andrew Lang came to agree with Weld and Wallace that Tylor had begged the question of the existence of spiritual realities.[106] Even in

---

[103] Tylor, *Primitive*, II, p. 190.   [104] Weld, 'Ancestors', pp. 78–106.

[105] Alfred R. Wallace, 'Physical Science and Philosophy', *Academy* 3 (15 February 1872), pp. 69–71.

[106] George W. Stocking, Jr. *After Tylor: British Social Anthropology, 1888–1951* (Madison: University of Wisconsin Press, 1995), pp. 56–60.

his festschrift tribute to him, Lang was not above just flat out mocking Tylor's deployment of the doctrine of survivals:

> Protestants in Germany, says Wuttke, get Catholic priests to lay ghosts for them. Why not, if the ghost be a Catholic priest? The Rev. Mr. Thomson of Ednam, father of the author of *The Castle of Indolence*, was slain by a ghost, obviously not Presbyterian…[107]

Marett was clearly embarrassed by Tylor's 'harsh' attitude towards religion and repeatedly noticed it with regret.[108] Here is Marett's exasperation at Tylor's habit of finding only literal and scientific meaning in any statement:

> One might even construct a myth of one's own to the effect that the first story-teller was interrupted in the middle of his moving recital by someone who asked, 'Was that really so?'; that he promptly slew the stupid fellow with his stone-axe; and that ever afterwards there has prevailed a certain tolerance of poetic licence.[109]

Eventually, the new school of functionalism swept away Tylor's notion of survivals. It rejected the assumption that any practice should be viewed as a now-pointless relic maintained by mere conservatism, insisting instead that these practices must be serving a contemporary function. An anthropologist's task, then, is to explore that current function and not to chase antiquarian Br'er Rabbit trails regarding how the practice initially arose. Anthropologists also abandoned Tylor's evolutionism. The First World War helped to dislodge the assumption that the human story was one of progress, as it were, on all fronts.[110]

Some of the difficulties in Tylor's theories may be highlighted by introducing a corollary notion of his to survivals, namely 'revivals'. He introduced it thus:

> Sometimes old thoughts and practices will burst out afresh, to the amazement of a world that thought them long since dead or dying; here survival passes into revival, as has lately happened in so remarkable a way in the history of modern spiritualism…[111]

---

[107] Thomas, *Anthropological*, p. 7.   [108] Marett, *Tylor*, pp. 72, 76, 146.

[109] Marett, *Tylor*, pp. 86–87.

[110] Kuklick, *Savage*, pp. 19–20, 95, 277. For a recent exploration of the limits of Tylor's thought, see Logan, *Victorian*, pp. 89–114. For a twenty-first century critique of Tylor's anthropological thought in relationship to religion, see Phillips, *Religion*, pp. 146–82.

[111] Tylor, *Primitive*, I, pp. 16–17.

The first thing to notice is that Tylor never offered a theory as to why revivals happen: he merely observed that they do happen. The second point is that revivals are in tension with his assumption that technological advance could be generalized to all-round progress. The point of the technological model was that advances, once made, were not unmade. A few quirky examples notwithstanding, if technology was the only field considered no category of revivals would have been needed: there are simply not enough cases of societies freely choosing to revert to more primitive technologies to necessitate the creating of a theoretical category for this phenomenon. 'Revival', of course, was a common word in Victorian society as a spiritual event, a term cherished by many Christians. It is therefore quite possible that Tylor chose it deliberately as a way of baiting believers. This suspicion is strengthened by the fact that as well as presenting revivals in his anthropological sense, Tylor also spoke with open abuse of revivals in the spiritual sense:

> Medical descriptions of the scenes brought on by fanatical preachers at 'revivals' in England, Ireland, and America, are full of interest to students of the history of religious rites … These manifestations in modern Europe indeed form part of a revival of religion, the religion of mental disease.[112]

* * *

Tylor's anthropological thought as a religious sceptic was littered with survivals (to adapt his parlance) from his Quaker past. Huxley waggishly referred to Comte's Religion of Humanity as 'Catholicism *minus* Christianity', and one might describe Tylor's mature views as Quakerism minus Christianity.[113] Most generally, he maintained a lifelong disdain for priests and saw every religious image as an idol. Quaker anti-ritualism was no doubt behind his judgement that the religion of the Native Americans 'expressed itself' in 'useless ceremony'.[114] The Friends were one of the very few Christian groups

---

[112] Tylor, *Primitive*, II, p. 421.

[113] Adrian Desmond, *Huxley* (London: Penguin, 1997), p. 373. The difference between Comte and Tylor is revealing on this point. Raised as a Catholic, Comte continued to think fondly of the ways that Catholic worship are expressed and wanted to retain them even in a post-theological context, while Tylor always maintained the disdain for the trappings of Catholicism which he had acquired in his Quaker formation, simply going on to expand this critique to include the basic tenets of Christian theology in all its forms as well.

[114] Tylor, *Primitive*, I, p. 31.

which did not observe the ordinances of baptism and communion, and one can read *Primitive Culture* as culminating in an attack on the sacraments. Quaker plainness continued to prompt Tylor to object to jewellery. He saw earrings as a savage survival: 'the women of modern Europe mutilate their ears to hang jewels in them.'[115] If no piercing was involved, then perhaps one had graduated a stage, but it was still uncivilized: 'our ladies keep in fashion barbaric necklaces of such things as shells, seeds, tigers' claws, and especially polished stones. The wearing of shining stones as ornaments lasts on.'[116]

The most dominant continuing Quaker attitude was Tylor's anti-militarism. Even in his anthropological textbook he could not refrain from offering an editorial opposing the existence of the military.[117] In *Primitive Culture*, Tylor insisted that one of 'the lessons' to be learned from studying savages was that order can be kept without the need for a police force.[118] War caused a society to regress back to an earlier stage.[119] And here is a rather peculiar definition: 'A constitutional government, whether called republic or kingdom, is an arrangement by which the nation governs itself by means of the machinery of a military despotism.'[120] Quaker traces continue to the end. The 'Christian Animism' chart in *The Natural History of Religion* betrays the fingerprints of Friends. For example, it includes 'Oath' and 'Religious Belief legally enforced', which in no way define Christianity but which loomed large for Quakers as issues that set them apart from other religious groups, while leaving out the sacraments (which have been far more universal and essential throughout Christian history, but are obscured in Quaker practice and thought).[121] While Tylor's Quaker mindset undoubtedly hindered his anthropological work when it came to reflecting on aspects of culture such as ritual and images, it also provided illumination. For instance, no British community was more attuned to questions of exogamy and endogamy than the Quakers.[122] Tylor's attentiveness to a chanting voice in worship was undoubtedly informed by his experience of the sing-song habit of Victorian Quaker preachers.[123] Finally, a book review reference might reveal that Tylor thought in a Quaker way even with

---

[115] Tylor, *Researches*, p. 1.   [116] Tylor, *Anthropology*, p. 243.
[117] Tylor, *Anthropology*, p. 228.   [118] Tylor, *Primitive*, II, p. 405.
[119] Tylor, *Primitive*, II, p. 414.   [120] Tylor, *Primitive*, vol. II, p. 434.
[121] Tylor, 'Natural', 'Christian Animism' section, p. 24.
[122] Tylor, *Researches*, p. 279.
[123] Tylor, *Anthropology*, p. 291; Tylor, *Primitive*, vol. I, p. 175. Isichei, *Victorian*, p. 95.

regards to his own apostasy from the Quaker way. Observing that the bishop of Manchester had conceded some ground to the views of biblical critics, he remarked: 'Having once "let in the reasoned" (as the old Quaker phrase goes), Dr. Fraser would probably feel obliged to admit…'.[124] This was a common Quaker expression for allowing doubt to undermine faith. Tylor himself had 'let the reasoner in', and he did find that there was no apparent way to stop scepticism from undermining religion as a whole thereafter.

One of the limitations of Tylor's notion of survivals was that, in practice, it seemed almost inevitably to become contaminated by the anthropologist's own prior disposition toward a practice or belief. Tylor could pronounce wearing necklaces barbaric and wonder that it continues on, but this was merely an expression of a personal preference. An emotionally distant person could just as well deem hugging a savage practice that had inexplicably survived into civilized culture. This arbitrariness may be illustrated by some details regarding the last period of Tylor's life. In 1912, Tylor was knighted. One might suspect that a progressive reformer would judge that knighthood was a survival that needed to be eliminated, but Tylor offered no such leadership on that front, underlining once again how exclusively he confined his concerted reforming agenda to religion. Relatedly, Edward and Anna Tylor had drawn closer to the Anglican world in their latter decades, presumably a manifestation of a desire for greater social prominence, ease, and respectability. The University of Oxford had Anglican worship woven into its fabric and in 1898 Tylor even lectured at the intentional Anglican community, Toynbee Hall.[125] In her diary, Anna took to noticing that things happened on days in the church calendar. For instance, 'Joe' died on 'Good Friday', and several years later 'Isabella' died on 'Easter Sunday'.[126] One might even go so far as to say that Tylor learned part of his anthropological methodology from the Quakers. For example, Friends rejected the traditional names of the days of the week as derived from pagan gods, substituting numbers instead. Tylor would have been trained to use this Quaker nomenclature, but reverted to the more traditional terms. One might see this as a classic revival of a survival. Moreover, day names are just

---

[124] [E. B. Tylor], 'Mythology Among the Hebrews', *Spectator* (21 April 1877), pp. 508–509.

[125] Tylor, 'Notebook', February 1898.

[126] Tylor, 'Notebook', 5 April 1901; 15 April 1906.

one of numerous such Friendly critiques of common practices. In other words, it was the Society of Friends that taught Tylor to think in terms of paganisms that have survived into the present, but which need to be purged.[127] Finally, no scholar has ever mentioned Tylor's funeral or apparently found a report of it. Nevertheless, it turns out that, in the end—presumably at his own request, and certainly with Anna's approval—Sir Edward Burnett Tylor received a spectacularly Anglican funeral: no fewer than three priests presided and the choirs of both Wellington Parish Church, Somerset and All Saints' Church sang.[128] In *Primitive Culture*, Tylor himself described what happens to a ghostly pagan soul that survives into a more respectable religious environment: 'the doleful wanderer now asks Christian burial in consecrated earth'.[129]

---

[127] There is also probably a negative influence as well. Marjorie Wheeler-Barclay has recently observed that because some Victorian Quakers retained outmoded ways such as archaic forms of speech and styles of dress, Tylor in all likelihood was observing practices in his own community that seemed unfortunate survivals. Marjorie Wheeler-Barclay, *The Science of Religion in Britain, 1860–1915* (Charlottesville: University of Virginia Press, 2010), p. 75.

[128] 'Edward Tylor', *Wellington*, p. 8.   [129] Tylor, *Primitive*, II, p. 29.

2

James George Frazer

Frazer is a tough nut to crack. He once wrote the preface to a book entitled *The Enigma of Jesus*, but what is to be made of the Sphinx-like riddle who was the author of *The Golden Bough*? One begins to suspect that a steady portion of his words and actions served as deliberate misdirection or perhaps were the fruit of a capacious propensity for self-deception. Reading a large quantity of Frazer's writings conditions one to thinking in terms of startling realities that lie hidden beneath an ostensibly calm surface. This was his standard scholarly method and the temptation to apply it to his own life and thought is well nigh irresistible. Frazer himself seemed to inhabit an idyllic classical scene: the serene Fellow of Trinity College, Cambridge, ensconced in ancient rooms lined with leather-bound tomes, quietly, meticulously, patiently dedicating all his time and strength to collating and interpreting arcane bits of knowledge. Like the grove of Nemi, however, one suspects that the tranquillity of this portrait is belied by something more emotive lurking in the shadows.

No man who went to Didsbury College ever forgot the place.[1] To come through the little gate into the Sundial Lawn was to step into a consecrated court where members of a brotherhood walked gravely, intent upon their sacred studies. To approach the holy and beautiful house was to be hushed by Grecian order set out reverently in

---

[1] Lest some readers should become disorientated, it should be noted that this paragraph is written somewhat playfully as a pastiche of the opening of *The Golden Bough*. Although it would therefore be distracting to include quotation marks and citations in this paragraph, the reader should also know that almost all of the descriptive words and phrases about Didsbury College [Manchester] have been taken directly from the following source: W. Bradsley Brash and Charles J. Wright (ed.), *Didsbury College Centenary, 1842–1942* (London: Epworth Press, 1942).

large hewn squares of sandstone. A lone figure in austere and simple clerical garb slowly ascends the elliptical staircase, clutching the
wrought-iron balustrade afresh after each step. He first goes to the
Prayer Room, with its silence, its strangely numinous and healing
presence. He bows his head in quiet meditation. The year is 1904—the
same one in which the medieval hamlet of Didsbury was incorporated
into the city of Manchester. The figure is a classical tutor who has dedicated his life to preparing these earnest young men to dispense the
sacrament of the Word. To assist in this cause he has written to James
Frazer beseeching him to give a course of lectures on comparative
religion. The anthropologist is thrown off balance by the invitation.
He tries to convince the college that they do not know what he actually stands for nor what his subject matter really is. They insist that
everything is quite clear on those points. He consults his friends and
they unanimously and enthusiastically reply that he should undertake
this task. And yet the Cambridge man will never cross the Sundial
Lawn, will never ascend the elliptical staircase. The questions to be
answered are two: first, why did Frazer seek reassurances from those
associated with Didsbury College and advice from his friends about
this offer, and, second, why after receiving those reassurances and the
encouragement of his confidants did he nevertheless still decline it?
The rest of this chapter will be an attempt to answer these questions.

* * *

James George Frazer (1854–1941) was born in Glasgow and obtained
an MA from the university of that city before matriculating at Trinity
College, Cambridge, where he studied classics.[2] A thesis entitled 'The
Growth of Plato's Ideal Theory' secured him a college fellowship in
1879. Thereafter, Frazer never fully abandoned either Trinity College
or classics. He fell under the spell of the young discipline of anthropology, however, and it would be in that field that he would achieve his
greatest fame. In the preface to the first edition of *The Golden Bough*
(1890) Frazer acknowledged the initial prompt for this: 'My interest
in the early history of society was first excited by the works of Dr. E. B.
Tylor, which opened up a mental vista undreamed of by me before.'[3]
Frazer's own anthropological work was in marked continuity with

---

[2] The standard life is Robert Ackerman, *J. G. Frazer: His Life and Work*
(Cambridge: Cambridge University Press, 1987).

[3] J. G. Frazer, *The Golden Bough: A Study in Comparative Religion*, 2 vols.
(London: Macmillan and Co., 1890), I, p. x.

Tylor's methodology and assumptions. Reading Frazer, one encounters survivals, animism, primitive philosophers, stadial progress, and the like. Most of all, Frazer was a flamboyant practitioner of the comparative method: the world was his parish. A typical Frazerian passage is a kaleidoscope of incidents from Zululand to Iceland that strike him as sharing common characteristics which reveal an underlying shared mentality. The continental leaps can be disconcerting. To take a minor example—confined entirely to one footnote—Frazer tracks activities that resemble the game of tug-of-war through southeast India, Pisa, Burma, Indonesia, Korea, French Guiana, Sri Lanka, the Eskimos, the Kamtchatkans (northeastern Russia), northwest India, Shropshire, Radnorshire, Yorkshire, and finally Normandy.[4] It is hard fully to concede Frazer's assumption that this helps to reveal a common conviction regarding the need to expel devils when one stops to ponder that even dogs have been known to play games resembling tug-of-war.

His relationship with Tylor can serve as a first (and not terribly strong nor significant) example of a pattern of ambivalence in Frazer's actions in which words of honour and praise on the surface seem to provide an outward covering that concealed more repugnant responses. They had a friendly relationship and met frequently for some years. On the basis of his letters, Robert Ackerman has discerned that Frazer developed a dislike for Tylor in 1898. The reason was Tylor's suggestion that Frazer had made use of the work of a Dutch scholar without fully acknowledging the extent of this debt. Frazer wrote a prickly missive. Tylor apologized in a letter that began: 'I am sorry that a remark in my last letter has been understood by you as imputation on your truthfulness.'[5] Frazer formally accepted this reconciliation in a letter that began: 'I must write just one letter to thank you for your last and to say what great relief it has given me.'[6]

---

[4] J. G. Frazer, *The Golden Bough: A Study in Magic and Religion*, 2nd. ed., 3 vols. (London: Macmillan and Co., 1900), III, pp. 95–96. I have simplified and modernized the spelling of some of these references. For example, 'French Guiana' is 'the Roocooyen Indians of French Guiana'.

[5] E. B. Tylor to J. G. Frazer, 19 October 1898: Robert Ackerman (ed.), *Selected Letters of Sir J. G. Frazer* (Oxford: Oxford University Press, 2005), pp. 131–32. I should also note that Ackerman observes Frazer's divided self as has, more recently, Marjorie Wheeler-Barclay, so the theme of this chapter is continuing in the trajectory of those insights. For the latter, see Marjorie Wheeler-Barclay, *The Science of Religion in Britain, 1860–1915* (Charlottesville: University of Virginia Press, 2010), pp. 181–214.

[6] J. G. Frazer to E. B. Tylor, 20 October 1898: Ackerman, *Selected Letters*, pp. 132–34.

Ackerman observes: 'henceforth, his private comments on Tylor are unremittingly negative.'[7] Indeed, Frazer was consistently snide about the author of *Primitive Culture*, his malice going so far to colour his judgement that he would repeatedly suspect that Tylor held an erroneous theory in a current anthropological dispute on the basis of no evidence whatever. For example, after discussing a scholarly disagreement with figures such as Andrew Lang and Frank Jevons, Frazer observes that Tylor has not yet addressed the issue, before scoffing: 'Is Saul also among the prophets?'[8] It would seem that Frazer was hoping for a neat polarity in which all the people he disliked were on the wrong side of the debate. In a perfect inversion to his consistently hostile private remarks, all of Frazer's public comments on Tylor continued to be laudatory. In 1907, he even contributed to the volume of essays in Tylor's honour.[9]

Frazer himself was a prophet with exceedingly great formal honour in his own generation. His work is generally, if not universally, dismissed today by anthropologists, but they are nonetheless saddled with the reality that *The Golden Bough* is the most popular and influential book in the history of the discipline in terms of its wider cultural impact.[10] Frazer began working on what would become *The Golden Bough* in the mid-1880s and it became the labour of a lifetime. The first edition (1890) appeared in Frazer's 36th year and *Aftermath: A Supplement to the Golden Bough* was published in 1936, when Frazer was 82 years old, making it in uniform sets thereafter the thirteenth and final volume of the third edition. Ostensibly an effort to explain the eponymous legend, *The Golden Bough* is a grand tour through human culture across time and space that defies easy summary. In the preface to the first edition, Frazer identified 'the central idea' of the work as 'the conception of the slain god'.[11]

The second edition appeared in three volumes in 1900. The subtitle of the first edition had been 'A Study in Comparative Religion',

---

[7] Ackerman, *Selected Letters*, p. 157.

[8] J. G. Frazer to E. Sindey Hartland, 19 April 1901: Ackerman, *Selected Letters*, p. 189.

[9] [Northcote W. Thomas (ed.)], *Anthropological Essays presented to Edward Burnett Tylor in honour of his 75th birthday Oct. 2 1907* (Oxford: Clarendon Press, 1907).

[10] For an exploration of its influence, see John B. Vickery, *The Literary Impact of The Golden Bough* (Princeton: Princeton University Press, 1973); Robert Fraser (ed.), *Sir James Frazer and the Literary Imagination* (London: Macmillan, 1990).

[11] Frazer, *Golden Bough* (1890), I, p. xi.

but this was now changed to 'A Study in Magic and Religion', signalling a new theoretical scheme that Frazer had developed. Furthermore, the second edition included for the first time a theory about the death of Jesus of Nazareth. Frazer speculates that the feast of Purim was actually just a Jewish borrowing of a Babylonian festival in which a man was treated as a king-god and then put to death. The idea of resurrection is also present, as this is a picture of the death of vegetation in the autumn and its return to life in the spring. The Roman Saturnalia also had some of these elements and blends into the scene. The Galilean was identified as 'the Haman of the year' and therefore his death was swept into the 'the ever-recurring drama of the divine resurrection and death'.[12] Frazer then observes that the 'devout Christian' would probably gloss these events in a type-and-fulfilment redemptive history scheme, while for 'the sceptic' these new findings by Frazer will serve to 'reduce Jesus of Nazareth to the level of a multitude of other victims of a barbarous superstition'.[13]

The new theoretical scheme was a three-stage human progression: magic, religion, and science. Magic is based on the assumption that particular actions inevitably produce certain results. These causal assumptions, however, are invalid. When magic is discerned to be erroneous, people turn to religion. This is marked by entreating spiritual beings and therefore accommodates the unpredictability of outcomes: prayers are offered, but one cannot know for sure whether or not the god will grant the request. In other words, Frazer claims that the most primitive peoples have no religion. Just as one can speak of a Stone Age before the Bronze Age so, he posits, 'everywhere' people had an 'Age of Magic' before an 'Age of Religion'.[14] Frazer believed that evidence from Australia confirmed that this was still the case for some savages in his own day. Most of the sources of evidence regarding primitive peoples, however, admittedly presented magical and religious elements mingled together. Sometimes Frazer attributed this to a later gloss. For example, on the explanation in Genesis 32:32 as to why the Israelites 'eat not of the sinew which shrank, which is upon the hollow of the thigh', Frazer averred: 'On this theory the narrative in Genesis supplies a religious sanction for a

---

[12] Frazer, *Golden Bough*, 2nd ed., III, pp. 191, 197.
[13] Frazer, *Golden Bough*, 2nd ed., III, p. 198.
[14] Frazer, *Golden Bough*, 2nd ed., I, p. 75.

rule which was originally based on sympathetic magic alone'.[15] Like a Protestant Reformer insisting that the original gospel was *sola fide*, so Frazer's dogma regarding primitive culture was *sola arte magica*. The practical failure of this demarcation when it comes to observing the evidence must speak poorly of the perspicacity of the ancients rather than of his scheme: 'Vagueness and confusion are characteristic of primitive thought, and must always be allowed for in our attempts to resolve that strange compound into its elements'.[16] After all, his definitions made the clear separation of magic from religion self-evident, however much the actual data seems to blur it: 'For while the logical distinction between magic and religion is sharp as a knife-edge, there is no such acute and rigid line of cleavage between them historically'.[17]

In this stadial triad, religion is the odd one out. Religion is wrong in both theory and practice, while magic is right in theory but merely wrong in practice. It is worth quoting Frazer at length on this point:

> Wherever sympathetic magic occurs in its pure unadulterated form, it assumes that in nature one event follows another necessarily and invariably without the intervention of any spiritual or personal agency. Thus its fundamental conception is identical with that of modern science; underlying the whole system is a faith, implicit but real and firm, in the order and uniformity of nature... Thus the analogy between the magical and the scientific conceptions of the world is close. In both of them the succession of events is perfectly regular and certain, being determined by immutable laws, the operation of which can be foreseen and calculated precisely; the elements of caprice, of chance, and of accident are banished from the course of nature... Hence the strong attraction which magic and science alike have exercised on the human mind; hence the powerful stimulus that both have given to the pursuit of knowledge... The fatal flaw of magic lies not in its general assumption of a succession of events determined by law, but in its total misconception of the nature of the particular laws which govern that succession.[18]

Frazer, of course, personally held this same belief in entirely predictable outcomes from the perspective of the third stage of science. In a rare autobiographical reflection he credited being a student of the physicist Lord Kelvin (1824–1907) at the University of Glasgow for

---

[15] James George Frazer, *Folk-Lore in the Old Testament: Studies in Comparative Religion, Legend and Law*, 3 vols. (London: Macmillan, 1918), II, p. 424.

[16] Frazer, *Folk-Lore*, II, p. 407.   [17] Frazer, *Folk-Lore*, III, p. 163.

[18] Frazer, *Golden Bough*, 2nd ed., I, pp. 61–62.

imparting to him 'a conception of the physical universe as regulated by exact and absolutely unvarying laws of nature expressible in mathematical formulas. The conception has been a settled principle of my thought ever since'.[19]

Clifford Geertz, in that punchy collection, *Works and Lives: The Anthropologist as Author*, has taught us to attend to the literary strategies that anthropologists deploy in order to create certain effects.[20] A short excursus on how Frazer reinforces this claim regarding the shared theoretical basis of magic and science in the way that he writes about the practices of savages is therefore in order. First, Frazer repeatedly explains magical rites with scientific analogies. Here is a typical example: 'accordingly in these cases the oath, or whatever the ceremony may be, is purely magical in character. The man absorbs the valuable properties of the stone just as he might absorb electrical force from a battery; he is, so to say, petrified by the stone in the one case just as he is electrified by the electricity in the other'.[21] And again from a different publication:

> it was viewed as a measure of self-deference, a moral quarantine, a process of spiritual purification and disinfection, and exorcism. It was a mode of cleansing the people generally and sometimes the homicide himself from the ghostly infection, which to the primitive mind appears to be something material and tangible, something that can be literally washed or scoured away by water, pig's blood, sheep's blood, or other detergents.[22]

Or to take an example from *The Golden Bough* itself: 'These taboos act, so to say, as electrical insulators to preserve the spiritual force with which these persons are charged from suffering or inflicting harm by contact with the outer world'.[23] In fact, Frazer was so committed to the theoretical unity of his first and third stage that he could collapse his stadial scheme and casually leave indeterminate as a matter of indifference whether the category of magic or science was applicable: 'the flesh and ashes of the victim were believed to be

---

[19] James George Frazer, *Creation and Evolution in Primitive Cosmogonies, and other pieces* (London: Macmillan, 1935), p. 124.

[20] Clifford Geertz, *Works and Lives: The Anthropologist as Author* (Stanford: Stanford University Press, 1988).

[21] Frazer, *Folk-Lore*, II, p. 407.

[22] James George Frazer, *The Devil's Advocate, a Plea for Superstition*, 2nd ed., rev. and expanded (London: Macmillan, 1927), p. 151.

[23] Frazer, *Golden Bough*, 2nd ed., I, p. 343.

endowed with a magical or physical power of fertilising the land'.[24] He could even conflate them in a phrase such as 'the magic wand of science'.[25]

The truly pervasive way that Frazer wrote this viewpoint into the fabric of *The Golden Bough* was by routinely using words such as 'infallibly' when describing magical rites. He would do this in a bald, factual tone rather than indicate this is merely the assumption or claim of the people being studied. It would be tedious indeed to quote even a tithe of such passages, but here are six to evoke this consistent pattern of presentation (all from just the first half of the first volume of the second edition):

> Among the Lkungen Indians of Vancouver Island an infallible means of making your hair grow long is to rub it with fish oil and the pulverised fruit of a particular kind of poplar (*Populus trichocarpa*).

> The votary of the Muses thereupon takes his baton and moves it twice down the right side and twice down the left side of the boy's body, after which he gives the lad some of his breakfast. That is an infallible way of making the boy a beautiful singer.

> [T]he Wawamba wash the precious stone, anoint it with oil, and put it in a pot full of water. After that the rain cannot fail to come.

> Thrice the axe is swung, and thrice the impending blow is arrested at the entreaty of the intercessor. After that the frightened tree will certainly bear fruit next year.

> If in the shape of a bird or an insect it was caught in the snare the man would infallibly die.

> Then bury it in the middle of a path where your victim is sure to step over it, and he will unquestionably become distraught.[26]

It hardly needs to be stressed that not only does Frazer not have a very profound grasp of the meaning of magic for its practitioners, but that his account of the origins of magic is highly improbable. He assumes that it begins with a false line of reasoning by a savage philosopher (some attributes can be transferred by touch, ergo the strength of a stone can be imparted to a person). This erroneous inference is then resolutely and persistently believed to

---

[24] Frazer, *Golden Bough*, 2nd ed., II, p. 245.
[25] Frazer, *Golden Bough*, 2nd ed., III, p. 39.
[26] Frazer, *Golden Bough*, 2nd ed., I, pp. 40, 55, 109, 174, 278, 282.

be an infallible way to achieve certain outcomes. Frazer on at least one occasion seemed aware that this second step might appear an unlikely one. He observes in passing as a way of making it more probable that the desired result does eventually happen—the crops do return.[27] That answer, however, even given the concession of not being able to control the timing, only accounts for certain types of magical acts—numerous others are performed in an effort to produce results that are by no means going to happen sooner or later in any event (one thinks, for example, of rites of healing—or even, to take one of the passages cited, not every boy does become a beautiful singer). The move from magic to religion occurs, in Frazer's scheme, because a few particularly perceptive people finally notice that these rites are not infallible after all.

Frazer's own authorial voice has often been referred to as fundamentally ironic, so perhaps it would not be unfitting to round off this section on Frazer's stadial scheme with a couple of ironies. First, Frazer was so desperate to side with science and progress that he sometimes ended up rejecting both. Although he lived until 1941, he always repudiated the theories of Albert Einstein, whom he dismissed as 'cloudy and confused to the last degree'.[28] Indeed, the very passage from 1932 in which he reminisced that Lord Kelvin taught him to believe in invariable natural laws is a set up—not to a condemnation of religion—but rather of the new physics:

> The conception has been a settled principle in my thought ever since, and now in my old age I am not disposed to exchange it for that conception of the ultimate indeterminism of matter which appears to find favour with some modern physicists…[29]

In Frazer's authorized biography—published while he was still alive— R. Angus Downie speaks apparently without intended irony of Frazer's 'dogmatic' dismissal of Max Planck's quantum hypothesis.[30] While one of the few scientific fields of study that most lay people know of today is Chaos Theory (which already existed in Frazer's time), in the triumphal conclusion of the second edition of *The Golden Bough*, Frazer insisted that anyone who spoke of chaos was *ipso facto* being

[27] Frazer, *Golden Bough*, 2nd ed., II, p. 115.
[28] Ackerman, *J. G. Frazer*, p. 317.
[29] Frazer, *Creation and Evolution*, p. 124.
[30] R. Angus Downie, *James George Frazer: The Portrait of a Scholar* (London: Watts & Co., 1940), p. 107.

unscientific.[31] The second irony is like unto the first: Frazer described magical practices and beliefs with such alluring vividness that some of his readers found themselves drawn to them rather than repelled as he had intended. As Mary Beard has wryly observed, if one hopes to go out shopping and find a copy of *The Golden Bough,* your best bet is to go to an occult bookshop.[32] Perhaps it is not too mischievous also to observe that although Frazer longed to be viewed as a man of science, in the one photograph of him in his authorized biography he looks like nothing so much as a stage magician.[33]

* * *

Judeo-Christian traditions are everywhere and nowhere in *The Golden Bough.* They are everywhere because Frazer is continually translating savage ways into Jewish and Christian categories, but they are nowhere because he ostentatiously refuses to focus on what in the minds of his readers is the most familiar and resonant example of the practice he is discussing. To take the most extreme case, 'scapegoat' is an English word that was coined specifically when the Bible was translated to provide terminology for the account given in Leviticus chapter sixteen. Frazer uses it as a word to describe rituals from across the globe and the centuries. In the third edition, *The Scapegoat* is the name of an entire volume which is 453 pages long. A major chapter is devoted exclusively to classical antiquity and another to Mexico. The Jewish ritual for which the term was created, however, is confined to literally one sentence! Moreover, this solitary sentence is tacked on as the last one of a paragraph the opening of which is summarized in the margin as discussing 'dogs as scapegoats in India, Scotland, and America'. The sentence immediately before the lone one on the Day of Atonement is about the Iroquois![34] While Frazer's unconvincing theory on Christ's crucifixion was relegated to an appendix and a disclaimer about its improbability had been added, Frazer had nevertheless contemplated entitling this volume not 'the Scapegoat' but rather 'the Man of Sorrows' (Isaiah 53:3—a text applied to Jesus in Christian biblical interpretation), thus in an even less subtle way

---

[31] Frazer, *Golden Bough,* 2nd ed., III, p. 459.

[32] Mary Beard, 'Frazer, Leach, and Virgil: The Popularity (and Unpopularity) of *The Golden Bough',* *Comparative Studies in Society and History,* 34, 2 (April 1992), p. 223.

[33] Downie, *James George Frazer,* frontispiece.

[34] James George Frazer, *The Scapegoat* (Part VI of *The Golden Bough,* 3rd ed.) (London: Macmillan [1913] 1951), pp. 209–10.

inviting readers to keep Christological convictions in view throughout this tour of savage ways.[35]

Just a few more examples will suffice of his transposing tendency.
Functionaries are particularly apt to receive this treatment. The elders
of the Njamus in East Africa, for example, are described as compara-
ble to 'the Levites of Israel'.[36] And seemingly every culture has its own
pope. To wit, on the Grand Lama of Lhasa: 'the tragic figure of the
pope of Buddhism—God's vicar on earth for Asia—looms dim and
sad as the man-god who bore his people's sorrows, the Good Shepherd
who laid down his life for the sheep'.[37] Human origins and deluge narratives were routinely correlated with the Bible: Frazer would speak
of 'the Hottentot Adam' or 'Deucalion, the Greek Noah', and so on.[38]
Categories such as 'new birth', 'born again', 'baptism', 'christening',
'sacrament', 'unclean' (which he often used as a synonym for taboo),
and the like are regularly imported into other contexts. Frazer would
even inject entire phrases from Christian contexts to create striking
juxtapositions. To take just one such example, intentionally poking at
those from his own Scottish Calvinist background, he would describe
a ritual among the Wachaga tribe in East Africa as forming 'a solemn
league and covenant'.[39] Frazer's commitment to this rhetorical strat-
egy was such that it sometimes brought him into conflict with the
fieldworkers who provided him with his ethnographic information.
The Australian anthropologist Baldwin Spencer, for example, wanted
to use a range of indigenous terms in his own monograph precisely
because he understood that using a word loaded with connotations
from another cultural context would be more likely to distort than
to aid understanding, but Frazer asked him to reconsider on the
grounds that it was an off-putting approach.[40] The fact that Frazer's
interest was more than merely avoiding being opaque and pedantic
is revealed in another exchange with Spencer a year later. Frazer had
transposed Spencer's account of the non-estrangement of the totem

---

[35] Wheeler-Barclay, *Science of Religion*, p. 205. Even Frazer's disciple Downie, who
was himself a religious sceptic, emphasized that Frazer's theory about Christ's crucifixion must be rejected as it has insurmountable internal difficulties: R. Agnus Downie,
Frazer and The Golden Bough (London: Victor Gollancz, 1970), p. 53.

[36] Frazer, *Folk-Lore*, II, p. 17.

[37] Frazer, *Golden Bough*, 2nd ed., III, p. 117.

[38] Frazer, *Folk-Lore*, II, p. 467; Frazer, *Creation and Evolution*, p. 5.

[39] Frazer, *Folk-Lore*, III, p. 396.

[40] J. G. Frazer to Baldwin Spencer, 13 July 1898: Ackerman, *Selected Letters*, p. 119.

into the resonant category for Christians of 'reconciliation'—arguing against Spencer's initial protest about this change that these were exactly equivalent. Moreover, Frazer was irritated when Spencer held his ground rather than giving way. Here is Spencer's plea:

> the only thing is that in Australia we have no ceremony which seems to suggest that the idea of 'reconciliation' is ever present in the man's mind…'Reconciliation' seems to me to stand in the relationship to 'non-estrangement' that 'cure' does to 'prevention'. From what I know of the Australian native I feel sure that the idea of 'reconciliation', which is so clearly seen among other savages, is never present in his mind.[41]

While Frazer was ostensibly engaging in these transpositions in order to make savage practices more familiar and understandable, his covert intention was in all likelihood the reverse: to make familiar religious practices that his readers had always accepted as understandable come to appear strange and savage.

Let us now return to Frazer's interpersonal relationships. (Frazer himself taught that before examining the work 'it may be well to look a little closer at the life and character of the writer, since these are always the determining factors in the composition of a book'.)[42] The dynamic between the Fellow of Trinity College and the anthropologist Andrew Lang has some parallels with that between him and E. B. Tylor. For years Frazer considered Lang both a personal friend and a co-labourer in the new discipline, working cooperatively and harmoniously along the same lines. Lang, however, thought the second edition of *The Golden Bough* was wrongheaded, and set out to expose its errors with great zeal and industry in a series of publications. Lang's mockery of the way that *The Golden Bough* relentlessly reduced the meaning of myths to agricultural statements was so delicious as to be oft-repeated: 'The solar mythologists did not share heroes like Achilles; they, too, were the sun. But the vegetable school, the Covent Garden school of mythologists, mixes up real human being with vegetation'.[43] Frazer was so churned up by Lang's attacks that, although

---

[41] Baldwin Spencer to J. G. Frazer, 10 July 1899: R. R. Marett and T. K. Penniman (eds.), *Spencer's Scientific Correspondence with Sir J. G. Frazer and Others* (Oxford: Clarendon Press, 1932), pp. 53–54.

[42] Frazer, *Creation and Evolution*, p. 86.

[43] Andrew Lang, *Magic and Religion* (London: Longmans, Green, and Co., 1901), p. 206.

a workaholic, he was unable to settle down to his tasks for several months.[44] Quite naturally, Frazer thereafter becomes snide about Lang in private comments to friends.[45] (It is also delightful to learn that flaming long predates the age of the internet: 'Lang has flamed out against me in the Fortnightly for June, but I only glanced at the article'.)[46] On the other hand, Frazer never criticized Lang in public or even attempted explicitly to reply to his critiques of his work. The preface to *Spirits of the Corn and of the Wild* (1912) (Part V of the third edition of *The Golden Bough*) is written in a defensive manner with Lang's barbs clearly providing the background explanation for these comments, but Lang himself is never cited or mentioned.[47] Likewise, Lang had demolished Frazer's theory on the crucifixion of Christ so effectively that Frazer admitted privately that he would probably need to remove it altogether, but when he did eventually relegate it to an appendix the closest he comes to acknowledging Lang's counter-arguments and evidence is to observe in a disclaimer footnote that his hypothesis 'has not been confirmed by subsequent research', without revealing to the uninformed reader where this new work might be found.[48] In a strong parallel with Tylor, Frazer went out of his way on Lang's death to make it known that he wished to be included in any plans to produce a volume in his honour, even going so far as to claim that he wanted to offer a more 'generous' and 'sympathetic' tribute than what had been contained in the official obituary.[49] In short, his

[44] Ackerman is sceptical about this claim (Ackerman, *J. G. Frazer*, pp. 171–74), but it is supported by two independent sources, not only Bronislaw Malinowski, but even Frazer's official biographer, a man who was such a disciple of the Master that he named his daughter Frazer (R. Angus Downie, *Frazer and The Golden Bough* [London: Victor Gollancz, 1970], p. 54). Moreover, Ackerman's defence includes the speculation that Frazer never read Lang's *Magic and Religion*. This in itself, however, would be a sign that Frazer felt emotionally unable to cope with this criticism. Frazer frequently claimed that his theories were provisional and that he welcomed criticisms that would help to improve his work so the fact that he stopped his ears against reasoned arguments for alterations (Frazer himself admitted that he refused to read Lang's later works) indicates that his personal feelings were undercutting his scholarly ideals in this case.

[45] See, for example, J. G. Frazer to E. Sidney Hartland, 18 March 1901: Ackerman, *Selected Letters*, p. 178.

[46] J. G. Frazer to A. W. Howitt, 24 July 1899: Ackerman, *Selected Letters*, p. 151.

[47] James George Frazer, *Spirits of the Corn and of the Wild* (Part V of the 3rd ed. of *The Golden Bough*), 2 vols. (London: Macmillan and Co. [1912] 1951).

[48] Frazer, *Scapegoat*, p. 412.

[49] Ackerman, *J. G. Frazer*, p. 175. (No such volume was ever organized, however.)

relationship with Lang is a prime illustration of Frazer's constitutional incapability of engaging in open conflict.

Frazer's relationship with William Robertson Smith, on the other hand, was one of wholehearted respect, admiration, and friendship. When Frazer spoke of Robertson Smith, the genuineness of his deep, unclouded affection for Smith is unmistakable. When Frazer referred to him in print as 'my revered master and friend' this was no mask for mixed emotions.[50] By inviting him to write the entries on 'Taboo' and 'Totemism' for the *Encyclopaedia Britannica*, Robertson Smith was the one who redirected Frazer's research life into anthropology. Frazer found Robertson Smith's own writings and conversation seminal and profound. One token of this personal and intellectual debt is that Frazer dedicated *The Golden Bough* 'To My Friend William Robertson Smith in Gratitude and Admiration'. And yet, and yet… When Frazer was asked after Robertson Smith's death to reminisce about him, he began by telling the story of their first substantial conversation. Frazer recalled hazarding an opinion on a subject only to have Robertson Smith demolish it: 'I never afterwards, so far as I remember, attempted to dispute the mastership'.[51] As Frazer's own point was that this encounter set the tone for their relationship, it is not unwarranted to agree that it expresses a key to the whole: Frazer navigated their differences of opinion by avoiding them. In the same document, Frazer observes: 'I confess I never understood his inmost views of religion…I never even approached, far less discussed, the subject with him'. Frazer understood perfectly well that Robertson Smith was not only an ordained minister in the Free Church of Scotland but also a sincere and devout Christian: what he apparently means is that he never understood how Robertson Smith could believe such things, but he never dared to bring their differences on the matter of religion out in the open to be examined and debated.

Moreover, after Robertson Smith's death in 1894, Frazer began constructing an imaginary view of his friend that minimized or removed their incompatible beliefs. This process began literally as soon as he was dead. In Frazer's obituary tribute to Robertson Smith not only did he leave the deceased's Christian identity so completely out of view that the uninformed reader could wonder if he had been an atheist

---

[50] Frazer, *Folk-Lore*, I, p. viii.

[51] J. G. Frazer to John F. White, 15 December 1897: Ackerman, *Selected Letters*, p. 102.

(this for a Christian minister!), but he even explained Robertson Smith's anthropological ideas in a way that suggested that their logical import was a rejection of any religious faith. Robert Ackerman has observed: 'That Frazer was able to turn the occasion of the death of his best friend to polemic purposes is, in emotional terms, extraordinary'.[52] The continuation of this process can be seen in an exchange in 1911 with Oxford anthropologist R. R. Marett. Frazer wrote to Marett telling him that he was mistaken in a claim he had made about Robertson Smith's views on the primacy of ritual over dogma, basing this judgement on the strength of 'intimate personal acquaintance as well as from a study of his writings'.[53] Marett simply provided the relevant citations from Robertson Smith's *Lectures on the Religion of the Semites*, thereby exposing the extent to which Frazer tended to excise mentally from his friend's works those pages which expressed views at variance with his own. A chastened Frazer was forced to reply: 'The passages of Robertson Smith to which you call my attention certainly support your interpretation of his view more fully than I had supposed'.[54] Frazer then more or less asserted that nevertheless if Robertson Smith was alive to weigh the arguments that the two of them had been advancing in this exchange, he would side with the author of *The Golden Bough*. Even in the closest friendship of Frazer's life one can therefore still discern a propensity to handle differences in a surreptitious or self-deceiving rather than forthright manner.

These relational patterns provide a context for evaluating Frazer's attitude toward his father and mother, Daniel and Katherine. His stereotypical habit was to refer to them as 'my dear and honoured parents'.[55] The fact that he relied upon this one trite, stock, unvaried phrase arouses suspicion. A key to Frazer's success as an author was his ability to paint a full and vivid scene with evocative details. He often did this gratuitously.[56] He was deeply gratified if he could describe something with such verisimilitude that readers erroneously assumed he must be writing as an eyewitness who had personally

[52] Ackerman, *J. G. Frazer*, p. 83.

[53] J. G. Frazer to R. R. Marett, 11 May 1911: Ackerman, *Selected Letters*, p. 307.

[54] J. G. Frazer to R. R. Marett, 17 May 1911: Ackerman, *Selected Letters*, p. 311.

[55] Frazer, *Creation and Evolution*, p. 117 (from a 1932 speech) and p. 131 (a separate article); J. G. Frazer to Edward Lyttelton, 19 June 1927: Ackerman, *Selected Letters*, p. 405.

[56] For an example of Frazer himself conceding that the scene he has painted is irrelevant to expounding his subject in hand, see Frazer, *Folk-Lore*, II, p. 520.

inspected the site of the drama.[57] It is therefore telling that after read-ing an entire article by Frazer entitled 'Memories of My Parents' one is still left with a blank impression.[58] By far what he most emphasizes is their religious convictions and pious habits as members of the Free Church of Scotland. It is worth quoting this part of the account at length, which begins with his father before turning to his mother:

> In religion he was a simple and devout Christian of unquestioning orthodoxy, who accepted the Bible in its literal sense as the inspired and infallible Word of God. In ecclesiastical matters he was a staunch Presbyterian and Free Churchman, with a large circle of clerical friends who were always welcome visitors to his house. In our household family worship formed part of the daily routine...The Sabbath was observed by us with the usual restrictions traditional in Scottish households. We never walked out of the house or the garden except to go to Church twice a day in the morning and afternoon...In the evening we children sang hymns at our mother's knee...Later in the evening our father read to us a good or edifying book....We learned the Shorter Catechism by heart, and accepted its teaching without question as the standard of orthodoxy...In religion she shared my father's child-like faith; on that sacred subject I cannot think that the shadow of doubt ever dimmed the clear surface of her mind or troubled her serene confidence in the merits of her Saviour.[59]

Suspecting that this might be over-read, Frazer also tries to com-municate that his parents did not approach faith fanatically or cre-ate a religious atmosphere that was oppressive. Beyond that, virtually everything he says is blandly factual in a who's who entry or amateur genealogical society sort of way. We learn that his father's distinctions included being a Justice of the Peace and a member of the Council of the Pharmaceutical Society, that his paternal uncle was a master printer, that his mother's family was grand enough to be associated with the estates of Daldowie, Langside, and Lanfine, and so on. Even these accounts of ancestors and relations are preoccupied with reli-gious matters, especially that an array of men on both sides of the family had been Christian ministers, but also an aunt who 'fell into a religious melancholy' and an uncle who had worked out to his own

---

[57] Downie, *Frazer and The Golden Bough*, pp. 75, 102–103.

[58] The article is published in Frazer, *Creation and Evolution*, pp. 131–51. This observation has also been made by others see, for example, Wheeler-Barclay, *Science of Religion*, p. 183.

[59] Frazer, *Creation and Evolution*, pp. 132–33.

satisfaction that a passage in the Old Testament prophesied the invention of steamboats.[60] There is not, however, a single detail about his
father that brings him alive as an individual or convinces the reader
that Frazer possessed genuine affection for him. The same is more or
less true of his mother. The only possible exception is this: 'she told
me that whenever she heard military music she felt moved to rush out
and plunge into the fray!'[61] That bolting heart of a would-be warrior is
the one glimpse we get of a real human being.

There are clues that Frazer, even as an adult, was unable to acknowledge to his parents that he had shed a Christian identity. We know
that his father did not allow him to go to Oxford for fear that he would
become High Church, from which we can generalize that the head
of the family was particularly anxious that Frazer maintain in his
manhood the faith that he had inherited from his parents as a child.
Ackerman credibly infers from the existing evidence that Frazer had
already traded Christianity for scepticism while still at the University
of Glasgow.[62] Obviously, the son had concealed this from his father
who otherwise would have realized that he had bigger issues to worry
about than the romance of Anglo-Catholicism. When Frazer became
a Cambridge student he would dutifully write home to his mother
an account of the sermon he heard during Sunday morning worship.
This strongly indicates that a pattern of deception continued—and
it is suggestive that Frazer's letters to his parents were deliberately
destroyed when they died.[63] Daniel Frazer lived into 1900, but we are
told that although James Frazer's writings had a sceptical drift 'his
father, enfeebled by age, had no longer the power to discern their
conclusions'.[64] Whether or not the details in that statement are literally true, its import is that Frazer managed to be a religious sceptic
for more than a quarter of a century without ever clearly confessing
his change of views to his devout parents. It is probable that having
become so used to behaving in this way Frazer continued it to a lesser
extent even after his parents' deaths: disguising his true identity, as it
were, to shield himself from the unwanted attentions of the ghost of

---

[60] Frazer, *Creation and Evolution*, pp. 138, 140.
[61] Frazer, *Creation and Evolution*, p. 141.
[62] Ackerman, *Selected Letters*, p. 18.
[63] Downie, *Frazer and The Golden Bough*, p. 21.
[64] Downie, *James George Frazer*, p. 7.

his father. One might object that his disguise was not very thorough, but ghosts are notoriously dim-witted about such matters.

* * *

As an adult, one of Frazer's best friends was the man of letters, Edmund Gosse (1849–1928). They had parallel lives to a certain extent as Gosse had also been raised in a home dominated by conservative Protestant beliefs and practices and had grown to despise his birthright. In *Father and Son* (1907), Gosse offered a damning portrait of his father as a religious fanatic who tried to smother him with faith, as well as an account of his own heroic and ultimately triumphant struggle to break free.[65] Philip Gosse is still one of the most widely ridiculed Victorian religious thinkers to this day for his risible attempt to square modern science with his literal interpretation of the book of Genesis by suggesting that the Almighty created the world complete with faux fossils. *Father and Son* is a minor classic and it is patent that it derives its emotional and therefore literary power from Edmund Gosse's unabated resentment of his deceased father. To preserve a fig leaf of Edwardian propriety, in an epilogue, Gosse made the absurd and disingenuous assertion that the value of his book 'consists in what light it may contrive to throw upon the unique and noble figure of the Father'.[66] James George Frazer is the only reader of *Father and Son* who has ever taken this little piece of cant at face value. Upon completing the volume, Frazer wrote to his friend: 'The portrait of your father which you have drawn is deeply interesting. One would like to know more of him. Has any memoir of him been published? If not, would you not give us one? He must have been a very high-minded man. His double devotion to science and religion was wonderful'.[67] This reaction is dumbfounding—not least because Frazer had made a career of discerning unpleasant realities beneath the smoothed-over surface of texts. Did his own unexamined, conflicted relationship with his father mean that he simply would not allow himself to see that the father in this portrait is meant to be loathed rather than admired? Or was pretending not to notice the animosity beneath the formal tribute, in Frazer's view, the best

[65] Edmund Gosse, *Father and Son* (London: Penguin [1907] 1983).
[66] Gosse, *Father and Son*, p. 236.
[67] J. G. Frazer to Edmund Gosse, 10 November 1909: Ackerman, *Selected Letters*, p. 294.

possible response—a way of reassuring himself as well as his friend that the double game could be played successfully?

It is worth gathering up here a few curious details about the rest of Frazer's family. All sources find the most important thing to say about Frazer's only brother Samuel is that he had a drink problem—this reality, of course, could well have no bearing on this discussion, but there is a possible connection as a painful childhood is a not-infrequent correlation with alcohol abuse. As to his two sisters, Isabella and Christina, Frazer might have been passing for a Christian with them as well. He would sometimes visit Isabella and her family over the Easter holiday and it would be in keeping with his behaviour elsewhere to assume that he was outwardly falling into line with a life of worship at this high point in the Christian calendar rather than that he was openly questioning the foundations of these cherished beliefs, let alone recusing himself. Christina died a spinster, but in 'Memories of My Parents' Frazer claimed of Isabella that her husband was 'my good friend and trusted brother-in-law' and that the couple had 'two good and dutiful daughters'.[68] Once again, this publicly conferred honour seems to shroud more mixed emotions. Downie reported on Lady Frazer's explanation as to why their wills were written so as to leave everything to Trinity College: 'The object of doing so, she explained to me quite openly, was to ensure that neither her family nor Sir James's should benefit in any way'.[69] The wording of this is revealing. It is not merely that Frazer was not close to his family and therefore he felt no impulse to make them beneficiaries: his good and dutiful nieces are keenly present in the couple's minds, indeed, the existence of these nieces is somehow the underlying motivating factor by way of repulsion.

These relational and personal dynamics shed light on why the second edition of *The Golden Bough* was noticeably more anti-Christian than the first. Frazer thought that even the first edition ought to undermine the possibility of faith for those who had the wit to follow its drift. He explained to George Macmillan, whom he hoped would agree to publish it, in 1889: 'The resemblance of many of the savage customs and ideas to the fundamental doctrines of Christianity is striking. But I make no reference to this parallelism, leaving my readers to draw

---

[68] Frazer, *Creation and Evolution*, p. 149.
[69] Downie, *Frazer and The Golden Bough*, pp. 123–24.

their own conclusions, one way or the other'.[70] Macmillan sent the manuscript to the agnostic John Morley for review, and he was in no doubt as to which direction the conclusion lay:

> He has (very wisely) been very careful to keep clear of any direct reference to the Christian mysteries of Atonement, Sacrifice, the Sacrament of Bread and Wine—but any reader with his eyes open will often be startled—almost painfully startled—by seeing before him the origins of these sacred things laid bare.[71]

Nevertheless, Frazer had maintained plausible deniability. The second edition was bolder in notable ways. First, as already mentioned, Frazer added the theory about Purim and Christ's crucifixion. Second, he added the three-stage scheme which made religion a misguided departure from belief in fixed, natural laws. This progression also reinforced the notion of a zero-sum struggle between religion and science: they are not two complementary facets of human insight and experience but rather competing explanatory views. Religion is wrong and science is right and therefore destined to replace it. The preface to the second edition even evokes military metaphors, thus all the more clearly situating *The Golden Bough* in the polemical warfare model of the relationship between faith and science.[72] Frazer observes of the comparative method:

> Well handled, it may become a powerful instrument to expedite progress if it lays bare certain weak spots in the foundations on which modern society is built—if it shows that much which we are wont to regard as solid rests on the sands of superstition rather than the rock of nature. It is indeed a melancholy and in some respects thankless task to strike at the foundations of beliefs in which, as in a strong tower, the hopes and aspirations of humanity through long ages have sought a refuge from the storm and stress of life. Yet sooner or later it is inevitable that the battery of the comparative method should breach these venerable walls... At present we are only dragging the guns into position: they have hardly yet begun to speak.[73]

---

[70] J. G. Frazer to George A. Macmillan, 8 November 1889: Ackerman, *Selected Letters*, p. 63.

[71] Ackerman, *J. G. Frazer*, p. 96.

[72] The warfare model had been championed in John William Draper, *History of the Conflict between Religion and Science* (New York: D. Appleton, 1874). Between the first and second editions of *The Golden Bough* an influential book had brought this way of thinking to the fore and increased its popularity: Andrew Dickson White, *A History of the Warfare of Science and Theology in Christendom* (New York: D. Appleton, 1896).

[73] Frazer, *Golden Bough*, 2nd ed., I, pp. xxi-xxii.

A major change that occurred between the first and second editions was the death in 1894 of William Robertson Smith. Frazer no longer had to concern himself with either the possibility that the Master might find his work insulting or the intimidating prospect of having Robertson Smith vanquish him in a dispute about these provocative ideas. Likewise, Frazer's mother died in 1899. Frazer had spent much of the 1890s working on *Pausanias*, a multi-volume effort in classical studies that was reassuringly innocuous. This was the kind of work he could bring home to mother: Frazer's *Pausanias* volumes, he tells us with satisfaction, 'may have been the last object on which her eyes rested at death'.[74] Daniel Frazer died on 10 January 1900.[75] Thus Frazer could increase the anti-religious tone and content of *The Golden Bough* for the second edition, safe in the knowledge that neither mentor nor mother nor father would ever read it or hear about it.

It is also possible that Frazer made stronger the critique of religion because he was disappointed that more readers had not come to anti-Christian conclusions themselves after reading the first edition. This would also fit a pattern. From a variety of clues, one can posit the possibility that Frazer was annoyed both when people accused him of intentionally seeking to undermine faith and when his intentions to undermine faith were not fulfilled. Perhaps his left hand did not always know what his right hand was doing. In 1901, by which time some reviews of the second edition had expressed indignation at his theory regarding Christ's crucifixion, Frazer was all startled innocence: 'Yet I was at some pains to put it in a form which should not give offence, and rashly flattered myself that I had succeeded, but the event has proved that I was wrong'.[76] Frazer must have been easily self-flattered (and self-deceived) as he had himself predicted this very outcome a couple months prior to its publication: 'There are things in it which are likely to give offence both to Jews and Christians, but especially, I think, to Christians. You see I am neither the one nor the other, and don't mind knocking them both impartially. But they will hardly thank me for it'.[77]

---

[74] Frazer, *Creation and Evolution*, p. 142.

[75] *Pharmaceutical Journal*, 20 January 1900, p. 61. Downie, on the other hand, rejected the theory that the death of Frazer's parents helps to explain the more anti-religious stance of the second edition: Downie, *Frazer and The Golden Bough*, p. 53.

[76] J. G. Frazer to Lorimer Fison, 14 July 1901: Ackerman, *Selected Letters*, p. 195.

[77] J. G. Frazer to Solomon Schechter, 22 September 1900: Ackerman, *Selected Letters*, p. 162.

Another part of the pattern is Frazer's frequent boast that he never engaged in controversy.[78] On one level, this claim is patently untenable. Frazer's writings were intended to advance contentious arguments in a range of emotive and contested subject areas. He was quite willing to play the provocateur and to attempt to refute the beliefs and theories of others in print. What he meant was that he never let himself be held accountable for these efforts by condescending to offer a reply to any substantive criticisms of his arguments. When someone wrote a book or article exposing a flaw in his handling of his sources or his theoretical scheme he would simply ignore it on the grounds that to take it into consideration would be to demean oneself by engaging in controversy! The most he would ever bend to such criticism would be to admit in a future edition or a subsequent publication on the same theme that his theory had been shown to be unlikely—while still continuing to include it nonetheless. This strange doubleness is a feature of Frazer's work: he doggedly persists in presenting a theory, but a disclaimer is added to the effect that the author is not so obstinate as to continue to defend it now that it has been so thoroughly called into question. Frazer praised his favourite English poet, William Cowper (1731–1800), for magisterially ignoring all critiques of his writings: 'He could afford to disregard them and to bide his time. *His* works will last with the English language: *their* criticisms have long been forgotten.'[79] While that might be a wise and dignified approach for an artist or literary author sometimes to take, Frazer purported to be undertaking scientific activity. One way to distinguish science from magic or religion might be that it is an on going process of trial and error, experimentation and evaluation, falsification and revision, in which corrections in the light of the criticisms and work of others is an essential part of the process. Still, Frazer's abstention from what he deemed to be the unpleasant possibility of being an active participant in a controversy accords well with his temperament. It is another example of his tendency to avoid an open dispute and of his desire to nudge people's thinking in a certain direction without

---

[78] To take an extreme example, he reiterated this stance in two letters to E. Sidney Hartland that were written within a couple days of each other: J. G. Frazer to E. Sidney Hartland, 27 March 1901 and 30 March 1901: Ackerman, *Selected Letters*, pp. 183–84.

[79] J. G. Frazer, *Letters of William Cowper*, 2 vols. (Freeport, NY: Books for Libraries Press [1912] 1969), I, p. lxxi.

being so explicit as to commit himself unequivocally regarding his own personal convictions.

* * *

Frazer's *Passages of the Bible chosen for their literary beauty and interest* was first published in 1895.[80] Ackerman observes that this project came out of the blue just four months after Robertson Smith's death and therefore views it as an expression of Frazer's grief for his friend.[81] The loss of Robertson Smith is certainly the right explanation for the timing, but it is possible to tease out additional reasons beside a state of mourning that trace connections between the death and the book. Frazer had been steeped in the Bible from childhood and his subsequent work makes readily apparent that he felt a deep urge to work through his relationship to this uniquely influential book.[82] He was itching to take it on. Robertson Smith, however, was a leading biblical scholar—as Frazer did not dare debate with him on any substantive issue, he would certainly not have wished to challenge Robertson Smith on his home terrain. Frazer, by contrast, did not even know Hebrew. Robertson Smith's death meant that Frazer could now write about the Bible without fear of having his views challenged by the Master. The theme of literary beauty also evaded other difficulties. It created an angle that allowed Frazer to write about the text even without being equipped to understand it in the original language: this linguistic incompetence effectively disqualified him from examining anything other than the literary merits of the English Bible if he wished to maintain his academic credibility. A literary focus also allowed Frazer to play his double game. Officially, the purpose of the volume was to admire the greatness of the Bible. The preface swelled to an effusive conclusion: 'it is noble literature; and like all noble literature it is fitted to delight, to elevate, and to console'.[83] Under this honorific cover, Frazer began to explore how ethnographic data could serve to destabilize scriptural authority. That his purposes are not confined to those announced in the title and preface is apparent in

---

[80] J. G. Frazer, *Passages of the Bible chosen for their literary beauty and interest* (London: Adam and Charles Black, 1895).

[81] Ackerman, *J. G. Frazer*, p. 119.

[82] For the dominant influence of the Bible in the British culture of Frazer's childhood, see Timothy Larsen, *A People of One Book: The Bible and the Victorians* (Oxford: Oxford University Press, 2011).

[83] Frazer, *Passages*, p. viii.

the forty-five pages of scholarly apparatus that he included. The very first note begins:

> The Biblical account of the creation of man agrees remarkably with some even more detailed accounts of the same event which have been handed down among rude peoples in various parts of the world. It may be not uninstructive to compare a few of these accounts with the Biblical narrative. Thus, for example, the Maoris say that Tiki made man after his own image...[84]

And so he continues on his Cook's world tour, stopping at Tahiti, the Pelew Islands, the Bank Islands, Borneo, southeastern India, Assam, Australia, Alaska, and Greece—all in the first endnote which is in turn attached to his very first text. What is striking is that this note—and many others like it which follow—is completely irrelevant to grasping the literary excellence of the text. Clearly Frazer hoped that readers would come away from *Passages from the Bible* with thoughts on other matters beside the artistic nobility of certain sections of scripture.

The desire to take on the scriptures continued to rumble along inside him for years. Almost a full decade after *Passages from the Bible*, Frazer decided to take the necessary plunge to do the thing properly and began to learn Hebrew. Half a century old, he nevertheless pursued this new task with tremendous dedication resulting in a marked measure of success. He was initially tutored by the Regius Professor of Hebrew at the University of Cambridge, the Revd Robert H. Kennett (1864–1932).[85] Frazer never attempted to learn any indigenous language of a savage culture in order to pursue his anthropological theories more effectively: the fact that he dedicated himself to learning the language of the Old Testament speaks to how much a priority grappling with the Bible had become for him. The first fruit of this labour arrived in 1907 as Frazer's contribution to Tylor's festschrift: 'Folk-Lore in the Old Testament'.[86] (As this essay was incorporated into Frazer's massive work of the same name, there is no need to explore its contents separately.) In 1909, appeared a second expanded edition of *Passages from the Bible*. Frazer opened the preface to this new edition by triumphantly reporting that he could now read the text in the original Hebrew.[87]

---

[84] Frazer, *Passages*, p. 419.   [85] Ackerman, *J. G. Frazer*, p. 183.

[86] J. G. Frazer, 'Folk-Lore in the Old Testament', in Thomas, *Anthropological Essays*, pp. 101–74.

[87] J. G. Frazer, *Passages of the Bible chosen for their literary beauty and interest*, 2nd ed. (London: Adam and Charles Black [1909] 1927), p. ix.

James Frazer spent the Great War studying the Good Book. Just after the armistice was signed in November 1918, *Folk-Lore in the Old Testament* came off the presses.[88] It was 1,706 pages long, spread over three volumes. In this work, Frazer's aim was to expose the savage beneath the sacred. Each chapter is devoted to a particular text: it is therefore a series of discrete treatments which are as long or as short as his material, insight, or fancy dictated. For example, some of the chapters such as 'The Waters of Meribath' and 'The Judgement of Solomon' do not even fill two pages, while 'Jacob's Marriage' might have been printed as a free-standing book, running as it does to 278 pages. Each of the texts were chosen because something in them caught Frazer's anthropological eye. By using the comparative method, he would then typically attempt to reveal some older reality that lay mostly hidden under a more recent gloss. For example, while the biblical text presents the mark of Cain as a divine warning to other people that it is not permissible to kill him, Frazer deduces that it was actually a disguise intended to hide Cain from the ghost of his dead brother.[89] Or again, Frazer gathers up various references to events happening near oak or terebinth trees in Old Testament narratives. With the support of comparative material, he then postulates that the original form of these stories included the worship of tree gods, but that these details were later airbrushed out in deference to the disapproval of such practices by the prophets.[90] One of the curious effects of Frazer's approach is to make it appear that there is absolutely nothing original or distinctive in Hebrew culture: everything is seemingly shared with others or borrowed from elsewhere. The quality of the chapters varies enormously, ranging from presenting clearly helpful information for understanding the cultural context of a text to unconvincing and strained speculative leaps to magpie material that has no obvious point whatever.

Once again, Frazer's implicit goal seems to be the inverse of his explicit one: while he is ostensibly taking incomprehensible parts of scripture and making them explicable, his actual aim would seem to be to make familiar and trusted parts of scripture suddenly appear alien and other. This suspicion is reinforced by the tone that Frazer frequently strikes. There are times when his voice approximates

---

[88] Frazer, *Folk-Lore*. As with *The Golden Bough*, the abridged edition of *Folk-Lore in the Old Testament* became a bestseller.

[89] Frazer, *Folk-Lore*, I, pp. 78–103. [90] Frazer, *Folk-Lore*, III, pp. 30–61.

the scoffing or denunciatory strains of figures such as Mark Twain or T. H. Huxley or the leader of organized atheism in late Victorian Britain, Charles Bradlaugh. As to the latter, Britain's Iconoclast wrote a series of 'new lives' which were character assassinations of biblical heroes.[91] This passage from Frazer would have fit in that series well as a *New Life of Samuel*:

> Dissatisfied with the rule of pontiffs who professed to govern them in the name and under the direct guidance of the deity, the people had clamoured for a civil king, and the last of the pontiffs, the prophet Samuel, had reluctantly yielded to their importunity and anointed Saul king of Israel. The revolution thus effected was such as might have taken place in the Papal States, if ever the inhabitants, weary of ecclesiastical oppression and misgovernment, had risen against the Popes, and compelled the reigning pontiff, while he still clutched the heavenly keys, to resign the earthly sceptre into the hands of a secular monarch. A shrewd man of affairs as well as an ecclesiastic of the most rigid type, Samuel had dexterously contrived not only to appoint but to nominate the new king on whom the hopes of Israel now centred.[92]

As for the Twain twang, this is from the chapter on the Fall: 'Having relieved his feelings by these copious maledictions, the irascible but really kind-hearted deity relented so far as to make coats of skins for the culprits.'[93] Here is Frazer on the shared colour of both flesh and clay, out of which human beings were made in the Genesis account: 'So remarkably does nature itself bear witness to the literal accuracy of Holy Writ'.[94] Or on the census:

> From two well-known narratives in the Book of Samuel and Chronicles we learn that at one period of his career Jehovah cherished a singular antipathy to the taking of a census, which he appears to have regarded as a crime of even deeper dye than boiling milk or jumping a threshold...every man paid half a shekel...On receipt of that moderate fee the deity was apparently assumed to waive the scruples he felt at the sin of a census.[95]

---

[91] For Charles Bradlaugh on the Bible, see Timothy Larsen, *Contested Christianity: The Political and Social Contexts of Victorian Theology* (Waco: Baylor University Press, 2004), pp. 97–112; Timothy Larsen, *A People of One Book: The Bible and the Victorians* (Oxford: Oxford University Press, 2011), pp. 67–88.

[92] Frazer, *Folk-Lore*, II, p. 517.   [93] Frazer, *Folk-Lore*, I, p. 46.

[94] Frazer, *Folk-Lore*, I, p. 29.

[95] Frazer, *Folk-Lore*, II, pp. 555, 563. (Frazer's discussion of the sin of the census seems almost wilfully obtuse. Committed to finding a strange superstition, he does not even consider the possibility that the purpose of the prohibition might have been

One could go on and on quoting such examples. Frazer's friend Edward Clodd (1840–1930), who was a public, forthright advocate of rationalism and opponent of religion, expressed his delight at Frazer's piety-puncturing prose. In response, Frazer was all innocent abroad: 'As to my irony, now that you have called my attention to it, I think there is perhaps more of it in the book than I had suspected…I can imagine you chortling over the passages, which other readers, less endowed with a sense of humour, might peruse with perfect gravity'.[96] It is almost as if Frazer would have preferred his friend to have written a letter like the one he himself had written to Gosse—what a deeply interesting study you have done, how wonderful a book the Bible is—and thereby display such good manners as to go along with the official version of the book's purpose. Indeed, the author of *Father and Son* was able to repay in kind. In his review of *Folk-Lore in the Old Testament*, Gosse claimed to have discovered in his careful reading of these three volumes that Frazer's goal was to distinguish the savage elements from 'the imperishable monument of spiritual religion' and that his 'attitude is reverent and pious in the highest degree'.[97]

More substantively, Frazer, in *Folk-Lore in the Old Testament* and elsewhere, could not refrain from making pronouncements about what he viewed to be the theological implications of his findings, despite it not being part of his stated brief (and indeed he would explicitly say that he was not addressing such matters). For example, the Fellow of Trinity College made the plausible claim that the Hebrew account of the Deluge was based on an earlier Babylonian narrative. He then irrelevantly insisted that this provenance is incompatible with any possible formulation of a doctrine of biblical inspiration: 'Dismissing, therefore, the theory of revelation or inspiration as irreconcilable with the known facts…'.[98] Surely it was for Christian believers to decide what the implications of these findings may or may

---

to guard against hubris or complacency. He even draws in as parallel taboos sayings about not counting chickens before they are hatched in this same determinedly esoteric manner.)

[96] Frazer Papers, Trinity College, Cambridge, Add. Ms. b. 35., J. G. Frazer to Edward Clodd, No. 1 Brick Court, Temple, 21 December 1918. (I am grateful to the Master and Fellows of Trinity College, Cambridge, for permission to quote from the letters in this collection.)

[97] This review in the *Sunday Times* was reprinted in Edmund Gosse, *Books on the Table* (New York: Charles Scribner's, 1921), pp. 91–93.

[98] Frazer, *Folk-Lore*, I, p. 334.

not have been for doctrine—such a discussion finds its natural place in a work of Christian theology (or, tellingly, a volume of anti-Christian polemics). At one point Frazer rails against the very concept of written sacred texts as inherently pernicious, the fierceness of his disdain for scripture making him sound almost like he regretted the very development of literacy:

> The publication of the Deuteronomic Code in written form marked an era in the history not only of the Jewish people but of humanity. It was the first step towards the canonization of Scripture and thereby to the substitution of the written for the spoken word as the supreme and infallible rule of conduct. The accomplishment of the process by the completion of the Canon in the succeeding centuries laid thought under shackles from which in the western world it has never since succeeded in wholly emancipating itself. The spoken word before was free, and therefore thought was free…a living growth had been replaced by a dead letter; the scribe had ousted the prophet…[99]

Frazer furthermore had an illogical tendency to ban the use of his own methods when they served to support traditional Christian views. He ruled out an extremely minor change to the received biblical text which would have allowed for the Deluge to have been local rather than universal even though it is known for certain not to have been in the original and could therefore quite reasonably be put down as a scribal error or guess:

> The textual change, it is true, is very slight, for it extends only to the vowel-points and leaves the consonants unaffected. But though the vowel-points form no part of the original text of the Scriptures, having been introduced into it not earlier than the sixth century of our era, they are not to be lightly altered…[100]

This is just bizarre. Frazer's standard approach in these three volumes is to treat the received text roughly on the assumption that its final form is not faithful to the original meaning. Now he sounds like a fanatically conservative biblical scholar who will not even allow the slightest detail of subsequent scribal additions to be altered: Frazer's desire for the biblical story to appear untenable is clearly trumping all else at this point. Similarly, Frazer was gleeful about an article in the *Hibbert Journal* which argued that New Testament texts on the virgin

---

[99] Frazer, *Folk-Lore*, III, p. 102–103.   [100] Frazer, *Folk-Lore*, III, p. 359.

birth and the Trinity were later interpolations that had been 'forged by the Church to support their doctrines'.[101] This is almost as peculiar. The obvious, intended deductions to make from Frazer's entire life's work are that notions such as supernatural conceptions and trinities are ubiquitous in primitive thought: they are pre-existing weeds that it is the task of a civilized culture finally to root out from its midst. For example, he claimed, 'The stories of miraculous births, which occur among all peoples, are merely isolated survivals of what was once the universal belief as to all human births'.[102] The idea that they are late developments after the era of the apostles also, however, has the potential to disconcert conservative Christian thinkers and Frazer therefore does not seem to mind which of these opposite-facing theories is being advanced just so long as orthodoxy is unsettled.

As a concluding unscientific postscript on Frazer and the Bible, it is worth observing his fascination with one particular text: the narrative of the witch of Endor (1 Samuel 28). In 1909, he included it in the second edition of *Passages from the Bible* even though no one else either before or since has ever considered it one of the portions of scripture that stands out 'in a great mass of other matter' as a 'gem' of literary beauty.[103] Frazer next included a chapter on the witch of Endor in *Folk-Lore in the Old Testament*. It begins with the unflattering portrait of Samuel, followed by a pointless survey of the landscape. The author of *The Golden Bough* then goes on to explain at length how séances in ancient Israel (and always and everywhere) were and are intentional acts of trickery in which cynical con artists dupe the gullible. This has the curious effect of making Frazer's account read like an evangelical commentary. Here is precisely the place in which he could disconcert orthodox Christians by emphasizing the otherness of this authoritative text from their own beliefs, but instead his own commitment to a certain unimaginative kind of scientific naturalism prompts him to side with them. The American philosopher and psychologist William James (1842–1910) happened to run into Frazer once and came away

---

[101] J. G. Frazer to Solomon Schechter, 22 December 1902: Ackerman, *Selected Letters*, p. 219.

[102] J. G. Frazer to Edward Clodd, 8 September 1905: Ackerman, *Selected Letters*, p. 252. As to the other doctrine mentioned: 'Thus it seems not impossible that the ancient Egyptian doctrine of the divine Trinity may have been distilled through Philo into Christianity'. Frazer, *Golden Bough*, 2nd ed., II, p. 4. Frazer would also find Hindu trinities, tree-god trinities, and so on.

[103] Frazer, *Passages*, 2nd ed., pp. v–vi (the quotations) and pp. 140–42 (the Witch of Endor section).

from their conversation flummoxed by how Frazer's rationalism blinded him, reporting bemusedly in a private letter that England's leading authority on primitive peoples 'thinks that trances, etc., of savage soothsayers, oracles and the like are all *feigned!*'[104] Indeed, Frazer's steady insistence on deliberate fraud throughout the witch of Endor chapter does not even accord well with the anthropological evidence it presents. He tells readers, for example, regarding the evocation of the dead among the Bataks of Sumatra: 'When the fit is over, the medium is often sick and sometimes dies'.[105] That's quite a trick! In his introduction to Paul Louis Couchoud's *The Enigma of Jesus*, despite the obscurity of this text, the New Testament theme of the task in hand, and the brevity of his contribution, Frazer nevertheless managed to steer the conversation toward 'the striking narrative of the ghost of Samuel and the witch of Endor'.[106]

As a septuagenarian, the light dramatically went out of Frazer's eyes when he was the speaker at a grand public banquet, and for the last decade of his life he was blind. During those final, dark years Sir James was largely housebound and assistants were hired to read to him. Like Tony Last in Evelyn Waugh's *A Handful of Dust* being held hostage and condemned to read Dickens aloud for the remainder of his days, so it is said that Lady Frazer insisted that her husband would be forced to listen to his own works read back to him for as long as they both should live. Two of these paid readers later wrote articles on what they experienced in the home of the aging anthropologist and both reported that he took the greatest delight in hearing the story of the witch of Endor from his *Passages from the Bible*.[107] What did this text mean to him? (Both assistants quip that he thought of Lady Frazer as the witch, but we can set that aside as more mischievous than insightful.) It seems more probable that Frazer viewed this text as the missing link that connected Christianity to witchcraft. In a traditional Scots-Calvinist worldview, to pursue witchcraft was the strongest and most sinister way imaginable to defy the God of

---

[104] William James to Frances Rollins Morse, 25 December 1900: Ackerman, *Selected Letters*, p. 176.

[105] Frazer, *Folk-Lore*, II, p. 546.

[106] Paul Louis Couchoud, *The Enigma of Jesus*, trans.Winifred Whale, with an introduction by Sir James Frazer (London: Watts & Co., 1924), p. xiii.

[107] Sarah Campion, 'Autumn of an Anthropologist', *New Statesman*, 13 January 1951, pp. 34–36; P. W. Filby, 'Life with the Frazers', *Cambridge Review*, 30 January 1984, pp. 26–30.

the Bible. There would be hardly a better way to spite the faith of his fathers than to insist that, at bottom, it was witchcraft.

* * *

Frazer's anthropological work was heavily dependent on information provided by missionaries. One of his best sources and a good personal friend was the Revd John Roscoe, Church Missionary Society missionary to Uganda, whose own writings were published in the *Journal of the Royal Anthropological Institute* and elsewhere.[108] In a private letter written in 1908 Frazer was already paying the highest tribute to Roscoe: 'I know no keener anthropologist than he'.[109] For the Australian context, another source, friend, and anthropologist in his own right was the Revd Lorimer Fison. The footnotes in *The Golden Bough* and Frazer's other anthropological works are littered with the works of missionaries which are being drawn on as reliable sources providing accurate information—even ones with confessional titles such as *The Gospel on the Banks of the Niger* and *Light in Africa*, and accounts given in periodicals such as *The Illustrated Missionary News* and *The Church Missionary Gleaner*.[110] When they reported things that substantiated his theories, Frazer would defend to the hilt missionaries as unrivalled ethnographic authorities. Here he is championing two missionaries: 'This explanation, while it has been rejected by theorists at home, has been adopted by some of the best observers of savage life, whose opinion is entitled to carry the greatest weight'.[111] On the other hand, if a missionary's evidence got in his way, then Frazer was not above dismissing them *en masse* as unreliable. For example, in *The Golden Bough* he sets aside a source thus: 'But as a Christian missionary Mr. Batchelor was perhaps not likely to hear of such a custom, if it existed'.[112] (The argument—which recurs as needed—is that indigenous peoples hide from missionaries those parts of their culture which they can anticipate these disapproving and dogmatic foreigners will dislike.) Another approach

---

[108] That this was a real friendship and not just Frazer being courteous in print is clear from their private correspondence: see, for example, Frazer Papers, Trinity College, Cambridge, Add. Ms. b. 35., John Roscoe to J. G. Frazer, 3 January 1928.

[109] J. G. Frazer to Baldwin Spencer, 5 February 1908: Marett and Penniman, *Spencer's Scientific Correspondence*, p. 107.

[110] Frazer, *Golden Bough*, 2nd ed., I, pp. 314, 390, 284; II, p. 352.

[111] Frazer, *Devil's Advocate*, pp. 84–85.

[112] Frazer, *Golden Bough*, 2nd ed., II, p. 377.

was to claim that missionaries were rigging the evidence on the basis of their theological convictions. This posture was taken in Frazer's dispute with Lang who had argued contra *The Golden Bough* that it was wrong to view certain tribes in Australia as not having any religious beliefs. Spencer continually reassured Frazer that the evidence Lang was using could be dismissed because it came from a Christian worker: beginning with a gentle hint that the missionary's report 'sounds rather Scriptural' and culminating five years later in a bluntness induced by exasperation with 'the differences between us are due to the fact that Strehlow is a missionary'.[113] (By 1970, even Frazer's disciple and authorized biographer was forced to report that anthropologists had unanimously decided that the Lang-Strehlow side in this debate was right and the Frazer-Spencer one had been mistaken.)[114]

Part of the wider context for Frazer's attitude toward his missionary sources was his desire for a well-defined division of labour between fieldworkers and theorists. Frazer boasted that he had never in his life met a savage—a claim that was augmented by others with the tale that as a child he had glimpsed 'The Wild Man of Borneo' at a fairground and ran away in terror.[115] Frazer was therefore entirely dependent on missionaries, colonial officials, and others on the spot to provide him with ethnographic data. Did this not at least potentially make him superfluous? Far from it, Frazer insisted that only anthropologists— strategically located at or near the metropole where the full range of comparative materials gravitated from every corner of the empire— were allowed to formulate theories. His was the armchair at the centre of the world. In an obituary tribute for Canon Roscoe, Frazer praised him not only for being unrivalled as a 'field anthropologist' but also for not having the presumption to attempt to explain his evidence with any theoretical statements.[116] (This tribute, alas, makes someone who was actually an astute ethnographer sound rather like he was Frazer's errand boy.) In his correspondence with Spencer, one can see the Fellow of Trinity College actively trying to keep this fieldworker in his place. Frazer expresses alarm at Spencer's suggestion that in his own writings he might want to address 'general questions', insisting firmly: 'What we want in such books . . . is a clear and precise statement

[113] Baldwin Spencer to J. G. Frazer, 22 September 1903 and 10 March 1908: Marett and Penniman, *Spencer's Scientific Correspondence*, pp. 96, 110.

[114] Downie, *Frazer and The Golden Bough*, p. 45.

[115] Downie, *Frazer and The Golden Bough*, p. 18.

[116] Frazer, *Creation and Evolution*, p. 77.

of facts (as far as they have been ascertained) concerning the particular people described—that and nothing else'.[117] The 'we', of course, is not the general reading public, but rather Frazer himself who wanted raw data for writing his own theoretical books and not rivals to them. One of the reasons for the sensational impact of *The Golden Bough* was the allure of its literary appellation: as one who had been bowled over by the book in her youth, Jane Ellen Harrison (1850–1928) testified in 1925 that 'Sir James Frazer has a veritable genius for titles'.[118] Frazer had arranged the publication of Spencer's *The Native Tribes of Central Australia* in 1899 and had been very involved in the process, although it is not clear if he chose its bland title. For Spencer's next volume, however, it is known that Frazer personally christened it, *The Northern Tribes of Central Australia*. Later, Frazer gave his blessing for Spencer to produce another monograph, letting him know that his naming genius had already decided what its title should be, 'The Native Tribes of Western Australia'.[119] Frazer was always careful to reassure his sources that their work—conveying as it did immutable facts—would endure, while his own theories would be superseded, and as this prophecy has been fulfilled to the letter their ghosts need not roam about aggrieved.[120]

On the other end of the spectrum from Frazer's ordained cronies were his rationalist companions. As has been shown, one of his best friends was Edmund Gosse who attempted to inscribe his personal loss of faith as the story of human progress in the modern age. More combative, however, was Frazer's close friend Edward Clodd, who served as chairman of the Rationalist Press Association and who was much more willing to attack religion openly. Frazer would even attend Clodd's house parties for like-minded rationalists. Trying to

---

[117] J. G. Frazer to Baldwin Spencer, 26 August 1898: Marett and Penniman, *Spencer's Scientific Correspondence*, p. 23.

[118] Robert Ackerman, *The Myth and Ritual School: J. G. Frazer and the Cambridge Ritualists* (New York: Garland Publishing, 1991), p. 92.

[119] J. G. Frazer to Baldwin Spencer, 21 August 1903 and 5 February 1908: Marett and Penniman, *Spencer's Scientific Correspondence*, pp. 85, 107.

[120] For a typical such prediction, see James George Frazer, *Man, God and Immortality: Thoughts on Human Progress* (New York: Macmillan, 1927), p. ix. Regarding his sources, this prediction is, of course, only fulfilled to the extent that they were perceiving and recording accurately. Ironically, the missionary Roscoe's work has stood the test of time rather well while Frazer's Australian sources who shared his religious scepticism have proved to be less able ethnographers: Ackerman, *J. G. Frazer*, pp. 269–70.

keep from signalling the religious import of his publications so decisively, however, Frazer refused Clodd's request to have an edition of
The Golden Bough appear under the imprint of the Rationalist Press
Association. In the third edition of his *magnum opus*, Frazer could
speak loftily of the hope of immortality, seeming to brush aside the
objections of grumpy secularists who would rule out such beliefs on
the grounds of insufficient evidence with the reassuring and affirming
disclaimer: 'if this is a dream, it is surely a happy and innocent one'.
When writing to Clodd privately, however, Frazer spoke of belief in
life after death as a 'tragedy'—people invest their hopes not realizing
'that all the lots in the lottery are blanks'.[121] While these two statements may not be inherently contradictory, 'happy' and 'tragic' certainly do place the emotional emphasis in incompatible places—yet
another example of Frazer's laudatory public voice masking his privately dismissive one.

Frazer was willing to provide a preface for Couchoud's *The Enigma
of Jesus* (1924) which was issued by the Rationalist Press Association.
He even identified the author as 'my esteemed friend'.[122] Couchoud's
thesis was that the origin of Christianity should be attributed to its
founding figures suffering from 'insanity', 'mental illnesses', 'madness'
or, at the very least, their being 'neurotic and subject to hallucinations'.[123] Frazer also singled out as 'one of our best friends' Albert
Houtin, an erstwhile Catholic priest who had been excommunicated
for his unorthodox views and who went on to publish an account
of his life with the rationalist publisher, Watts & Co.[124] Lady Frazer

---

[121] James George Frazer, *The Dying God*, 3rd Part of 3rd ed. of *The Golden Bough*
(London: Macmillan [1911] 1951), p. vi. Frazer Papers, Trinity College, Cambridge,
Add. Ms. b. 35.: J. G. Frazer to Edward Clodd, Trinity College, 5 January 1925. On
another occasion, however, Frazer was willing to express in print his conviction
that belief in the immortality of the soul has been fundamentally pernicious: James
George Frazer, *Psyche's Task: A Discourse Concerning the Influence of Superstition on
the Growth of Institutions* (London: Macmillan, 1909), p. 52.

[122] Couchoud, *Enigma*, p. vii.

[123] Couchoud, *Enigma*, pp. x–xi. (Couchoud also argued that there was no such
person as Jesus of Nazareth and Frazer demurred from this claim while raising no
objection to the thesis that the apostles were madmen.) Frazer said he would not consider the possibility of a project on 'Folk-Lore in the New Testament' until after a
book appeared by a French scholar who was a friend of his which would present 'a
very important discovery concerning the early history of Christianity': Frazer Papers,
Trinity College, Cambridge, Add. Ms. b. 35., J. G. Frazer to Edward Clodd, Temple, 11
April 1919. Presumably this is a reference to Couchoud's work. For whatever reason,
Frazer never did attempt a New Testament sequel.

[124] J. G. Frazer to Edward Clodd, 22 June 1924: Ackerman, *Selected Letters*, p. 398.

was French and the couple often spent time in France where their circle of friends were religious sceptics including 'deep-dyed rationalists of the Renanian persuasion'.[125] Another friendly contact of Frazer's was Grant Allen (1848–99), the author of the Rationalist Press Association's popular *The Evolution of the Idea of God*. Frazer's authorized biography was published when the author of *The Golden Bough* was still alive by the avowedly agnostic firm Watts & Co., the publisher for the Rationalist Press Association. Moreover, its author, Frazer's disciple R. Angus Downie, with a forthrightness that his master lacked in his own publications, declared frankly in the very first paragraph of the preface that he personally was a religious sceptic.[126]

In continuity with Tylor, Frazer frequently made statements to the effect that anthropology was a reformer's science—that the material he was presenting should prompt people to seek actively to discard those parts of their thinking and culture that he had exposed as arising from faulty logic. In the preface to the second edition of *The Golden Bough* (as has already been observed), Frazer used military imagery in order to speak of the task of destroying the foundations and walls of contemporary society that the comparative method had proven to be built upon sand. Likewise, in a preface to one of the volumes in the third edition he asserted that this work would serve in 'directly assisting us to replace what is effete by what is vigorous, and what is false by what is true'.[127] Another book of Frazer's was dedicated to such reformers: 'To all who are engaged in Psyche's Task of sorting out the seeds of good from the seeds of evil I dedicate this discourse'.[128] In the private letter to the like-minded Spencer in which Frazer first aired his three stages of magic, religion, and science, he made it explicit that this was not merely a descriptive scheme but rather a prescriptive call to action: 'It is for those who care for progress to aid the final triumph of science as much as they can in their day'.[129]

* * *

---

[125] Ackerman, *Selected Letters*, p. 339.

[126] Downie, *James George Frazer*, p. v.

[127] James George Frazer, *Taboo and the Perils of the Soul*, Pt II of the 3rd ed. of *The Golden Bough* (London: Macmillan and Co. [1911] 1951), p. viii.

[128] Frazer, *Devil's Advocate*. (The original edition of this work was entitled *Psyche's Task*, but Frazer abandoned this conceit as it had proved too confusing for the reading public.) In a more cautious mood, Frazer now admits that one should not be too rash about assaulting even faulty foundations (p. vii).

[129] J. G. Frazer to Baldwin Spencer, 28 November 1898: Marett and Penniman, *Spencer's Scientific Correspondence*, p. 42.

Fundamental to Frazer's work is the conviction that the reason why some of the foundational timbers of culture are rotten is because they are soaked in blood. J. G. Frazer viewed much of Western popular culture as thoroughly intertwined with religion; he viewed religion as inherently drawn to violence; and he viewed such violence as typified by a universal impulse in the religious frame of mind toward human sacrifice. *The Golden Bough* is relentless in this regard. Frazer argues that the Jewish Passover was really a ritual of human sacrifice: the use of a lamb is a modified survival of something much more awful. It is a sly substitution which dupes 'the bloodthirsty but near-sighted deity'.[130] Likewise, when examining the Jewish feast of Purim 'we should expect to find traces of human sacrifice lingering about it' (and, of course, our expectations are not disappointed).[131] And it is well known that once a creature gets a taste for human blood they never can shake it: therefore 'we may hesitate to dismiss as idle calumnies all the charges of ritual murder which have been brought against the Jews in modern times'.[132] As for Christianity, Frazer speculates, Christmas was once a festival in which a man was sacrificed 'in the character of the Yule Boar'.[133] The blood at the bottom of things is such a persistent theme that one comes away from *The Golden Bough* wondering if European peasants have any quaint customs which are untainted by it. Has there never been an innocent festival or tradition? Seemingly every celebration of the coming of spring, however cheerful and bright it might appear now, every harvest festival, however simple and culinary, every festive fire—whatever it is—finds its origins in some earlier compulsion to slaughter one's own children and one's neighbours. After reading Frazer, one can hardly eat a gingerbread man without wondering who the poor bloke was whose blood was shed before this mitigated form was devised. Moreover, the violent logic which undergirds these could experience a revival. The sinister truth is that beneath 'a thin veneer' of civilization, 'to this day the peasant remains a pagan and savage at heart'.[134] The second

---

[130] Frazer, *Golden Bough*, 2nd ed., II, p. 49–50.

[131] Frazer, *Golden Bough*, 2nd ed., III, p. 172.

[132] Frazer, *Golden Bough*, 2nd ed., III, p. 175.

[133] Frazer, *Golden Bough*, 2nd ed., II, p. 287.

[134] James George Frazer, *Balder the Beautiful: The Fire-Festivals of Europe and the Doctrine of the External Soul* (Pt VII, 3rd ed. of *The Golden Bough*), 2 vols. (London: Macmillan and Co. [1913] 1951), I, pp. viii–ix. Frazer's assumption that peasant ways still reflect primitive culture often makes him naïve about influences. In a Frazerian frame of mind, if contemporary peasants fast during Lent that is not

edition of *The Golden Bough* ends by identifying magic with the colour black (befitting the darkness of its ignorance and the evil of its effects), science with white (symbolizing the light of its knowledge and its inherent goodness), and religion with red (portraying its defining propensity to shed innocent blood). This colour scheme is rounded off with a little sermonic warning that the triumph of the side of progress is not automatic: it must be chosen. Religion will not just naturally die on the vine: it must be purposefully rooted out.[135]

This monomania is yet more evident when one includes Frazer's other writings. For example, in the memoir in his collection of the letters of William Cowper, Frazer mentions that a notion Cowper had during a period of mental disturbance and suicidal depression was 'the insane idea that God required him to offer himself up as a sacrifice after that approved style of Abraham and Isaac'.[136] Clearly Frazer saw that detail as revealing not so much the extent to which Cowper's mind was deranged as the quickness with which a religious preoccupation reconnects to its bloody fount. When the reactions to the second edition of *The Golden Bough* began to appear, Frazer confided to Lorimer Fison: 'The orthodox here have been dragging me over metaphorical coals (and some of them I daresay would like to drag me over real hot coal in the good old style) for my theory on the Crucifixion'.[137] Nothing more unpleasant had happened than his ideas being critiqued in print, but Frazer instinctively assumed that orthodox Christians were hankering for blood. Sounding deranged himself, this conspiracy theory was baldly put forward in another private missive earlier that same year. This is a portion of the final paragraph of that letter, including its first and last sentences:

> I am much interested to learn that Grant Allen threw out a suggestion that the Passion may have been a piece of periodical ritual in Judea...I was told some little time ago that human sacrifices are said still to be secretly offered in a cave in one of the Greek Islands. Stupidly enough I did not make a note of it at the time and am not sure who my informant was. I think it was a Cambridge man who had been travelling and studying with a scholarship in Greece...Our religious friends do not

evidence that they have been influenced by Christianity, but rather that Lent is actually a primitive practice that pre-dates Christianity—and so it goes on and on.

[135] Frazer, *Golden Bough*, 2nd ed., III, p. 461.
[136] Frazer, *Letters of William Cowper*, I, p. xxx.
[137] J. G. Frazer to Lorimer Fison, 14 July 1901: Ackerman, *Selected Letters*, p. 195.

change their principles. They are only prevented at present from carrying them into practice by police. Will they always be so prevented? I hope so, but do not feel sure of it.[138]

This is a heady blend of gullibility and paranoia. Frazer himself had lucidly taught that legislation is merely an expression of the general sentiments of a community and a codification of what the people have already been doing voluntarily for a long time.[139] It should have been painfully obvious to him that the police would not allow human sacrifice because a Christian populace had enacted its long-standing repugnance for such vile practices into law. Frazer's animus against his religious heritage, at its worst, could tempt him toward a blood libel against both Jews and Christians.

At the other extreme from the smell of blood, however, is the sound of bells. This is Frazer at his most nostalgic, wistful, and affirming. *The Golden Bough* famously ended on this note:

> But Nemi's woods are still green, and at evening you may hear the church bells of Albano, and perhaps, if the air be still, of Rome itself, ringing the Angelus. Sweet and solemn they chime out from the distant city, and die lingering away across the wide Campagnan marshes. *Le roi est mort, vive le roi!*[140]

This was a deeper truth than merely a descriptive one: Frazer acknowledged in the preface to the second edition that he was retaining it in defiance of the pedant who had informed him that his evocation of the Eternal City was an auditory impossibility.[141] Tellingly, Frazer borrowed this trope from Ernest Renan (1823–92) as he had noticed it allowed him to express a more appreciative sound that would raise him above the mere 'arid rationalism' of some other religious sceptics.[142] That admission, of course, makes it yet harder to discern the degree to which Frazer actually had such warm sentiments himself versus the extent to which he was merely shrewd enough to know that undiluted rationalism could be experienced by readers as unpalatable. Whatever the motivation, Frazer loved to ring this bell. The massive three volumes of *Folk-Lore in the Old Testament* likewise end

[138] J. G. Frazer to E. Sidney Hartland, 2 April 1901: Ackerman, *Selected Letters*, pp. 187–88.

[139] Frazer, *Folk-Lore*, II, p. 235.

[140] Frazer, *Golden Bough* (1890), II, p. 371.

[141] Frazer, *Golden Bough*, 2nd ed., I, p. xxii.

[142] Frazer, *Folk-Lore*, III, p. 453.

in the same way with a chapter on 'The Golden Bells', evoking church bells in Europe as a sound which 'has endeared itself to so many pious hearts by its own intrinsic sweetness and its tender associations'.[143] In an earlier chapter, Frazer had discussed the Israelite reforms that eliminated local shrines. He tried to awaken sympathy for the peasantry who lived through this upheaval by asking readers to imagine the reaction of common people in their own day if the churches were removed: 'How often would they listen in vain for the sweet sound of Sabbath bells chiming across the fields and calling them to the house of prayer, where they and their forefathers had so often gathered to adore the common Father of all!'[144] In his tribute to his parents, Frazer averred that although they enforced a strict Calvinist Sunday, he did not chafe against it: 'I never found this observance of the Sabbath irksome or wearisome. On the contrary, I look back to those peaceful Sabbath days with something like fond regret, and the sound of Sabbath bells, even in a foreign land, still touches a deep chord in my heart'.[145] (As his parents were always 'dear and honoured', so it is suspicious that church bells are almost invariably 'sweet'.)

Frazer evoked his 'dear and honoured parents' once again in a letter to the clergyman Edward Lyttleton. One can infer from this reply that Lyttleton was a kind soul who had gently pressed Frazer as to his attitude toward Christianity. In response, although admitting that he is not personally religious, Frazer nevertheless honours his father and mother and testifies: 'I have a tenderness for the old faith and for those who hold it'.[146] He goes on to admit, 'Hardly anything offends me as much as the confident dogmatism of some rationalists'. Once again, it is hard to judge to what degree this is a true confiding, especially as Frazer then proceeds to assert that he has 'not seriously studied the great historical religions of the civilized peoples', and to intimate that the implications of his work are confined to primitive contexts, both

---

[143] Frazer, *Folk-Lore*, III, pp. 466–67. One of the ethnographic questions Frazer wanted those in the field to seek answers for was: 'Do they make use of bells or gongs in any religious or superstitious rites?': J. G. Frazer, *Questions on the Customs, Beliefs, and Languages of Savages*, third impression (Cambridge: Cambridge University Press, 1916), p. 48.

[144] Frazer, *Folk-Lore*, III, p. 106.

[145] Frazer, *Creation and Evolution*, p. 133.

[146] J. G. Frazer to Edward Lyttelton, 19 June 1927: Ackerman, *Selected Letters*, pp. 405–406. Ackerman only had access to excerpts from this letter that were printed in a book dealer's catalogue. The original letter is now apparently in private hands. I tried to track it down, but was not successful.

of which statements are clearly cant. The Fellow of Trinity College admired French philosopher Nicolas de Condorcet (1743–94) greatly, but nevertheless chided him for falling into the trap that Renan had avoided with his bells. Condorcet was surely right about the great evil that religious faith has done, but he failed to grasp that from the same source has also flowed 'spiritual comfort and consolation', 'inspiring hopes', and 'active beneficence'.[147]

It seems more probable that these positive statements were sometimes expressions of heartfelt sentiments rather than always merely a masking tactic. Frazer himself cautioned that when studying others the fluid boundaries between 'belief or disbelief, of faith or of scepticism' were not easy to discern: 'they melt and shade off into each other by graduations as fine and imperceptible as the hues of the rainbow'.[148] When an elderly Frazer heard read back to him some of his own sentences in *The Golden Bough* such as, 'How do such wild ravings and blasphemous pretentions contrast with the simple and sober claim of the carpenter of Nazareth to be the Creator and Governor of the universe!', perhaps even he could not finally decide whether or not he was being ironic.[149] He was certainly repulsed by thoroughgoing efforts to eradicate religion in the name of modernity and progress such as those undertaken in the French and Russian revolutions.[150] Although Frazer was willing to avow that he was not a Christian when the situation seemed to call for that level of candour, he nevertheless would sometimes be drawn to Christian worship. Even after his parents were dead and he had relocated for a while to London, Frazer would decide some Sunday mornings that he and Lady Frazer should attend church.[151] This tender part of Frazer's heart for the old faith is probably the clue to the deeply evangelical William Cowper being his favourite English poet—a crasser, more defiant, religious sceptic might have made a point of celebrating Shelley or Byron instead. The excuse of the project on folk-lore in the Old Testament allowed Frazer to read the Bible habitually at the start of each new day.[152] This is, of course, a standard practice of evangelical piety: his formal ideology may have undergone a transformation from the beliefs of the Free Church of

---

[147] Frazer, *Creation and Evolution*, pp. 104–105.
[148] Frazer, *Folk-Lore in the Old Testament*, II, p. 551.
[149] Frazer, *Golden Bough*, second edition, I, p. 151.
[150] Frazer, *Creation and Evolution*, p. 85.
[151] Downie, *Frazer and The Golden Bough*, pp. 21, 27–28, 66.
[152] Ackerman, *J. G. Frazer*, p. 265.

Scotland to rationalism, but what an anthropologist notices is that while the explanation for the behaviour is now different, the ritual carries on more or less the same. Peter vehemently denies Christ, but continues to follow him at a distance.

* * *

Although it seems that we have sometimes strayed far afield, we are now in a position to examine the incident of the college at Didsbury. This institution was the oldest existing one in Britain for training Methodist ministers. The invitation to fill a chair in comparative religion had been extended through the classical tutor J. H. Moulton (1863–1917), a leading authority on Zoroastrianism. After a positive conversation about this possibility had taken place in person, here is a portion of Frazer's follow-up letter to Moulton seeking reassurances:

> I said I might do so on certain conditions. But I am in two minds about it. I have begun to doubt whether, with my views on religion in general and Christianity in particular, it would be right for me to accept a teaching post in a Theological faculty instituted by Christians for Christians, in particular for men training for the Christian ministry.[153]

Frazer consulted J. S. Black, the biographer of William Robertson Smith. Black replied that he would take 'the liveliest satisfaction and delight' in Frazer's accepting this post. Black argued that the college was to be encouraged in its desire to have an unbeliever teach this material: 'No, my dear Frazer: you must *not* refuse the opening' if your only reason is that you are falsely imagining that Christianity is stuck in 'the old way' when it is clear from the very offer that it is not.[154] Had not Frazer been insisting that Christians needed to not evade but rather face squarely the implications of anthropological evidence for their own beliefs and practices? Now they were asking him to help them do that. A few days later Frazer consulted the classical scholar Henry Jackson (1839–1921). In this letter Frazer clearly sounds like he wants to find grounds for refusing:

> I am not a Christian, on the contrary I reject the Christian religion utterly as false.…I should be implicitly bound to conceal my own firm belief of the falseness of Christianity…Certainly I would not attack Christianity openly, even if I had given no pledge or implied promise

[153] J. G. Frazer to J. H. Moulton, 10 April 1904: Ackerman, *Selected Letters*, p. 233.
[154] J. S. Black to J. G. Frazer, 14 April 1904: Ackerman, *Selected Letters*, pp. 234–35.

to abstain from doing so. Such attacks are repugnant to my feeling and I regard them as bad policy besides. But the facts of comparative religion appear to me subversive of Christian theology…[155]

Jackson replied that the Didsbury people understood quite clearly that he was not a Christian—adding with dry understatement that this fact was 'hardly a secret' in British society at large. If he stuck to the approach to religion he had taken in *The Golden Bough*, that was all he would need to do to act responsibility. It mattered not that Frazer was convinced that the implication of these facts was that Christianity was false. Others did not agree. Jackson regarded himself as a Christian, his extensive study of anthropology notwithstanding.[156] With no one accepting his concerns and arguments, Frazer was therefore reduced to asserting naked personal revulsion: 'with the views I have as to religion, I could not reconcile myself to accepting a teaching post in what is practically a seminary for the training of Christian clergy. The feeling may be unreasonable, but I could not rid myself of it'.[157]

In the light of Frazer's life and work, what is to be made of this refusal? His initial confusion was augmented by the fact that this offer did not fit into his standard way of thinking about Christians as opponents who would like to persecute him if they could. Far from wanting to murder him, they hope to hire him. In writing his disclaimers, it is as if he is hoping that they will reject him as unsuitable. When they do not reject but rather continue to welcome him, Frazer is left with the confusing narrative that perhaps it is he that is the bigot rather than them. He is forced to admit that maybe he is the one motivated by irrational feelings—he is the one being 'unreasonable'. Moreover, with his official concern that his unbelief and his anthropological evidence will be unacceptable dispelled, one senses that his deeper fear was the reverse: perhaps his covert efforts to undermine faith were not effective. It was cold comfort for Henry Jackson to reassure him that if the worst he had to offer was what he had presented in *The Golden Bough*

---

[155] J. G. Frazer to Henry Jackson, 18 April 1904: Ackerman, *Selected Letters*, p. 236.
[156] Henry Jackson to J. G. Frazer, 19 April 1904: Ackerman, *Selected Letters*, pp. 239–40.
[157] J. G. Frazer to Henry Jackson, 2 May 1904: Ackerman, *Selected Letters*, p. 241. A parallel case was Frazer's needless concern (later overcome) that giving the Gifford Lectures (which E. B. Tylor had already done) might somehow compromise his opposition to religion: J. G. Frazer to Lorimer Fison, 14 July 1901: Ackerman, *Selected Letters*, p. 196.

then the faith of the young ordinands in his charge would be safe. Perhaps Frazer's real fear, the unreasonable one which he dared not face, was that after teaching comparative religion to the rising generation they would be largely untroubled by this material and still go on to be faithful ministers of the gospel.

3

E. E. Evans-Pritchard

The preface to *Aftermath*, the final volume of the third edition of J. G. Frazer's *The Golden Bough*, is dated 13 August 1936. Just five months later in January 1937, Edward Evan (E. E.) Evans-Pritchard (1902–1973) penned the preface to his landmark study, *Witchcraft, Oracles and Magic among the Azande*. One can imagine scholars and perhaps even book reviewers for learned journals endeavouring to keep up with the discipline, with copies of both books stacked in the pile of fresh material they needed to read through. The leap from Frazer to Evans-Pritchard is an athletic one in terms of method, theory, practice, and personal convictions, but it must be kept in mind that it is a short or even overlapping space in terms of chronology. Perhaps it is longer in structural than calendar time.

Evans-Pritchard's position at the top of the discipline in his day is undisputed. David F. Pocock testified: 'Evans-Pritchard was the most distinguished British social anthropologist of his generation'.[1] *The International Dictionary of Anthropologists* (1991), also has entries on everyone else that might be considered a credible rival claimant, and yet is quite willing to declare unequivocally: 'Evans-Pritchard is the most important social anthropologist of post-World-War-II Britain'.[2] If anything, this uncontested crown seems to be especially bestowed by those criticizing his work. Richard Fardon, for example, in a piece arguing that Franz Steiner's writings hold up better in the new millennium, avers: 'Evans-Pritchard has good claim to being simply *the*

[1] David F. Pocock, 'Sir Edward Evans-Pritchard 1902–1973: An Appreciation', *Africa: Journal of the International African Institute*, 45, 3 (1975), p. 327.
[2] T. O. Beidelman, 'E. E. Evans-Pritchard', in Christopher Winters (ed.), *International Dictionary of Anthropologists* (New York: Garland, 1991), p. 185.

pre-eminent social anthropologist of the mid-twentieth century, the late twentieth-century discipline is hardly thinkable without him'.[3]

It has been common for contemporary anthropologists—again not least those who disliked him or disagreed with him—to reflect that 'E-P' (as he was called) was the greatest of their generation.[4] Raymond Firth, whose relationship with the Oxford anthropologist was complicated, nevertheless generously conceded: 'he was, I think, beyond doubt the most brilliant of all of us in theory as well as in exposition'.[5] Even Edmund Leach, whose relationship with Evans-Pritchard was one of straightforward, mutual antagonism, was heard to concede, 'But Evans-Pritchard was the brightest of us all'.[6] Evans-Pritchard's books will be discussed later in this chapter, but it should be observed here that several of these have often been given places of pre-eminence or fountainhead status in the discipline. To take just one example, Fredrik Barth has identified *The Nuer* as 'probably the most influential monograph ever published in anthropology'.[7] Moreover, this is even sometimes true of his shorter works and articles. To wit, his two-part article 'The Zande Corporation of Witchdoctors', which appeared in 1932–33 in the *Journal of the Royal Anthropological Institute*, did not end up on essential reading lists in the discipline, yet John W. Burton deems it to be 'probably the first example of "thick description" in modern anthropology'.[8]

Extraordinarily, nine separate edited volumes were published in Evans-Pritchard's honour—going fantastically beyond the noble

---

[3] Richard Fardon, 'Religion and the anthropologists revisited: Reflections on Franz Baermann Steiner, E. E. Evans-Pritchard, and the "Oxford School" at their Century's End', in Jeremy Adler, Richard Fardon, and Carol Tully (eds.), *From Prague Poet to Oxford Anthropologist: Franz Baermann Steiner Celebrated* (München: Iudicium, 2003), pp. 21–22.

[4] Those who knew him typically refer to him as 'E-P' and he would often sign his own letters that way. I intend mainly to use 'Evans-Pritchard' in this chapter so as not to affect an acquaintanceship I did not possess, but will use E-P occasionally in the interests of a writing style with more variation.

[5] David Parkin, 'An Interview with Raymond Firth', *Current Anthropology*, 29, 2 (April 1988), p. 335.

[6] Piero Matthey, 'A Glimpse of Evans-Pritchard through his correspondence with Lowie and Kroeber', *Journal of the Anthropological Society of Oxford*, 27, 1 (1996), p. 30.

[7] Fredrik Barth, 'Britain and the Commonwealth', in Fredrik Barth et al. *One Discipline, Four Ways: British, German, French, and American Anthropology* (Chicago: University of Chicago Press, 2005), p. 33.

[8] John W. Burton, *An Introduction to Evans-Pritchard* (Studia Instituti Anthropos 45), (Fribourg: Fribourg University Press, 1992), p. 64.

standard for successful and beloved scholars of a festschrift or two by colleagues and former students. An entire volume was created by the Department of Social Anthropology at the University of Manchester even though Evans-Pritchard had never studied or taught there.[9] Even some who acknowledged his greatness thought matters had gone too far when Evans-Pritchard was selected as a subject for the Fontana Modern Masters series, thus making him the one anthropologist from the entire English-speaking world in the whole history of the discipline worthy of being in the company of figures deemed to be so eminent that they are identified in the book titles by only their last names—Darwin, Einstein, Freud, Marx, and so on.[10]

If most of that is somewhat subjective, the concrete positions he held and honours he accrued are more than sufficient to sketch Evans-Pritchard's place as a towering presence in the discipline during his own lifetime. For most of his career he held the prestigious University of Oxford chair in anthropology which came with a Fellowship at All Souls College.[11] In 1949–51 he served as president of the Royal Anthropological Institute. He was the founding and animating force of the Association of Social Anthropologists which, in turn, eventually formally acknowledged his pre-eminence by appointing him Life President.[12] He was elected a Fellow of the British Academy. He was selected to give a range of named lectureships, was awarded medals, and accumulated honorary doctorates. He was inducted into several of the most prestigious learned bodies in other countries and even made a Chevalier of the Légion d'honneur. As to his own country's honours system, Evans-Pritchard was knighted by the Queen in 1971. This was still such a rare distinction in the discipline of anthropology at that time that even a figure as eminent as

[9] Max Gluckman (ed.), *The Allocation of Responsibility* (Manchester: Manchester University Press, 1972).

[10] Mary Douglas, *Evans-Pritchard* (Brighton: Harvester Press, 1980). (This edition—the one I was able to consult—was done 'by agreement with Fontana Books'.)

[11] To return to the subjective, Evans-Pritchard's occupancy of this chair 'is often regarded as the Classical or Golden Age of Oxford social anthropology'. Introduction by Peter Rivière in Peter Rivière (ed.) *A History of Oxford Anthropology* (Oxford: Berghahn Books, 2007), p. 7.

[12] An official ASA publication described Evans-Pritchard in its dedication to him as 'Founder and First President of the Assocation of Social Anthropologists'. If this was to exaggerate his unique pre-eminence at the founding, it is no less telling that he came to loom so large that this became the official view. Mary Douglas (ed.), *Witchcraft, Confessions and Accusations* (London: Tavistock Publications, 1970).

Bronislaw Malinowski had not gained it (but Tylor and Frazer had). When two festschriften appeared in 1972, they proudly emblazoned on their covers that they contained essays 'presented to Sir Edward Evans-Pritchard'—the only living British anthropologist who could be addressed with that title.[13]

* * *

Edward Evan Evans-Pritchard was the son of a Church of England clergyman, the Revd Thomas John Evans-Pritchard. He thought fondly of his father's Christian ministry: as an adult, at his home in Oxford the anthropologist kept in a bowl on the mantelpiece of his study a newspaper clipping which praised his father for the power of his preaching.[14] Evans-Pritchard remembered his mother Dorothea as 'a sentimental kind of Christian.'[15] (One scholar has spoken of 'those special gems of paradoxical obfuscation for which Evans-Pritchard is justly famous,'[16] and on another occasion—presumably not having the case of his mother in mind—he aphorized: 'I am so sentimental myself that I don't like sentimentality.'[17]) Evans-Pritchard had one sibling, an elder brother Thomas, who was a highly talented classicist as a student, but who began manifesting the symptoms of schizophrenia as a young man and spent the rest of his life in a mental institution. Someone who knew them when Thomas and Edward were still youths

---

[13] André Singer and Brian V. Street (eds.), *Zande Themes: Essays presented to Sir Edward Evans-Pritchard* (Oxford: Basil Blackwell, 1972); Ian Cunnison and Wendy James (eds.), *Essays in Sudan Ethnography presented to Sir Edward Evans-Pritchard* (London: C. Hurst & Company, 1972). Evans-Pritchard led the way: Firth was knighted the year after (1973) and Leach in 1975.

[14] I have interviewed in person, by telephone, or email a dozen or more people who knew Evans-Pritchard personally, including three people who lived with him for a year or more—his son Ambrose, his research assistant André Singer, and Bruce Ross-Smith, his neighbour and confidant who came to live with the family, who is still close to the children, and who is the keeper of Evans-Pritchard's personal photographs and some of his personal papers. I am grateful to them all for their helpfulness and frankness. Bruce Ross-Smith and his wife Sally, and their children, hosted me for Sunday lunch and—through the kindness of the current owners—Bruce gave me a tour of Evans-Pritchard's home, The Ark, where he used to live with E-P and the children.

[15] E. E. Evans-Pritchard, 'Fragment of an Autobiography', *New Blackfriars* (A monthly review edited by the English Dominicans), 54, 632 (January 1973), p. 36.

[16] J. A. Barnes, 'Edward Evan Evans-Pritchard', *Proceedings of the British Academy*, 73 (1987), p. 481.

[17] T. O. Beidelman, 'Sir Edward Evan Evans-Pritchard (1902–1973): An Appreciation', *Anthropos*, 69 (1974), p. 556.

living at home recalled that the family would spend their mealtimes energetically debating the issues of the day.[18]

Evans-Pritchard was proud of his Welsh blood (his father could and did preach in Welsh as well as English), but he was universally regarded as 'a great Englishman nonetheless'.[19] This has much to do with his elite education and the socialization into the ruling class that came with it. When Leach wrote an exposé of the secret influence of class distinctions in the careers of anthropologists, he identified the Fellow of All Souls College as the quintessential well-bred gentleman: 'At one extreme stands Evans-Pritchard, a very English Englishman despite his Welsh name, educated at the ultra-prestigious Winchester College (founded in 1387) and Exeter College, Oxford, where he read history'.[20] The Oxford anthropologist himself traced this educational pedigree even earlier: 'I went before the age of six to one of the best and oldest preparatory schools in England, The Grange, at Crowborough in Sussex. I say one of the best in a social sense...'.[21] He would attribute his ability to take down Zande texts in the field in the days before tape recorders to having been 'brought up on Greek and Latin'.[22] Another sign of his social position: fieldwork was made easier by the fact that he received £300 per annum from a family endowment.[23] Evans-Pritchard thought of anthropology as translating 'them' to 'us' and his 'us' was specifically the English—even when it came to Nuer cattle, the comparison point was the milk of 'English cows' and the ways of 'English dairy farmers'.[24]

---

[18] Bernard Nightingale to Mary Douglas, 1 July 1980, Evans-Pritchard Papers, 2/2/10, Tylor Library, Institute of Social and Cultural Anthropology, University of Oxford.

[19] John Davis, 'Edward Evan Evans-Pritchard: A Great Englishman Nonetheless', in William Roger Louis (ed.), *Penultimate Adventures with Britannia* (London: I. B. Tauris, 2008), pp. 169–84.

[20] Edmund R. Leach, 'Glimpses of the Unmentionable in the History of British Social Anthropology', *Annual Review of Anthropology*, 13 (1984), p. 16.

[21] Edward Evans-Pritchard, 'Genesis of a Social Anthropologist: An Autobiographical Note', *New Diffusionist*, 3, 10 (January 1973), p. 18. (The Grange was indeed serving a refined social world, but the claim that it was one of the oldest foundations is an improbable one.)

[22] E. E. Evans-Pritchard, 'Some Reminiscences and Reflections on Fieldwork', *Journal of the Anthropological Society of Oxford*, 4, 1 (1973), p. 10.

[23] E. E. Evans-Pritchard, 'Some Recollections of Fieldwork in the Twenties', *Anthropological Quarterly*, 46, 4 (October 1973), p. 236.

[24] E. E. Evans-Pritchard, *The Nuer: A Description of the Modes of Livelihood and Political Institutions of a Nilotic People* (Oxford: Clarendon Press, 1940), p. 23.

Evans-Pritchard had already chosen history as his special subject while at Winchester and that is what he read at Exeter College, Oxford (1921–24). In his own telling of it, he broke the monotony of an unvaried diet of historical scholarship 'by taking an interest in books like Tylor's *Primitive Culture* and Frazer's *Golden Bough*' and thus began his migration to anthropology.[25] No doubt another influence was that the university's leading anthropologist at that time, R. R. Marett (1866–1943), was also at Exeter. At Oxford and in his early twenties in London Evans-Pritchard ran in aesthetic, bohemian cliques in that determinedly frivolous, high-spirited way of the young elite in the period after the horrors of the Great War. As an undergraduate he was a member of the Hypocrites Club as were the novelists Evelyn Waugh (1903–66) and Anthony Powell (1905–2000) during this period. There is a photograph of Evans-Pritchard at a fancy-dress party sponsored by the Hypocrites in which he is in Arab dress looking like T. E. Lawrence (1888–1935).[26] One suspects that Lawrence was something of a role model. Evans-Pritchard once observed that he decided to become an anthropologist because fieldwork held out the promise of a life of adventure rather than merely reflection. Robin Maugham provided anecdotes of Captain E. E. Evans-Pritchard in this persona during the war. As a way of putting a tediously boastful sheik in his place, he takes his pistol out and—without altering his relaxed, lounging position in a deck chair—coolly shoots all the empty beer bottles left on a balcony. He sends an ornate dagger to a French general as a gift with a note attached. Maugham assumes that it was the English captain's awkward French which made the indignant general think that his expressed hope that he would know what to do with it was a hint that he should commit suicide, but it is more likely that the Frenchman had successfully discerned E-P's Zande *sanza*.[27] Evans-Pritchard also stole some secret military documents of anthropological interest which were not supposed to be declassified until 2019.[28] It seems fitting that in the Coffee Room at All Souls

[25] Evans-Pritchard, 'Genesis', p. 18.

[26] Anthony Powell, *Infants of the Spring* (memoirs volume 1), (London: Heinemann, 1976), pp. 148–55.

[27] Robin Maugham, *Nomad* (New York: Viking Press, 1948), pp. 27–28, 34–34, 47. For *sanza*, the Zande art of expressing one's resentment in veiled language, see E. E. Evans-Pritchard, *Social Anthropology and Other Essays* (New York: The Free Press, 1962), pp. 330–54.

[28] They are *A Note on the Alawites* and *A Note on the Druzes*. When the Institute realized long after Evans-Pritchard's death that they were in possession of these items

College the photographs of Lawrence and Evans-Pritchard are displayed side by side.

Having been awarded his BA in Modern History from the University of Oxford in 1924, Evans-Pritchard went on in that same year to pursue postgraduate studies in anthropology at the London School of Economics (LSE). He chose the LSE because it had a programme where the faculty members had field experience.[29] C. G. Seligman (1873–1940) became his PhD supervisor. This was a pivotal connection as Seligman was an Africanist and this would become Evans-Pritchard's own area of expertise. Seligman had gone on the pioneering Torres Straits expedition and to other far-flung parts of the world before doing research for two to three years in the Sudan. This was an incomparable advance from Tylor and Frazer who merely sat in their studies reading accounts written by others, but it fell well short of what would become the new, expected standard of intensive participant observation. Rather, Seligman and his wife Brenda primarily conducted surveys through an interpreter before rapidly moving on to another location. Evans-Pritchard also served as his research assistant in the field and collected some data for him. Retrospectively, he wryly reported that Seligman was so old-fashioned as to be preoccupied with collecting bodily measures of natives and that he initially acquiesced in this as well.[30] This Victorian legacy is discernable in Evans-Pritchard's photographs from the field which are heavily populated with what are identified as specimen images: 'Nuer type'; 'Male type'; 'Female type'; 'Man—back view'; 'Man—front view'; 'Man—side view'; and on and on.[31]

they wrote to the Ministry of Defence which replied with the official declassification date, but allowed them to keep them nonetheless. Evans-Pritchard Papers, 1/10/61, Tylor Library, Institute of Social and Cultural Anthropology, University of Oxford.

[29] Evans-Pritchard always acknowledged that the adaption of 'experimental fieldwork is clearly one of the most important movements in social anthropology in this century': E. E. Evans-Pritchard, *The Position of Women in Primitive Societies and other Essays in Social Anthropology* (London: Faber & Faber, 1965), p. 31. A 1935 conference paper in which he commended fieldwork as the future of the discipline was read by another anthropologist in his absence. In it, he was able to declare, 'I write this paper in my camp in Kenya'. E. E. Evans-Pritchard, 'Anthropology and the Social Sciences', in J. E. Dugdale (ed.), *The Social Sciences: Their Relations in Theory and in Teaching* (London: Le Play House Press, 1937), p. 63.

[30] Evans-Pritchard, 'Some Recollections', p. 242.

[31] Evans-Pritchard Papers, Pitt Rivers Museum, Oxford. I am grateful to Dr Christopher Morton, Head of Photography and Manuscripts Collections, for being so helpful and attentive while I was researching at the museum. Those interested in Evans-Pritchard and visual culture should seek out Dr Morton's own publications,

Bronislaw Malinowski (1884–1942), a former student of Seligman's, had recently joined him as a colleague at the LSE. Malinowski had spent years carefully studying the Trobriand Islanders and others in New Guinea and to him goes the credit for pioneering modern anthropological fieldwork. Evans-Pritchard and Firth were in Malinowski's first seminar—a gathering which 'became a virtual rite of passage for aspiring anthropologists'.[32] If so, perhaps like the Nuer initiation of boys, it was the kind of rite of passage that left men with permanent scars.[33] A pattern has been observed of his male students needing to make a somewhat bitter break from Malinowski.[34] It is certainly true that Evans-Pritchard's relationship with Malinowski became and remained antipathetic. It can be seen to be turning sour as early as February 1928 when Evans-Pritchard responded explosively to Malinowski's suggesting that he had 'cooked' his evidence from the field. [35] Evans-Pritchard thought better of a permanent breach at that time and wrote a fulsome apology. By 1931, Malinowski is on record as saying that he would thwart any attempt to get Evans-Pritchard appointed at the LSE on the grounds that he could not work with him, and it has been surmised that E-P had to take his first appointment in Cairo because Malinowski blocked him in Britain altogether. (Years later, Evans-Pritchard found it delicious to contemplate that Malinowski was only able to occupy the Yale chair because he himself had been offered it first but turned it down.) The impression of some of the other scarred men was that Malinowski wanted to take credit for their work and to exalt himself into a position of unrivalled ascendancy by keeping them down. Evans-Pritchard would make general charges that Malinowski was a bully who would belittle his students and so on. Although he was doing

a recent one of which is: Christopher Morton, 'Double Alienation: Evans-Pritchard's Zande and Nuer Photographs in Comparative Perspective', in Richard Vokes (ed.), *Photography in Africa: Ethnographic Perspectives* (Woodbridge: James Currey, 2012), pp. 35–55.

[32] Burton, *Introduction*, p. 19.

[33] The Nuer initiation involved cutting lines in the forehead. For a photograph that shows the scars, see Evans-Pritchard, *The Nuer*, plate XXIII (between pp. 256–57).

[34] George W. Stocking, Jr., 'Radcliffe-Brown and British Social Anthropology' in George W. Stocking, Jr. (ed.), *Functionalism Historicized: Essays on British Social Anthropology* (Madison: University of Wisconsin Press, 1984), p. 176. There were women in the seminar as well and some went on to be eminent anthropologists, but Stocking discerns 'the universal Oedipus complex' at work in the relationship between Malinowski and some of the men he taught.

[35] Christopher Morton, 'Evans-Pritchard and Malinowski: the Roots of a Complex Relationship', *History of Anthropology Newsletter*, 34, 2 (December 2007), pp. 10–14.

fieldwork at the time, Evans-Pritchard needed to come home in 1929 to deal with two family tragedies that came hard together: the death of his father and the necessity of institutionalizing his brother. One of the proofs he would later offer that his former professor was contemptible was that the short sympathy note he received purportedly from Malinowski personally was typed out and unsigned. While never failing to acknowledge that he did not like him, late in life Evans-Pritchard's comments on Malinowski as an anthropologist were mixed—occasionally generous ('I learnt more from him than from anyone'), but sometimes breathtakingly dismissive (he 'was in any case a futile thinker').[36] As good as any summative word of his own view is his 1970 assessment that Malinowski was 'a cad, a swine, a shit—and a genius'.[37]

* * *

Therefore, to Evans-Pritchard goes the credit for being the first professional anthropologist to do proper, participant observation fieldwork in Africa. Moreover, as that continent would come to preoccupy British anthropologists for decades to come (it is not a coincidence that the rest of the figures studied in this volume were all Africanists), he was the trailblazer for what would become the main path during his lifetime.[38] From 1926 to 1945 Evans-Pritchard was repeatedly in Africa for long stays. Counting his war service (during which he did research that he was able to turn into a scholarly book on the Cyrenaican Bedouin) and his first teaching appointment in Cairo, Evans-Pritchard spent over ten years in Africa. He studied a range of different groups in the southern Sudan. His Frazer lecture, for example, was on the Shilluk.[39] Delightfully, his notes on the Dinka are

---

[36] Evans-Pritchard, 'Genesis', p. 19; Edward Evans-Pritchard, *A History of Anthropology Thought*, ed. André Singer (London: Faber & Faber, 1981), p. 199.

[37] George W. Stocking, Jr. *After Tylor: British Social Anthropology, 1888–1951* (Madison: University of Wisconsin Press, 1995), p. 436. Evans-Pritchard also derided Malinowski for allegedly being willing to make pure research subservient to applied work in order to obtain grant money by referring to the LSE as £.S.D.: Adam Kuper, 'Alternative Histories of British Social Anthropology', *Social Anthropology*, 13, 1 (2005), p. 53. While Evans-Pritchard had pioneered fieldwork in Africa, the LSE came to controlled the flow of funding for African studies: Henrika Kuklick, 'The British Tradition' in Henrika Kuklick (ed.), *A New History of Anthropology* (Oxford: Blackwell, 2009), p. 71.

[38] For an account of this shift, see Jacky Goody, *The Expansive Moment: Anthropology in Britain and Africa, 1918–1970* (Cambridge: Cambridge University Press, 1995).

[39] E. E. Evans-Pritchard, *The Divine Kingship of the Shilluk of the Nilotic Sudan* (Cambridge: Cambridge University Press, 1948).

on the Cunard White Star stationery of the RMS *Queen Mary*.[40] His intensive participant observation fieldwork, however, was with the Azande (with whom he spent twenty months in total) and the Nuer (a year in total).

Evans-Pritchard's first book, *Witchcraft, Oracles and Magic among the Azande* (1937), became a seminal classic in the discipline and beyond.[41] *The International Dictionary of Anthropologists* testified in 1991: 'it remains the single most important empirical work in the sociological analysis of the thinking of preliterate peoples'.[42] No attempt will be made in this chapter to present all the themes, theories, or achievements in any of Evans-Pritchard's major works—or his career in general for that matter. Those features will be emphasized that most help to illuminate the focus of this study upon anthropologists and the Christian faith. To begin—lest Evans-Pritchard's distinctive contribution be over-read—one needs to keep in mind that he is quite clear that the Azande are fundamentally in error about most of these matters: 'Witches, as Azande conceive them, cannot exist'.[43] As to the second heading in the title, although the Azande do not discern this, actually 'their oracles tell them nothing'.[44] (Their main oracle involved observing how a chicken reacted to ingesting a particular poisonous substance.)[45] And to complete the triad, 'the futility of their magic' is also demonstrable.[46] So far, Frazer. What made Evans-Pritchard's monograph so groundbreaking, however, was his argument that all this notwithstanding, the Azande were no less rational than their European contemporaries. It was wrong to assume as Tylor and Frazer had done, and as Lucien Lévy-Bruhl (1857–1939) had expounded, that the thinking of primitive people was 'pre-logical' and thus fundamentally different from our own. This mistake was made by exaggerating both the extent to which Europeans are rational and the extent to which primitive people are irrational.

---

[40] Evans-Pritchard Papers, Pitt Rivers Museum, Oxford.

[41] E. E. Evans-Pritchard, *Witchcraft, Oracles and Magic among the Azande* (Oxford: Clarendon Press, 1937).

[42] T. O. Beidelman, 'E. E. Evans-Pritchard', p. 185.

[43] Evans-Pritchard, *Witchcraft*, p. 63.

[44] Evans-Pritchard, *Witchcraft*, pp. 337–38.

[45] To see a demonstration of this practice and for a visual depiction of Evans-Pritchard's anthropological work in general, see a film directed by André Singer, *Strange Beliefs: Sir Edward Evans-Pritchard* (Princeton: Films for the Humanities & Sciences, Inc, 1990).

[46] Evans-Pritchard, *Witchcraft*, p. 475.

First, Azande explanations do not contradict natural ones. We would explain an injury by saying that it happened because the wood was rotten and therefore the shelter collapsed. When Azande say that it was because of witchcraft they are not denying this explanation but rather accepting it before moving on to another level of enquiry. Witchcraft is their explanation for a question we do not even ask: why did it collapse at the particular time when it would injure me and not at some other time? Indeed, Evans-Pritchard never tired of observing that primitive people could not possibly survive if they did not have a keen understanding of the natural world which was grounded in observation and experimentation. Secondly, 'their mystical notions are eminently coherent, being interrelated by a network of logical ties, and are so ordered that they never too crudely contradict sensory experience but, instead, experience seems to justify them'.[47] They are thinking logically within a closed system: 'Within the limits set by these patterns they show great intelligence...they reason excellently in the idiom of their beliefs, but they cannot reason outside, or against, their beliefs because they have no other idiom in which to express their thoughts'.[48] All three parts of the mystical triad named in the title comprised an intellectually coherent system. Evans-Pritchard's conclusion was that Zande notions were neither illogical nor even uncritical, but rather marked by intellectual consistency. He even dryly observed:

> I always kept a supply of poison for the use of my household and neighbours and we regulated our affairs in accordance with the oracles' decisions. I may remark that I found this as satisfactory a way of running my home and affairs as any other I know of.[49]

This wry remark allows us to pick up the comparison from the other end. Vilfredo Pareto had argued that European thought was also largely 'non-logico-experimental'.[50] In the light of Evans-Pritchard's work on the Azande, many scholars have roguishly relished applying this insight to specific aspects of Western thought. For example, Ely Devons (1913–67), a professor of applied economics, claimed that economic statistics function for us in the same way that oracles did

---

[47] Evans-Pritchard, *Witchcraft*, pp. 319–20.
[48] Evans-Pritchard, *Witchcraft*, pp. 337–38.
[49] Evans-Pritchard, *Witchcraft*, pp. 260–70.
[50] E. E. Evans-Pritchard, *Theories of Primitive Religion* (Oxford: Clarendon Press, 1965), p. 92.

for the Azande.[51] Also drawing on Evans-Pritchard's monograph, the intellectual Michael Polanyi (1891–1976) observed that Marxism and Freudian theory were also closed, circular systems resulting in those working within them being blind to inconsistencies obvious to outsiders.[52] These applications of the argument of *Witchcraft, Oracles and Magic among the Azande* can also serve to underline how extraordinarily influential that book was even well beyond the discipline of anthropology.[53]

During 1932–34, Evans-Pritchard taught at Fuad I University (what is now Cairo University), but he returned to Oxford as Research Lecturer in African Sociology in 1935. His Lawrence-of-Arabia side was undiminished and when the war came he eagerly joined the Welsh Guards. The university had this squashed, however, by insisting that he was in a reserved occupation. Not to be thwarted, Evans-Pritchard set off for Africa, ostensibly to do fieldwork, but once there he was able to obtain a commission in the Sudan Auxiliary Defence Force (Oxford retaliated by dismissing him from his lectureship). He and his men hampered and fought Italian forces. He later ended up in the Middle East, finally spending a couple years as a Tribal Affairs Officer among the Bedouin of Cyrenaica (Libya)—work which included military intelligence. On St Michael's Day (29 September) 1944, Edward Evan Evans-Pritchard was received into the Roman Catholic Church in the cathedral at Benghazi.

*   *   *

Some academics found this action so against the grain of what a great anthropologist ought to be and do as to be almost unable to absorb it. Perhaps only a psychological theory of denial can explain how T. O. Beidelman—who had discussed his life with Evans-Pritchard at length and made a special study of the Oxford professor's contribution to the discipline—could write that he was 'converted to Roman Catholicism' at 'the close of his career'.[54] (He was only 42 years old

---

[51] Gluckman, *Allocation of Responsibility*, p. xiii.

[52] Michael Polanyi, *Personal Knowledge: Towards a Post-Critical Philosophy* (Chicago: University of Chicago Press, 1958), pp. 287–92.

[53] It was also influential for the discipline of history. The eminent historians Peter Brown and Keith Thomas both contributed to Mary Douglas (ed.), *Witchcraft, Confessions and Accusations* (London: Tavistock Publications, 1970).

[54] Beidelman, 'E. E. Evans-Pritchard', p. 186. Beidelman had known for decades the precise year that Evans-Pritchard had become a Catholic: T. O. Beidelman (ed.), *A Bibliography of the Writings of E. E. Evans-Pritchard* (London: Tavistock, 1974), p. 3.

and still two years away from being appointed to the Oxford chair that he would occupy so influentially for a quarter of a century!) Anthropologists have often emphasized a human tendency toward dual organization or binary thinking—the sacred and the profane, the right and the left, the sky and the earth, and so on. As the preface to an Evans-Pritchard festschrift affirmed: 'We have not lost the preoccupation with dichotomies that characterized writing at the end of the nineteenth century—in fact this interest runs through the volume'.[55] It has come as a comfort to some, therefore, to be able to reflect that Evans-Pritchard was a bad Catholic—secular is better than religious, Protestant is better than Catholic but—saved without a moment to spare—bad Catholic is better than good Catholic: E-P might have been a Catholic, they muse, but at least he was a bad Catholic. It was actually Evans-Pritchard who initially labelled himself in this manner. His article in response to the question, 'Why did you become a Catholic?', concluded with these words: 'I have no regrets. Bad Catholic though I be, I would rather be a bad one than not one at all'.[56] This was published in the year of his death in the journal *New Blackfriars* (yes, he was the kind of 'bad' Catholic who has his spiritual autobiography printed in a publication of the English Dominicans).

What might people have in mind when Evans-Pritchard is referred to as a bad Catholic? Perhaps that he would engage in behaviour that official Catholic teaching deemed sinful. Anthropology is a relentlessly gossipy profession. It was Evans-Pritchard's own instinct to improve a tale in the telling and he has certainly reaped what he sowed. My experience of researching this chapter has been that those who are in the least position to know are the ones that confidently tell these urban legends (or even put them in print)—some of which are not just exaggerated but simply demonstrably false. There is no need for me to attempt to sort this laundry here—conceding it all for the purpose of argument makes no difference to the theme of this chapter. In particular, it is patently obvious that Evans-Pritchard drank too much. This habit got sufficiently out of hand that he was pulled over by the police for drunk driving—an incident that was reported in the *Telegraph*.[57] (Touchingly, the institutional memory at All Souls is that he promptly went to the Warden and offered to resign his fellowship.)

---

[55] Robin Horton and Ruth Finnegan (eds.), *Modes of Thought: Essays on Thinking in Western and Non-Western Societies* (London: Faber & Faber, 1973), p. 15.

[56] Evans-Pritchard, 'Fragment', p. 37.   [57] Burton, *Introduction*, p. 15.

One thinks of Evans-Pritchard's obituary tribute for Jack Driberg: 'His was a rare spirit and his weaknesses were consistent with the heroic in his personality and further endeared him to his friends. The gods give us faults to make us men'.[58] On the strength of his salty conversation in a New York taxi cab, Beidelman relished portraying Evans-Pritchard as a 'dirty old man'.[59] One might therefore be tempted in good binary fashion, and with no less a twinkle in one's eye, to counter with Evelyn Waugh's revelation towards the end of *Brideshead Revisited*, in which 'a very holy old man' discerns Sebastian Flyte's holiness, were it not that someone would no doubt read such a statement woodenly and accuse one of trying to turn E-P into a saint.[60] (It is generally agreed as best practice among anthropologists that tales of sinfulness, however improbable, should be accepted piously on faith, whilst saintliness demands rigorous scientific proof.) It is enough to say, as Evans-Pritchard did in order to warn against underestimating the importance of their religion to the Bedouin of Cyrenaica: 'piety and holiness, as we have often been admonished, are not the same'.[61]

Godfrey Lienhardt (1921–93) is perhaps the key disseminator of the bad Catholic trope (which he expressed in the more delicate form that Evans-Pritchard 'was not what is called a "good Catholic" ').[62] By this Lienhardt seems to have had in mind the fact that E-P did not attend Mass regularly. The literary scholar and writer J. R. R. Tolkien (1892–1973) tried to no avail to recruit Evans-Pritchard to join him in supporting their local Catholic parish church. Instead, Evans-Pritchard chose to worship corporately at the Dominican house in Oxford, Blackfriars. Timothy Radcliffe OP, who continues to serve at Blackfriars, can still remember seeing Evans-Pritchard at Mass, but his testimony accords with the general report that E-P was the kind of Catholic who one would see in the congregation mostly at Christmas and Easter.[63] Were we not obliged to think in binary terms, one might be tempted to say that this would make him a typical

[58] E. E. Evans-Pritchard, 'Obituaries: Jack Herbert Driberg: 1888–1946', *Man*, 47 (January 1947), p. 12.

[59] T. O. Beidelman, 'Sir Edward Evan Evans-Pritchard (1902–1973): An Appreciation', *Anthropos*, 69 (1974), p. 556.

[60] Evelyn Waugh, *Brideshead Revisited: The Sacred and Profane Memories of Captain Charles Ryder* (Boston: Little, Brown and Company, 1945), pp. 305–306.

[61] E. E. Evans-Pritchard, *The Sanusi of Cyrenaica* (Oxford: Clarendon Press, 1949), p. 63.

[62] Godfrey Lienhardt, 'E-P: a Personal View', *Man*, n.s. 9, 2 (June 1974), p. 303.

[63] Timothy Radcliffe OP to Timothy Larsen, email, 25 April 2012.

Catholic. Moreover, Evans-Pritchard was active in Catholic intellectual venues, including giving the Aquinas lecture, and writing and
reviewing for *New Blackfriars*. The editor of the venerable Catholic
newspaper, the *Tablet*, so took Evans-Pritchard's support for granted
that he once sent him a book to review without even bothering to
first inquire whether or not he would be willing to do it; as assumed,
he was.[64]

One would be quite mistaken, however, to infer from 'bad Catholic'
that Evans-Pritchard was not a sincere Catholic or that he did not give
genuine intellectual assent to the principal, historic doctrines of the
Christian faith. Yet some have sought to relieve the tension of a great
anthropologist choosing as an adult to be received into the Church
by imagining that it was so. Thus Michael G. Kenny has written: 'But
why a Catholic? Evans-Pritchard said that he had no taste for the catechism nor much for dogma; in this he was not only a bad Catholic
but indeed a rank heretic.'[65] In a lifetime of writing about religion,
the only evidence Kenny found that Evans-Pritchard was a 'rank heretic' was that he once expressed a preference for *creatio ex deo* over
creatio ex nihilo. This is an area of thought where Christians in good
standing have been given to speculation (it is not addressed in the historic creeds) and it is certainly not the kind of statement that could be
equated with having a heretical view of the doctrine of the Trinity or
the person and work of Jesus Christ. Kenny goes on to assert: 'I think
that he was a Catholic on emotional and esthetic grounds.'[66] Again,
this is simply wrong and, moreover, the precise point of this erroneous view seems to have been a desire to be able somehow to dismiss
the idea of Evans-Pritchard having actually believed the creed.

Bruce Ross-Smith remembers his friend E-P as someone with
an unabashed commitment to historic Christian doctrines—not
least the resurrection of Jesus Christ—right to the end of his life.
This testimony accords well with Evans-Pritchard's published writings which make it abundantly clear that he thought that attempts
to make Christianity more acceptable to the modern world by mut-
ing or abandoning its key doctrinal claims were both unnecessary

---

[64] Evans-Pritchard to John Cumming, June and July 1973, Tablet Publishing
Company Records, Burns Library, Boston College.

[65] Michael G. Kenny, 'Trickster and Mystic: The Anthropological Persona of E. E.
Evans-Pritchard', *Anthropology and Humanism Quarterly*, 12, 1 (1987), p. 13.

[66] Kenny, 'Trickster and Mystic', p. 14.

and counterproductive. In his *A History of Anthropological Thought*, Evans-Pritchard's disdain is palpable as he covers figure after figure, judging for each in turn that while they maintained a Christian social identity—sometimes even a Catholic one—they had so drained away the intellectual content of the faith that they would be better labelled a deist.[67] Here is his explicit rejection of such accommodating attempts: 'An even greater embarrassment were the desperate efforts to save the ship by jettisoning its entire cargo. Overboard went prophecies, miracles, dogma, theology, ritual, tradition, clericalism, and the supernatural.'[68] Evans-Pritchard himself was quite willing to affirm God's power and prerogative to do miracles. Far from such a pious conviction denying the consistent, orderly working of nature that is the foundation of modern science, it actually presupposes it: 'there cannot be a stronger assertion of natural law than belief in miracles.'[69] Becoming a Catholic was not merely an aesthetic affinity but rather a deliberate siding with full-blooded Christian belief in the judgement that: 'Protestantism shades into Deism and Deism into agnosticism, and that the choice is between all or nothing, a choice which allows of no compromise between a Church which has stood its ground and made no concessions, and no religion at all.'[70]

* * *

Evans-Pritchard never tired of pointing out that the vast majority of leading anthropologists, past and present, did not have a religious faith. In a 1947 article in *The Listener* he averred: 'It would therefore be useless for me to pretend that social anthropology is not predominantly rationalist in outlook. It has been so from its beginnings, was yesterday among my teachers, and is today among my colleagues.'[71] In a 1950 essay he observed: 'anthropology has always been mixed up with free-thought and has been considered, not unjustly, as anti-religious in tone, and even in aim'.[72] He developed this point systematically in his 1959 Aquinas lecture, naming names as he worked his way from

[67] Evans-Pritchard, *History of Anthropological Thought*, pp. 3–4, 13, and 19.

[68] E. E. Evans-Pritchard, *Social Anthropology and Other Essays* (New York: The Free Press, 1962), p. 167. (This is from his 1959 Aquinas lecture, 'Religion and the Anthropologists'.)

[69] Evans-Pritchard, *Social Anthropology*, p. 169.

[70] Evans-Pritchard, *Social Anthropology*, p. 171.

[71] E. E. Evans-Pritchard, 'Does Anthropology Undermine Faith?', *The Listener* (8 May 1947), p. 714.

[72] Evans-Pritchard, *Social Anthropology*, p. 113.

the eighteenth-century precursors of the discipline to the present. The early figures were 'agnostics and hostile to religion': belief in God was an illusion for both Tylor and Frazer. Indeed, 'The purpose of *The Golden Bough* was to discredit revealed religion'.[73] (He had earlier dismissed Frazer's assumption that a religious idea could be invalidated by showing that it was also believed by savages as 'a piece of ethnocentric arrogance'.[74]) Moreover, this is an area of continuity in the discipline:

> All the leading sociologists and anthropologists contemporaneous with, or since, Frazer were agnostics and positivists—Westermarck, Hobhouse, Haddon, Rivers, Seligman, Radcliffe-Brown and Malinowski; and if they discussed religion they treated it as superstition for which some scientific explanation was required and could be supplied. Almost all the leading anthropologists of my own generation would, I believe, hold that religious faith is total illusion, a curious phenomenon soon to become extinct and to be explained in such terms as 'compensation' and 'projection' or by some sociologistic interpretation on the lines of maintenance of social solidarity...Religion is superstition to be explained by anthropologists, not something an anthropologist, or indeed any rational person, could himself believe in.[75]

Later that same year he wrote to Alfred L. Kroeber, Professor Emeritus of Anthropology at the University of California, Berkley, asking him to confirm that no American anthropologist adhered to any religious faith.[76] In the introduction of *Theories of Primitive Religion* (1965), Evans-Pritchard yet again observed a common feature of the theorists under discussion:

> with one or two exceptions, whatever the background may have been, the persons whose writings have been most influential have been at the time they wrote agnostics or atheists...They sought, and found, in primitive religions a weapon which could, they thought, be used with deadly effect against Christianity...Religious belief was to these anthropologists absurd, and it is so to most anthropologists of yesterday and today.[77]

[73] Evans-Pritchard, *Social Anthropology*, p. 161.

[74] Evans-Pritchard, 'Does Anthropology Undermine Faith?', p. 715.

[75] Evans-Pritchard, *Social Anthropology*, p. 162.

[76] E. E. Evans-Pritchard to Alfred L. Kroeber, 15 November 1959: Matthey, 'A Glimpse', p. 43.

[77] E. E. Evans-Pritchard, *Theories of Primitive Religion* (Oxford: Clarendon Press, 1965), pp. 14–16.

Other observers agreed. To take one, his collaborator for the influential *African Political Systems* and ally in the profession, the Cambridge anthropologist Meyer Fortes (1906–83), confirmed the accuracy of this point.[78] Various voices testify that Evans-Pritchard's faith commitment, especially in the years immediately after he became a Catholic, led to some personal opposition from some of his fellow anthropologists. Ahmed Al-Shahi, for example, reports: 'his conversion to Catholicism was regarded as a kind of defection from the mainly rationalist, agnostic or "humanist" principles of his pre-war friends at LSE'.[79] Evans-Pritchard himself credited his Anglican mother with supporting him when: 'I became a Catholic and had to face some personal difficulties, as many of us have had to do'.[80]

Evans-Pritchard's response to the widespread belief by anthropologists that the findings of their discipline exposed religious belief as false was to attempt to hoist them with their own petard. As to the leading theorists who assumed that religion was an illusion, again and again his judgement on their own work was that it was not based in research and it was not scientific. His unsparing attacks often seemed to have been the mirror image of the complaints that these figures made about religious beliefs. To wit:

> Durkheim was an evolutionary fanatic who wished to explain social phenomena in terms of pseudohistorical origins. Hence arose one of his most serious blunders, a blunder in both logic and method…a whole string of unsupportable, even stupid, assumptions…We have, I fear, come down decisively against Durkheim and to conclude that he may not in any sense be regarded as a scientist…He broke every cardinal rule of critical scholarship, as well as of logic…[81]

As for *The Golden Bough*: 'I conclude therefore that Frazer's theories of the similarity between magic and science and of their historic

---

[78] M. F. C. Bourdillon and Meyer Fortes (eds.), *Sacrifice* (London: Academic Press for the Royal Anthropological Institute of Great Britain and Ireland, 1980), p. vi. For the view that Evans-Pritchard played a significant part in the drafting of the influential introduction to *African Political Systems*, see Goody, *Expansive Moment*, p. 77.

[79] Ahmed Al-Shahi, 'Evans-Pritchard, Anthropology, and Catholicism at Oxford: Godfrey Lienhardt's view', *Journal of the Anthropological Society of Oxford*, 30, 1 (1999), p. 70.

[80] Evans-Pritchard, 'Fragment', p. 36. Sympathetic to such difficulties, Evans-Pritchard donated money to the Converts' Aid Society for the assistance of clergy and religious received into the Catholic Church.

[81] Evans-Pritchard, *History of Anthropological Thought*, pp. 161, 168.

stages are unsupported by either sound evidence or logic and that they have little heuristic value'.[82] While the standard theorists had hitherto looked upon the mystical behaviour of primitive people as so illogical that it was difficult for those who think like us to understand it at all, Evans-Pritchard not only demonstrated that the Azande were actually quite rational, but he completed the inversion by claiming that it was the ideas of figures such as Tylor and Frazer that were 'contrary to common sense', 'ludicrous', or even just plain 'silly'—'the interpretations that satisfied Victorian and Edwardian anthropologists now appear so lacking in understanding that we are surprised that anyone could ever have thought them adequate'; 'explanations which now seem to us remarkable for their triviality but which were widely accepted at the time'.[83] Damning it as the 'intellectualist (English) interpretation', as far back as 1933 Evans-Pritchard had explained that the mystical beliefs which so convinced Tylor and Frazer that primitive people did not know how the natural world works actually in themselves proved that they already possessed such knowledge: 'You cannot have agricultural or hunting magic unless you have agriculture and hunting'.[84] One imagines Evans-Pritchard took mischievous delight in identifying the religious mystic Emanuel Swedenborg (1688–1772) as 'that remarkable scientist', while Darwin, Marx, Freud, Frazer, and Comte are 'the great myth-makers'.[85] He could even turn this assault on his contemporaries. Evans-Pritchard's review of Theodor Reik's *Myth and Guilt* was entitled 'Just-So Stories', and he often claimed that theories purporting to be scholarly were just yarns spun from pure imagination like Rudyard Kipling (1865–1936) entertaining us with a fanciful account of how the leopard got his spots. Reik, he avers, draws on discredited and out-of-date material (such as Tylor) and though he imagines he is offering 'a scientific discovery' it would take more faith to believe in it than to accept literally the account of the Fall in the book of Genesis.[86]

[82] Evans-Pritchard, *History of Anthropological Thought*, p. 146.

[83] Evans-Pritchard, *Theories*, pp. 4–5; Evans-Pritchard, *Social Anthropology*, p. 36; E. E. Evans-Pritchard et al., *The Institutions of Primitive Society: A Series of Broadcast Talks* (Oxford: Basil Blackwell, 1954), p. 9; Evans-Pritchard, *Social Anthropology*, p. 161.

[84] E. E. Evans-Pritchard, 'The Intellectualist (English) Interpretation of Magic', *Bulletin of the Faculty of Arts* (Cairo), 1, 2 (1933): I have been able to consult a reprint of this article in the *Journal of the Anthropological Society of Oxford*, 1 (1970), p. 136.

[85] E. E. Evans-Pritchard, 'Some Reflections on Mysticism', *Dyn*, 1 (1970), p. 101; Evans-Pritchard, *Theories*, p. 1.

[86] E. E. Evans-Pritchard, 'Just-So Stories' (review of Theodor Reik, *Myth and Guilt*), *The Tablet*, 8 March 1958, pp. 229–30.

Furthermore, it is their very lack of religious beliefs which tempted these theorists into many of these unscientific and absurd views.[87] To wit:

> I think it is significant that Durkheim was a militant atheist, not just an unbeliever but a propagandist for unbelief. Religion therefore presented a challenge to him. He had to find some sort of explanation of what is a universal phenomenon in both time and space, and could only do so in terms of the sociological metaphysic to which he had irretrievably committed himself.[88]

The conclusion of *Theories of Primitive Religion* dismisses the whole lot of them in this way:

> I would further suggest that this followed from their assumptions that the souls and spirits and gods of religion have no reality. For if they are regarded as complete illusions, then some biological, psychological, or sociological theory of how everywhere and at all times men have been stupid enough to believe in them seems to be called for. He who accepts the reality of spiritual beings does not feel the same need for such explanations...[89]

Imagine how different Evans-Pritchard's *The Nuer* would have been if he had proceeded on the assumption that cattle are purely imaginary creatures and then attempted to find some way—however far-fetched—to explain why they were nonetheless so central to the thinking and actions of this Nilotic people. This is what it is like to read Tylor, Frazer, and company on primitive religion: 'After all, it does make a difference whether one thinks that a cow exists or is an illusion!'[90] In a 1947 article entitled, 'Does Anthropology Undermine Faith?', Evans-Pritchard gave his summative statement that all the attempts to imply that his discipline had findings which ought to make a thinking person abandon Christian beliefs had themselves been exploded as false: 'There is certainly nothing in its subject-matter which should make faith more

---

[87] Evans-Pritchard repeatedly remarked that the best textbook on anthropology when he was a student was Robert Lowie's *Primitive Society* (1920) and one wonders if part of the reason why he was less critical of it was because Lowie never even attempted to discuss religion in it. E. E. Evans-Pritchard, 'Some Recollections', p. 241.

[88] Evans-Pritchard, *History of Anthropological Thought*, p. 157.

[89] Evans-Pritchard, *Theories*, p. 121.

[90] E. E. Evans-Pritchard, 'Some Reminiscences', p. 5. See also, Matthew Engelke, 'The Problem of Belief: Evans-Pritchard and Victor Turner on "the inner life"', *Anthropology Today*, 18, 6 (December 2002), pp. 3–8.

difficult'.[91] Moreover, this was also his judgement on geology, biology, and all the other disciplines which it was claimed in the nineteenth century had made discoveries which discredited Christianity. This entire crisis of faith was simply a Protestant muddle: they had made the Bible into 'a fetish' and confused the idea of it being literally true throughout (which it is not) with the credibility of 'Christian theology' itself.[92] E-P dismissed half a century of attacks on the intellectual viability of Christianity with a yawn: 'I must confess that I find the whole period when these controversies were at their height exceedingly tedious'.[93]

* * *

E. E. Evans-Pritchard did not think that religious convictions could be proved in an objective, scientific manner. To say that religion was the product of 'faith and sentiment' rather than 'experiment and reasoning', however, was simply to place it at the heart of what human beings value most: 'the same may be said of most of our ideas and actions; our morals, our loyalties to our families and countries, and so forth'.[94] Evans-Pritchard was quite confident of his own awareness of the reality of God. The fact that other people denied the Almighty's existence did not make him doubt his own apprehension: it merely caused him to reflect that just as there are those who are colour-blind or tone deaf so some are deprived of a spiritual sense which most people possess.[95] Evans-Pritchard once even went so far so to claim that religious unbelief was a 'disease' which 'makes its victims blind'.[96] His framing of Darwin's doubt is suggestive: 'Darwin slowly lost his faith, and with it all taste for the arts, during his forty years as a neurotic invalid'.[97] In an interview in 1970—the year of his retirement—he said that one of his projects for this new phase of his life would be a book on 'religious mysticism'. It would seem, he remarked, that mystics are using different language to express the same thing: 'If that is true, then there is a certain objectivity in it because all these people must have

---

[91] Evans-Pritchard, 'Does Anthropology Undermine Faith?', p. 715.

[92] Evans-Pritchard, *Social Anthropology*, p. 165. Catholics, by contrast, he averred, were able to think in terms of 'different modes, or levels, of interpretation in the Bible'.

[93] Evans-Pritchard, *Social Anthropology*, p. 166.

[94] Evans-Pritchard, *Theories*, p. 97.

[95] Evans-Pritchard, *Theories*, p. 121.

[96] Evans-Pritchard, 'Does Anthropology Undermine Faith?', p. 715.

[97] Evans-Pritchard, *Social Anthropology*, p. 160.

had the same experience...they can't for hundreds and even thousands of years, have been completely fooling themselves.'[98]

Despite this being such a robust, polemical claim that the divine is real (mystics testify that they 'have incontroversible knowledge of God...this knowledge is experiential and therefore verifiable'),[99] it also made faith a rather private affair in the sense that it conceded that if an interlocutor professed not to share this perception then one had straight off reached an impasse. Christianity for Evans-Pritchard was mystical in the sense that one could experience it as an immediate apprehension of the presence of the Almighty but—if one did not—then the only way to belief was forever barred by an angel with a flaming sword. Thus while they placed Evans-Pritchard in the 'bad Catholic' category, Lienhardt nevertheless also thought of him as 'a contemplative' and Kenny as 'a mystic'.[100] Many have observed that Evans-Pritchard tended to hold in reserve what was most important to him, especially from those who did not already have an affinity with it. He was apt to deflect attention away with a joke from the things he took most seriously. His son Ambrose observed: 'My father always disguised his deepest thoughts behind layers of self-irony, mischief, and intellectual barricades, which could make him seem irreverent. That was clearly not the case'.[101] (As the Azande say, 'One cannot see inside a man as one can see into an open-wove basket'.)[102] Nevertheless, at the end of his Oxford career Evans-Pritchard put his spiritual side on display in a refracted way with a public lecture entitled, 'Some Reflections on Mysticism'.[103] After he delivered it, E-P remarked to Meyer Fortes: 'It must have been apparent to you, if not to them, that this is my inner life'.[104] In the lecture, he observed that to understand whereof they speak one has to 'experience what it is

---

[98] 'Oxford Scientists: Professor E. E. Evans-Pritchard', *Zenith*, VII, 3 (1970), pp. 20–21. (I read a copy of this article which is in the Mary Douglas Papers, Northwestern University Archives, Evanston, Ill. I have taken the citation details from Beidelman's *Bibliography*.)

[99] Evans-Pritchard, 'Mysticism', p. 115.

[100] R. G. Lienhardt, 'Sir Edward Evan Evans-Pritchard (1902–1973)' in Robert Blake and C. S. Nicholls (eds.), *The Dictionary of National Biography: 1971–1980* (Oxford: Oxford University Press, 1986), p. 298; Kenny, 'Trickster and Mystic', pp. 9–15.

[101] Mr Ambrose Evans-Pritchard to Timothy Larsen, email, 18 March 2010.

[102] Evans-Pritchard, *Witchcraft*, p. 250.

[103] Evans-Pritchard, 'Mysticism', pp. 101–15.

[104] Barnes, 'Edward Evan Evans-Pritchard', p. 480.

the mystics say they have experienced' since it is 'incommunicable in words'.[105] Mysticism is:

> the intuitive, inward, imaginative, poetic, and therefore personal and highly subjective, element in religion in contrast to the formal, external, conventional, institutional, dogmatic, ritual and liturgical side of it. These are not opposites.[106]

This non-oppositional contrast is the context for understanding many things that Evans-Pritchard thought, said, and did regarding his own life of faith. The contrast was real. His own lackadaisical approach to corporate worship was at least partially because he saw it as the formal side of religion and he preferred the inward side. Thus his insight into the seemingly slack religious practices of the Bedouin: they had chosen primarily a mystical expression of their faith to compensate for official Islam's tendency 'to be a cold and formalistic religion'.[107] Evans-Pritchard was evoking the same contrast when he claimed that the catechism was not the essence of the faith for him. Nevertheless, it is wrong to over-read this as oppositional: 'Indeed it has generally been recognized by the great mystics themselves that, if not anchored to institutional religion, any form of mystical exercises can be both futile and dangerous'.[108] Evans-Pritchard preferred to experience God in this highly subjective way, but while moving about on the surface as the winds of the Spirit blew, he was careful to remain tethered to the Church Catholic.

Most of the lecture covertly reveals Evans-Pritchard's own inner life by presenting the devotional resources that meant the most to him. He evokes a whole range of great Catholic mystics. Evans-Pritchard did his own private prayers daily with earnest concentration. He regularly read the Bible, the Missal, and books by spiritual authors such as the Desert Fathers which would be stacked on his bedside table. He frequently sang hymns to himself and declaimed the religious poetry that meant so much to him. These personally prized treasures became

---

[105] Evans-Pritchard, 'Mysticism', p. 101.

[106] Evans-Pritchard, 'Mysticism', p. 102.

[107] Evans-Pritchard, *Sanusi*, p. 1. The research for this book took place alongside his military duties. See also, Major E. E. Evans-Pritchard, *Biographical Notes on Members of the Sanusi Family*, 'by H.Q.B.M.A. (Cyrenaica) for the use of offices of the Adminstration', n.d. Evans-Pritchard Papers, 1/9, Tylor Library, Institute of Social and Cultural Anthropology, University of Oxford.

[108] Evans-Pritchard, 'Mysticism', p. 102.

the storehouse of illustrations he raided. For example, in the lecture he connected poetry with mysticism and the first poet he mentioned was Henry Vaughan (1621–95). Not only did Evans-Pritchard have Vaughan's poem 'Peace' (which is doctrinally specific enough to speak of the rule of 'One born in a manger') memorized, but he would frequently quote it aloud for his own edification.

Evans-Pritchard destroyed his private papers, but this side of his life has even managed to leave a trace or two in the professional papers of his that made it into archives at the Institute of Social and Cultural Anthropology. In the notebook on 'Egypt & Lebanon' there is one solitary newspaper clipping. It is from the *Egyptian Gazette*, 19 October 1938: 'The Crisis that Changed my Life' by H. W. (Bunny) Austin (1906–2000), a Cambridge graduate and society figure who was famous for being a highly successful gentleman tennis player. This article was Austin's testimony of Christian conversion and his appeal for others to seek a divine transformation: 'We can only change ourselves by the help of God. But God cannot help us unless we are willing first to surrender our wills to His...He will help us if, in stillness, we know that He is God'.[109] The file 'Notes on Nilotic Religion' has attached to it a Catholic devotional card: 'Saint Winefride Pray for us'.[110] One suspects that Evans-Pritchard might have had a soft spot for Winefride as she is a Welsh saint. But one must not tax readers any further in this vein. As Evans-Pritchard himself observed: 'If Lévy-Bruhl had wished to arouse an Englishman's worst suspicions, he could not have done better than he did by the use of the word "mystical"'.[111]

As to his anthropological work, perhaps the final volume in his trilogy on the Nuer might be seen as Evans-Pritchard's own attempt to answer the question: what hath St Winefride to do with leopard-skin priests? While this monograph was a new departure, it is worth observing that there are continuities as well. The first in the series, *The Nuer* (1940), was published several years before Evans-Pritchard became a Catholic. Still, it is not without its own connections to Christianity. After the title page, the first thing one reads is the dedication: 'To

---

[109] Evans-Pritchard Papers, 1/10 'Egypt & Lebanon', Tylor Library, Institute of Social and Cultural Anthropology, University of Oxford.

[110] Evans-Pritchard Papers, 1/8 'Notes on Nilotic Religion', Tylor Library, Institute of Social and Cultural Anthropology, University of Oxford.

[111] Evans-Pritchard, *Theories*, p. 83.

the Staff of the American Mission at Nasser'.[112] It is hard to imagine Malinowski dedicating a book to missionaries. Evans-Pritchard, however, as Mary Douglas observed, credited missionaries in his writings with a 'punctiliousness' that was almost ostentatious.[113] This was the case even with his first book on the Azande: the acknowledgements thanked the staff of four different mission stations as well as Canon E. C. Gore who had read the entire manuscript and pointed out errors in it.[114] At various points in the main text, Evans-Pritchard acknowledges that he is gratefully dependent on good scholarly work done by missionaries. Most notably, he gives effusive credit to Father De Graer, a Dominican missionary, when discussing Azande medicine.[115] Evans-Pritchard also expressed a wish that his own research would be of use to missionaries in Zandeland. Even in 1972—by which time missionaries were thoroughly a despised foil for the vast majority of anthropologists—Evans-Pritchard was quite willing to write for *Bible Lands*, a publication of the Church of England mission to Jerusalem and the Middle East.[116] One can sense his desire to not have the contribution of missionaries edited out of the record in comments such as his praise for Adam Ferguson (1723–1816): 'He gives a good account, based on Jesuit sources, of what was then known of the American Indians'.[117] Evans-Pritchard could also be critical of some missionaries, of course, but he did not criticize the aim of Christian missions, but only their inept attempts to achieve it.[118]

The American Mission at Nasser was the work of evangelical Presbyterians. Evans-Pritchard thanked in particular one of its missionaries, Cora Blanche Soule. In a letter in which she also mentioned that she was on her way to the influential conservative evangelical Holiness annual gathering in England, the Keswick Convention, she noted with pleasure that 'the Anthropologist' had donated twenty pounds sterling to the mission.[119] In the letter which Evans-Pritchard sent with this

[112] Evans-Pritchard, *The Nuer*.

[113] Douglas, *Evans-Pritchard*, pp. 29–30.

[114] Evans-Pritchard, *Witchcraft*, p. viii.

[115] Evans-Pritchard, *Witchcraft*, pp. 481–82.

[116] E. E. Evans-Pritchard, Review of Brian Hugh MacDermot, *Cult of the Sacred Spear: The Story of the Nuer Tribe in Ethiopia*, in *Bible Lands*, 18, 8 (autumn 1972), pp. 247–48.

[117] Evans-Pritchard, *History of Anthropological Thought*, p. 26.

[118] E. E. Evans-Pritchard, 'The Perils of Translation', *New Blackfriars* (December 1969), pp. 813–15. It is significant that he chose to place this article criticizing some missionary efforts in a Christian publication.

[119] Cora Blanche Soule to Dr Anderson, 28 January 1932, Cora Blanche Soule Papers, Presbyterian Historical Archives, Philadelphia, RG 209-14-12. I am grateful to Dr Edward Miner of the University of Iowa.

cheque in 1931 (that is, well over a decade before he was received into the Catholic Church) he had observed:

> I shall be indebted to you if you will allow me to show my apprecia-
> tion of your work in this manner. People in the Sudan often say that
> I am against Christian missions. It is largely true that I am against mis-
> sions, but not against Christian missions, and by that I mean missions
> which regard it as a privilege to work among Africans and realize that
> Christianity is a spirit which can permeate any culture and not a body of
> ready-made and repressive rules of conduct which a native must accept
> in exchange for a higher social status. Yours is the only station I have
> ever been at where I felt that the Europeans were really at one with the
> natives and treated them as brothers and sisters.[120]

A missionary at this same station in the post-Second World War period, Eleanor Vandevort, a graduate of Wheaton College, Illinois, wrote an account of her ministry among the Nuer entitled *A Leopard Tamed* (1968).[121] The preface was written by the most famous evangelical missionary of that era, her friend Elisabeth Elliot (1926–). Evans-Pritchard wrote to the publisher to say that he had found the book 'most moving and even beautiful'.[122]

After this dedication to missionaries, the next page in *The Nuer* is a rather gratuitous passage from the Bible (Isaiah 18:1-2) which serves as an epigraph. In the introduction, he tells us that the Nuer are 'about 200,000 souls'.[123] Across his writings over the decades Evans-Pritchard was apt to use this old-fashioned construction and one wonders if he liked it as a kind of quiet, personal, and somewhat playful affirmation that human beings do indeed have souls. It was apparently distinctive. For example, in the edited volume *African Political Systems*, the chapters generally include population estimates, but all others— Max Gluckman on the Zulu, Isaac Schapera on the Ngwato, Audrey Richards on the Bemba, S. F. Nabel on the Kede, Günter Wagner on

---

[120] E. E. Evans-Pritchard to Cora Blanche Soule, American Presbyterian Mission at Nasir, 24 December 1931, Cora Blanche Soule Papers, Presbyterian Historical Archives, Philadelphia, RG 209-14-12. For Evans-Pritchard praising these missionaries in a letter to a colonial officer, see Douglas H. Johnson, 'Evans-Pritchard, The Nuer, and the Sudan Political Service', *African Affairs*, 81, 323 (April 1982), pp. 231–46.

[121] Eleanor Vandevort, *A Leopard Tamed: The Story of an African Pastor, his People, and his Problems* (New York: Harper & Row, 1968).

[122] E. E. Evans-Pritchard to Laura Paull, Religious Books Department, Harper & Row, 8 February 1968, Nuer Field Notes Collection, Indiana University Library Digital Program.

[123] Evans-Pritchard, *The Nuer*, p. 3.

the Bantu, and Meyer Fortes on the Tallensi—do this without reference to 'souls' which only occur in the parts of the volume written or
co-written by Evans-Pritchard.[124] There are also biblical references in
the main text of *The Nuer*. The hostile relationship between the Nuer
and the Dinka, for example, is explained by them with a myth 'like
that of Esau and Jacob'.[125] Or again: 'This rite and the mark of Cain
on the arm are known as *bir*'.[126] As Evans-Pritchard's appreciation for
this Nilotic people will be evident in *Nuer Religion* it is perhaps also
worth noting that *The Nuer* chronicles the rocky start of this relationship. The British had recently subdued them and therefore, in the eyes
of the Nuer, Evans-Pritchard was one of the enemy. His attempts to
elicit information from them were met with a stonewalling technique
of which he gives a hilarious specimen. This was so frustrating that it
drove him into a state that he described as 'Nuerosis'. When they did
become loquacious he faced the problem of the unreliable narrator: he
once spent a whole day taking down the details of a lineage, only to
be told on the morrow by his informants that they had just been jok-
ing with him and had made it all up! While not cooperating with his
inquiries, the Nuer would nonetheless allow him no privacy: he seems
to have been unable to escape observation even to defecate. Sprinkled
into his anthropological account are, as it were, dry glimpses into what
his life was like such as, 'It at once strikes a European that the condition
of drinking water at periods of the dry season leave much to be desired,
especially if he has to drink it himself'.[127] The second volume in the trilogy, *Kinship and Marriage among the Nuer*, also carefully credits missionaries and uses 'souls' to describe population estimates.[128] The title
pays tribute to a monograph by one of the rare founding figures of the
discipline who also believed Christian faith claims, William Robertson
Smith, *Kinship and Marriage in Early Arabia* (1885).

* * *

[124] M. Fortes and E. E. Evans-Pritchard (eds.), *African Political Systems*
(Oxford: Oxford University Press, 1940). Henrika Kuklick has observed of this volume: 'It is generally agreed that this book heralded and inspired a generation of
anthropologists'. Henrika Kuklick, *The Savage Within: The Social History of British
Anthropology, 1885–1945* (Cambridge: Cambridge University Press, 1991), p. 269.

[125] Evans-Pritchard, *The Nuer*, p. 125.

[126] Evans-Pritchard, *The Nuer*, p. 152.

[127] Evans-Pritchard, *The Nuer*, p. 33.

[128] E. E. Evans-Pritchard, *Kinship and Marriage among the Nuer* (Oxford: Clarendon
Press, 1951), pp. vi, vii, 69.

Evans-Pritchard was interested in the religious beliefs of the people he studied from the very beginning of his career. Even before his first book appeared, he had already published an article on 'Zande Theology'.[129] This was, however, unpropitious terrain: 'I have never been able to elicit any interest in, and have found that Azande are frankly bored by, questions about the Supreme Being'.[130] Their deity, Mbori, was a god-of-the-gaps, evoked simply as a way of saying that they did not know. The divine name was often voiced as a thought-less expletive—something not to be confused with a pious utterance. When a prince named his son 'Mbori has closed my lips', he was not testifying to the workings of divine providence in his life: the poor flummoxed father had simply responded when asked what they should call the child that he could not think of a name.[131]

Not so the Nuer. The Zande were a magical people, but the Nuer were a religious one. Moreover, magic is fundamentally false while religion is fundamentally true. While the intended inference of Tylor and Frazer's work was that not only is savage religion erroneous but so is civilized religion, Evans-Pritchard's implicit message was the inverse: not only is Christianity sophisticated, insightful, and true, but so is Nuer theology. Evans-Pritchard initially made the case for Nuer religion in no less a high-profile way than at his presidential address for the Royal Anthropological Institute.[132] (As the material in that lec-ture would be incorporated into the monograph, however, there is no need to analyse that address separately.)

One immediately knows what kind of book *Nuer Religion* is: on the very first page Evans-Pritchard discusses the term *kwoth* ('spirit') in relation to the equivalents in what in traditional Catholic teaching are the three sacred languages: the Latin *spiritus*, the Greek *pneuma*, and the Hebrew *ruah*.[133] In the preface, Evans-Pritchard asserted that Nuer and Dinka religions 'have features which bring to mind the Hebrews of the Old Testament' and therefore he defiantly warned readers that the Bible would be a recurring point of reference.[134] It would be tedious

[129] E. E. Evans-Pritchard, 'Zande Theology', *Sudan Notes and Records*, XIX (1936), pp. 5–46.

[130] Evans-Pritchard, 'Zande Theology', p. 38.

[131] Evans-Pritchard, 'Zande Theology', p. 20.

[132] E. E. Evans-Pritchard, 'Some Features of Nuer Religion (Presidential Address)', *Journal of the Royal Anthropological Institute of Great Britain and Ireland*, 81 (1951), pp. 1–13.

[133] E. E. Evans-Pritchard, *Nuer Religion* (Oxford: Clarendon Press, 1956), p. 1.

[134] Evans-Pritchard, *Nuer Religion*, p. vii.

to chronicle all the times this is done, but it is worth quoting a couple of striking examples to illustrate the general effect. When they compare themselves to ants, Evans-Pritchard reflects: 'We are reminded of Isaiah's likening of men to grasshoppers (xl. 22)', while on the very next page we read: 'I cannot convey the Nuer attitude better than by quoting the Book of Job: 'the Lord gave, and the Lord hath taken away; blessed be the name of the Lord' (I. 21)'.[135] A whole series of specific stories are referenced—Jacob and Esau, Elijah and the priests of Baal, the burning bush in Midian, the garden of Eden, and so on. Moreover, while even Evans-Pritchard seems to have found no scholarly warrant for bringing the New Testament explicitly into it, he does sometimes seem to have deliberately constructed his material in order to invite the reader to do so. Thus we have Pauline theology: 'There is in the idea a suggestion of the natural man being changed into the spiritual man'.[136] And also arguably an evocation of Johannine theology: 'We see here again the implicit metaphor, which runs through Nuer religion, of light and dark'.[137] Another way to present this would be through the citations given in the first chapter. No anthropologist is cited for matters of theory or broader interpretation, though a few make it in as ethnographers with data to report from fieldwork or for their expertise on African languages. Most of the notes, however, acknowledge biblical scholars and missionaries. There are even citations of a theological work (Rudolf Otto, *The Idea of the Holy*), the text of the Vulgate translation of the Bible, and Archbishop R. C. Trench (1807–86) on the New Testament. Evans-Pritchard would also deploy terms from the rich tradition of Catholic biblical exegesis, speaking of Nuer interpretations as 'allegorical' and even as reading 'anagogically'.[138] When he translated Nuer prayers he would use archaic forms such as 'thy' which are common in Christian liturgical contexts in English but had no justification in the original.[139]

Nor have we yet waded into the deep waters. Evans-Pritchard was determined to reveal Nuer religious thought to be as sophisticated as formal Christian theology. He did this by continually transposing and juxtaposing. At the simplest level, this involved recourse to the

---

[135] Evans-Pritchard, *Nuer Religion*, pp. 12–13.
[136] Evans-Pritchard, *Nuer Religion*, p. 60.
[137] Evans-Pritchard, *Nuer Religion*, p. 97.
[138] Evans-Pritchard, *Nuer Religion*, pp. 26, 9.
[139] My source on the Nuer language on this point is Douglas Johnson: Dr Douglas Johnson to Timothy Larsen, email, 21 March 2012.

Latin terminology used by Christian theologians: *ex nihilo, ex opere operato, deus absconditus,* and so on. As lapsing into Latin was a tic of his generation of British scholars, however, what is even more startling is the advanced theological categories he wields. He repeatedly identifies Nuer spiritual beings as 'hypostases of the modes and attributes of a single God'—a technical term used in Trinitarian and Christological formulas.[140] Several descriptions are reminiscent of the Chalcedonian Definition. For example: '*Deng* has several forms but they are all the same *deng*...each of whom is *deng,* without *deng* being in any way divided'. Or, soundly like an articulation of the hypostatic union of Christ's two natures: 'Twins are two *pwony* but a single *ran*'.[141] Evans-Pritchard even uses the Aristotelian categories incorporated into Thomistic theology of accidents and substance.[142] Nor does he always leave it to the reader to infer these connections: '*Tie* corresponds to the *anima* in scholastic writings'.[143] At one point, Nuer religious thought is put in conversation with 'the fourth-century neo-Platonist Sallustius'.[144] To state the matter plainly: 'The Nuer are undoubtedly a primitive people by the usual standards of reckoning, but their religious thought is remarkably sensitive, refined, and intelligent. It is also highly complex'.[145] The famous last words of *Nuer Religion* are:

> Nuer religion is ultimately an interior state. This state is externalized in rites which we can observe, but their meaning depends finally on an awareness of God and that men are dependent on him and must be resigned to his will. At this point the theologian takes over from the anthropologist.[146]

Contemporaries who were not fond of the book were apt to quip that the theologian had actually taken over much earlier. Certainly this ending brings one back full circle to the preface in which Evans-Pritchard acknowledged that 'even in a descriptive study' it made a noticeable difference whether the interpreting scholar is 'an agnostic or a Christian'.[147] His friend and colleague Godfrey Lienhardt

---

[140] Evans-Pritchard, *Nuer Religion,* p. 49.
[141] Evans-Pritchard, *Nuer Religion,* pp. 52, 157.
[142] Evans-Pritchard, *Nuer Religion,* pp. 125–26.
[143] Evans-Pritchard, *Nuer Religion,* p. 155.
[144] Evans-Pritchard, *Nuer Religion,* p. 275.
[145] Evans-Pritchard, *Nuer Religion,* p. 311.
[146] Evans-Pritchard, *Nuer Religion,* p. 322.
[147] Evans-Pritchard, *Nuer Religion,* p. vii.

observed that unusually for a work of social anthropology, *Nuer Religion* was 'written from an explicitly theistic viewpoint'.[148]

Not everyone liked the book—and some of the negative reactions seem to correlate with personal disbelief in religion. Leach, no doubt refracting his own dismissive view, claimed that 'cynics have remarked that it exhibits the Nuer as first-class Jesuit dialecticians'.[149] Beidelmann was also surely expressing his own opinion and with *Nuer Religion* as the prime case in point when he averred: 'Some consider that his conversion accounts for a falling off in Evans-Pritchard's analytical acuity'.[150] Something had certainly changed, but those who were sympathetic would probably have said that it reflected his humanistic turn and therefore, far from marking a decline, it was actually leading the discipline forward in an exciting and fruitful way. In his 1950 Marett lecture, Evans-Pritchard had caused a sensation in the discipline by announcing that he had given up on viewing anthropology as akin to the natural sciences (and therefore a social science) and instead now thought of it as most like social history (and therefore one of the humanities).[151] *Nuer Religion* certainly reflects this move. Even in the Marett lecture, however, Evans-Pritchard insisted that anthropologists understood natives better than they understood themselves. He offers as an unobjectionable analogy that a trained linguist can perceive the structure of someone else's mother tongue better than a native speaker. Nevertheless, as the reaction against colonialism waxed strong in the discipline, this assumption increasingly began to feel arrogant, imperialistic, and condescending.[152] It is not likely that such matters were on Evans-Pritchard's mind when he wrote *Nuer Religion* but, nevertheless, his desire in that book was to present what the Nuer themselves believed and not to go behind it to find reasons they knew not of: 'Here we have to take them as given. We are interested not in the structural

[148] Lienhardt, 'Sir Edward Evan Evans-Pritchard', p. 298.

[149] Edmund Leach, 'Cairo Essays' (review of Mary Douglas, *Evans-Pritchard*), *London Review of Books*, 2, 23 (4 December 1980), pp. 24–25.

[150] T. O. Beidelman, 'E. E. Evans-Pritchard', p. 186.

[151] E. E. Evans-Pritchard, 'Social Anthropology: Past and Present' (The Marett lecture, 1950), *Man*, No. 198 (September 1950), pp. 118–24. This stance allowed Evans-Pritchard to approach the *New Diffusionist* with sympathy as he rejected the kind of functionalism that made historical development irrelevant in principle to understanding a society: E. E. Evans-Pritchard, 'Recollections and Reflections', *New Diffusionist*, 2 (1971), pp. 37–39.

[152] Take, for example, this unvarnished statement: 'Africans have no objective knowledge of the forces determining their social organization and actuating their social behaviour'. Fortes and Evans-Pritchard, *African Political Systems*, p. 17.

aspect of the interdictions'.[153] Or again: 'the Nuer conception of God cannot be reduced to, or explained by, the social order... I have tried also to describe and interpret it as a system of ideas and practices in its own right'.[154] For some, Evans-Pritchard was lauded for guiding the discipline from an emphasis on function to one on meaning.[155] The career of the Oxford-trained anthropologist Talal Asad is instructive in this regard. His fieldwork led him to decide that *The Nuer* was a less helpful model than he thought. On the other hand, Evans-Pritchard's move toward a humanistic approach and toward meaning struck a chord. Eventually, he even found himself enamoured with the sophistication of medieval theology.[156] Moreover, even if Evans-Pritchard's reason for this shift in *Nuer Religion* was simply that he thought their beliefs happened to be true to a certain extent, it did become a new approach he pursued more generally. He began publishing Zande texts, confessing that the older anthropology did not place inherent value upon the reflections of pre-literate peoples: 'I have myself erred in this respect and this volume is an act of penance... in my study of the Azande I took less interest in their tales for their own sake than I should have done'.[157] Thus *Nuer Religion* was not merely an eccentric, personal project by an anthropologist who also happened to be a mystic, but rather an influential study in the discipline. J. A. Barnes observed that it 'became a model and inspiration to many younger anthropologists' and it is common to see it identified as a classic.[158]

* * *

---

[153] Evans-Pritchard, *Nuer Religion*, p. 189.

[154] Evans-Pritchard, *Nuer Religion*, pp. 320–21.

[155] J. H. M. Beattie and R. G. Lienhardt (eds.), *Studies in Social Anthropology: Essays in Memory of E. E. Evans-Pritchard by his former Oxford colleagues* (Oxford: Clarendon Press, 1975), pp. 333–34. Towards the end of his life, Evans-Pritchard himself was increasingly pessimistic about the future of the discipline. In 1972, Claude Lévi-Strauss (1908–2009) wrote in reply to a letter from Evans-Pritchard, observing that they had in common 'a dim outlook on the future of Anthropology in England as well as in France where the situation is hardly more encouraging than the one which you describe'. Claude Lévi-Strauss to E. E. Evans-Pritchard ('Sir Edward'), postcard, 24 December 1972. The Evans-Pritchard papers in the possession of Bruce Ross-Smith.

[156] David Scott and Charles Hirschkind (eds.), *Powers of the Secular Modern: Talal Asad and His Interlocutors* (Stanford: Stanford University Press, 2006), pp. 244–88. Also, Talal Asad to Timothy Larsen, email, 20 January 2012. I should also add that Asad's personal impression of Evans-Pritchard was mainly an unfavourable one.

[157] E. E. Evans-Pritchard (ed.), *The Zande Trickster* (Oxford: Clarendon Press, 1967), p. 15.

[158] Barnes, 'Edward Evan Evans-Pritchard', p. 468.

Whether Evans-Pritchard had any direct influence on fellow anthropologists becoming Catholics is the subject of a minor dispute. In
a clever construction, one unsympathetic anthropologist took to
referring to the Institute as the Oxford Oratory. The general claim
was asserted in print in Adam Kuper's book-length account of
mid-twentieth century British anthropologists. After outlining how
Oxford anthropology fostered a distinctive approach to the discipline,
Kuper went on:

> These tendencies may have been related to the odd fact that several of
> the members of the department were converts to Roman Catholicism,
> including Evans-Pritchard himself. In many cases students coming to
> Oxford were converted first to the vogue theoretical position, and sub-
> sequently to Roman Catholicism; and the professor acted as godfather
> at their baptism.[159]

It is telling that Kuper would choose the pejorative-tinged adjective
'odd'. It is certainly true that the Institute did bring together several
Catholic anthropologists—sometimes comprising a significant per-
centage of the faculty as a whole at a particular time—and that Mary
Douglas (whose time there was brief) was apparently the only one
who was a cradle Catholic. (Those most often named as Catholic converts are Evans-Pritchard, Godfrey Lienhardt, Peter Lienhardt, and
David Pocock.) Godfrey Lienhardt, the most influential Catholic at
the Institute after E-P himself, was anxious to refute Kuper's claim.
Lienhardt's primary concern seems to have been that it created the
wrong impression: Evans-Pritchard was not remotely proselytizing in
his personal relationships and the ethos of the Institute in no way
included a theological agenda. It was certainly a wild exaggeration
for Kuper to say that there were 'many cases' of students swimming
the Tiber. On the other hand, Lienhardt's desire to get the impression right led him to deny the evidence that did exist, averring: 'As
far as I know, E-P was not anyone's "godfather" '.[160] The South African

---

[159] Adam Kuper, *Anthropologists and Anthropology: The British School 1922–1972*
(New York: Pica Press, 1973), p. 158.

[160] Ahmed Al-Shahi, 'Evans-Pritchard, Anthropology, and Catholicism at
Oxford: Godfrey Lienhardt's view', *Journal of the Anthropological Society of Oxford*, 30,
1 (1999), p. 71. It is possible that part of Lienhardt's concern was that people might
assume that Evans-Pritchard had arranged for him to be appointed to the Oxford faculty at such an early stage in his career because he was a Catholic. On this appointment, see Goody, *Expansive Moment*, p. 81; Barth, *One Discipline*, p. 45.

anthropologist David Brokensha, who had been raised in a secular household, not only credited Lienhardt with helping to awaken his interest in Catholicism, but also proudly records that his two sponsors when he was received into the Roman Catholic Church were Leinhardt and Evans-Pritchard.[161] Still, Brokensha goes on to say that Evans-Pritchard had never had a conversation with him on matters of faith, and it would be absurd to assert that E-P and Leinhardt were attempting to recruit people for the Church or even that 'the Institute favoured RCs'.[162] While it is wrong, therefore, to think of the Institute during these years as directed by some kind of scheming Catholic cabal, it does seem fair to observe that it did have an ethos which made it affirming of religious belief and experience. It is also telling—to take two other anthropologists who were at the Institute for a time—that Franz Steiner (1909–52) rediscovered Judaism, and that M. N. Srinivas (1916–99) was a Hindu.[163] Wendy James was not personally attracted to faith but as an anthropologist she nevertheless found the openness to religion at the Institute more intellectually exciting than the too-pat positions that were then held in the departments at Manchester and the London School of Economics.[164] To take a wider perspective, one wonders to what degree personal views regarding religion were sometimes a factor in the relationships between anthropologists in Britain more generally. This is hard to discern as personal dislike and professional rivalry also clearly played large parts. Still, to evoke just one example, Edmund Leach and Evans-Pritchard loathed one another and in the mix of this bad blood is the fact that Evans-Pritchard was

[161] David Brokensha, *Brokie's Way: An Anthropologist's Story* (Cape Town: Amani Press, 2007), pp. 148–51.

[162] Brokensha, *Brokie's Way*, p. 151.

[163] Steiner defiantly argued that it was those anthropologists who lacked religious experience who were more likely to be unreliable: 'one is inclined to make reservations of the kind one would make when asked to read a treatise on sexual psychology composed by a eunuch': Franz Baermann Steiner, *Taboo, Truth, and Religion: Selected Writings Volume 1*, Jeremy Alder and Richard Fardon eds. (Oxford: Berghahn Books, 1999), p. 213. Srinivas reflected: 'Hinduism's appeal to me is at least partly due to my dissatisfaction with a materialist view of the universe. While science is essential, and needed desperately in a country such as India, it does not ask or answer questions which are asked in religion or theology… "Scientific humanism", the credo of agnostic and liberal intellectuals, is not only anaemic but arbitary': M N. Srinivas, 'Why I Am a Hindu', *Illustrated Weekly of India*, 17 November 1974, pp. 9–10.

[164] Personal conversation with Professor Wendy James, Oxford, 24 April 2012. Likewise, Cambridge had a 'more secular, scientific, rationalist flavour': preface by Alan Macfarlane in Rivière, *A History of Oxford Anthropology*, p. xiv.

an adult convert and—one might say—a Catholic intellectual, while Leach had shed decisively a highly religious childhood and gone on— one might even say—to become a secularist intellectual, serving as the president of the British Humanist Association.[165]

Throughout Evans-Pritchard's work there are sprinkled references to influential theologians from across the centuries from Augustine of Hippo (354–430) to Freidrich Schleiermacher (1768–1834) and Ernst Troeltsch (1865–1923). In other publications beside *Nuer Religion*, he also drew on works by contemporary theologians such as Rudolf Otto (1869–1937) and Martin Buber (1878–1965), as well as biblical scholars. A particular influence was *Agape and Eros* by Anders Nygren (1890–1978), the full English translation of which appeared as a single work in 1953.[166] Around the time he became a Catholic, Evans-Pritchard was doing serious reading in medieval theology and church history and he later reflected that this material provided a crucial background that made possible his *The Sanusi of Cyrenaica*.[167] Conversely, he claimed that anthropologists of religion would not have developed such misguided theories if they had studied 'Christian theology, history, exegesis, apologetics, symbolic thought and ritual'.[168] Certainly one result of Evans-Pritchard's work was that it opened up an interdisciplinary conversation between anthropologists on the one hand, and theologians and biblical scholars on the other. Evans-Pritchard himself would supervise theses from the Faculty of Theology and he would review books by theologians with anthropological interests such as John Mbiti (1931–).[169] Theologians responded in kind. Cornelius Ernst OP, wrote an article on *Nuer Religion* in which he claimed that through this anthropological monograph 'a Catholic can enlarge his personal understanding of God', and expressed his conviction that Evans-Pritchard's work would play a part 'in any

---

[165] Stanley J. Tambiah, *Edmund Leach: An Anthropological Life* (Cambridge: Cambridge University Press, 2002), esp. pp. 3, 15–18, 72–74. Curiously, after his death, Leach's widow Celia was received into the Roman Catholic Church. (Information provided in a personal conversation with a friend of the Leaches, the Very Revd John Drury, All Souls College, Oxford, 30 April 2012.)

[166] Anders Nygren, *Agape and Eros*, trans. Philip S. Watson (London: SPCK, 1953). Douglas, *Evans-Pritchard*, p. 92.

[167] Evans-Pritchard, 'Some Reminiscences', p. 1.

[168] Evans-Pritchard, *Theories*, pp. 16–17.

[169] E. E. Evans-Pritchard, 'Social Anthropology at Oxford', *Journal of the Anthropological Society of Oxford*, 1, 3 (1970), p. 108; E. E. Evans-Pritchard, Review of John S. Mbiti, *African Religions and Philosophy*, *Journal of Religion in Africa*, 2, 2 (1969), pp. 214–16.

theological revival which we may be fortunate enough to see'.[170] Even in a festschrift with such a specific focus as *Zande Themes* there was an article by the Catholic religious Michael Singleton (of the Order of the White Fathers) which put Zande theology in conversation with the then-fashionable secular theology and sparkled with references to Pierre Teilhard de Chardin (1881–1955), John Henry Newman (1801–90), Karl Barth (1886–1968), and so on.[171] How this trend waxed strong in the years after Evans-Pritchard's death may be seen by a 1979 conference on the theme of sacrifice which was sponsored by the Royal Anthropological Institute and designed as an interdisciplinary meeting 'between social anthropologists and Christian theologians'.[172] A co-convener was Simon Barrington-Ward (1930–), who would go on to become an Anglican bishop, and Evans-Pritchard's legacy looms large in Meyer Fortes's preface to the resulting volume.

* * *

On 3 September 1939 Edward Evan Evans-Pritchard married Ioma, the daughter of the Right Hon. George Heaton Nicholls, who would later be appointed High Commissioner for South Africa. Ioma had been studying anthropology when they met. In 1941 their first child died soon after birth; their daughter Shineen was born in Bagdad in 1942. Four more children followed, including twins Nicky and John. In 1950 Ioma published a whimsical children's story, *Bong and Wong*. It is dedicated to Shineen and recounts how twin boys, inspired by the conversation of their anthropologist father, set off on a tour of various African peoples, their adventures hingeing on the different beliefs and practices regarding twins of each group. When they are dissatisfied with the Zulu, they solicit advice from home and receive a cable which says: 'TRY THE NUER—LOVE—DADDY'.[173] At some point Ioma began to develop symptoms of some kind of psychological disorder. Evans-Pritchard loved her dearly, and one imagines this turn of events also recalled for him his brother's promising life gone awry.

---

[170] Cornelius Ernst OP, 'The Relevance of Primitive Religion', *New Blackfriars*, 38, 452 (November 1957), pp. 526, 528.

[171] Michael Singleton, 'Theology, "Zande Theology" and Secular Theology' in Singer and Street, *Zande Themes*, pp. 130–57.

[172] M. F. C. Bourdillon and Meyer Fortes (eds.), *Sacrifice* (London: Academic Press for the Royal Anthropological Institute of Great Britain and Ireland, 1980), p. 1.

[173] Ioma Evans-Pritchard, *Bong and Wong* (Prairie City, Ill: Decker Press, 1950), p. 21.

While they were on a family vacation in Cornwall in September 1959, Ioma committed suicide. On 15 November Evans-Pritchard wrote to Alfred L. Kroeber: 'Last year my mother died and this year my wife died also, after a long and depressing illness. I now have to cope with five children between the ages of 1½ and 17'.[174] Many observers have commented that they felt he never recovered from this tragic loss. The royalties for one of the festschriften were donated to 'the Ioma Evans-Pritchard Scholarship Fund, at St Anne's College, Oxford, which was established in the memory of the wife of Sir Edward Evans-Pritchard'.[175] As a way of marking his retirement, the plan had been for colleagues to create a fund in his own name, but he requested that it honour his late wife instead.[176]

Another source of distress in Evans-Pritchard's life was his combat experience. His son Ambrose recalls: 'He suffered from terrible feelings of guilt over what happened in the war, and would wake up screaming in the night. The memories tortured him'.[177] When Godfrey Lienhardt was among the Anuak he heard eyewitness accounts of Evans-Pritchard killing Italian soldiers.[178] He apparently at least once killed someone at quite close quarters. Evans-Pritchard himself wrote a military history of part of his war service. In it, he incidentally reveals that an assault he led—in addition to killing seventeen soldiers and wounding numerous others—also resulted in some civilian casualties: 'Unfortunately, five women, wives of Galla, and a child, who were in the trenches were killed also'.[179]

This brings us back to the question so often asked, 'Why did E-P become a Catholic?' Evans-Pritchard discerned that the question itself often arose from a secularist bias: 'The suggestion being that there must be some explanation to account for such a strange, even

[174] E. E. Evans Pritchard to Alfred L. Kroeber, 15 November 1959: Matthey, 'A Glimpse', p. 43.

[175] Cunnison and James, *Essays in Sudan Ethnography*, p. [v].

[176] Wendy James, ' "A Feeling for Form and Pattern, and a Touch of Genius": E-P's Vision and the Institute, 1946–70', in Riviére, *A History of Oxford Anthropology*, p. 114.

[177] Mr Ambrose Evans-Pritchard to Timothy Larsen, email, 18 March 2010. (Bruce Ross-Smith's account of living with the family also included this information.)

[178] Burton, *Introduction*, p. 55.

[179] Edward Evans-Pritchard, 'Operations on the Akobo and Gila Rivers 1940–41', *Army Quarterly*, 103 (1973), p. 477. Clifford Geertz's treatment of this article would have benefited from knowing that Evans-Pritchard's memories of the war were not as breezy as he imagined they were: Clifford Geertz, *Works and Lives: The Anthropologist as Author* (Stanford: Stanford University Press, 1988), pp. 49–72.

a remarkable, lapse from rational behaviour on the part of one supposed to be some sort of scientist'.[180] To counter that it should be
recalled that it was not uncommon in this period for intellectuals to
take Christian beliefs seriously—one thinks, for example, of T. S. Eliot,
W. H. Auden, Dorothy Sayers, and C. S. Lewis—and for some this was
in the form of Catholicism (J. R. R. Tolkien) or led to Catholicism
(Graham Greene and E-P's contemporary at Oxford, Evelyn Waugh).
The influences that ultimately led to Benghazi Cathedral began early
for Evans-Pritchard: a clergyman father followed by schooling in the
Anglo-Catholic atmosphere at Winchester. (He spoke of Winchester
Cathedral, where the students would sometimes go for corporate
worship, as a place where he could sense the presence of God.) At
Oxford he became friends both with Catholics and Anglicans who
would become Catholics, including Viscount Clonmore, later the
Earl of Wicklow, who was received into the Roman Catholic Church
in 1932. As a young man, Evans-Pritchard already had yearnings in
this direction. He twice tried to become a Catholic, but when he went
to study the Church's teachings on matters typically of concern for
Protestants such as the authority of the pope and doctrines regarding
the Virgin Mary he found he was not able to accept them. He eventually decided that 'if you want the pearl of no price you have got to take
the oyster with it'.[181] Looking back he saw this as a long, slow process.
He seems to have always believed in God, and thus it was a journey
specifically to Rome. It was certainly an emotional and existential
spiritual event in his life when it finally happened. He described it as
'rapture'.[182] He credited 'a long camel ride through the desert' as providing the meditative space to lead him to 'the final plunge'.[183] What
has been said so far is a full, sufficient explanation this side of heaven,
yet if one is looking for a more specific prompt, it could be surmised
that perhaps it included a longing to receive divine forgiveness for
his sins in this concrete act of reconciliation and that this wish might
have been related to his feelings of guilt resulting from the fog of war.
Evans-Pritchard confessed that his road to this event involved 'accu-
mulating much sin'.[184] In *Theories of Primitive Religion* he spoke of

---

[180] Evans-Pritchard, 'Fragment', p. 35.
[181] Evans-Pritchard, 'Fragment', p. 37.
[182] Evans-Pritchard, 'Fragment', p. 37.
[183] Evans-Pritchard, 'Fragment', p. 37.
[184] Evans-Pritchard, 'Fragment', p. 37.

his own religion in terms of the significance of hearing Christ say to us: 'My peace I give unto you' (John 14:27).[185] This is best revealed in a poem which has never before been published or even seen by any scholar writing about Evans-Pritchard. He wrote it just eight days before he was received into the Roman Catholic Church:

> *On My 42nd Birthday*
> No harvest have I gathered in
> Except a few chance grains of truth
> That ripened mid the tares of sin
> I scattered in the years of youth;
> No store of sacramental grace,
> No merit won by constant prayer,
> Nothing garnered with which to face
> The bitter winters of despair.
> And yet, I thank thee, Lord of years,
> This day of retrospective shame,
> This day of memories and tears,
> That faith now burns a stronger flame.
> From this dull spark thou hast fanned
> With wings of sorrow and of pain;
> Till I can place in thine my hand
> And feel today a child again.[186]

* * *

The drinking was a nightly pattern toward the end of his life. He found he was not able to fall asleep without the aid of whisky. The very real prospect of having nightmares about the war would have made going to sleep that much more difficult, as would the absence of Ioma and thoughts of her breakdown and suicide. Evans-Pritchard was particularly distressed on the anniversaries of their wedding and of her death. Nevertheless, his faith was still burning a stronger flame. André Singer, who lived in the house for a year, reports that Evans-Pritchard thought of him as a Jewish agnostic and certainly did not try to impose religion on him. Nevertheless, it was important to E-P that Singer read the article he had recently written recounting

---

[185] Evans-Pritchard, *Theories*, p. 120.
[186] E. E. Evans-Pritchard, 'On My 42nd Birthday', 1944. This poem is among the Evans-Pritchard papers in the possession of Bruce Ross-Smith. Evans-Pritchard's forty-second birthday was on 21 September 1944.

his spiritual journey. Singer's general impression was that 'thoughts about faith I think were becoming increasingly important to him'.[187] In 1972 Evans-Pritchard told Fortes that after his seventieth birthday later that year he planned to 'give most of my time to religious thought and duties'.[188] At times, the guilt, the whisky, and the faith all seem to have blended together. He remarked: 'I won't look after myself. What is the use of trusting in God if you can't leave it to him'.[189] After a few drinks, Evans-Pritchard would sometimes reveal that he was looking forward to going to heaven where he would be able to ask Ioma to forgive him for anything he had done wrong that had made her life harder. A week before he died he wrote to Beidelman: 'though it may seem odd to you, I have always taken it for granted that any contribution I have made to knowledge is not mine but God's through me. *Nisi dominus*'.[190] Evans-Pritchard died at his home while taking a bath on 11 September 1973. E-P RIP.

---

[187] Dr André Singer to Timothy Larsen, emails, 14 February 2012 and 22 February 2012.

[188] Barnes, 'Edward Evan Evans-Pritchard', p. 480.

[189] Barnes, 'Edward Evan Evans-Pritchard', p. 481.

[190] Barnes, 'Edward Evan Evans-Pritchard', p. 555.

4

Mary Douglas

A Jewish anthropologist, a Hindu anthropologist, and a Catholic anthropologist walk into a bar on a Friday night. The barmaid takes their drink orders and then says, 'We have a special today on ham sandwiches. Would anyone like one?' The first replies, 'I never eat ham, I'm Jewish'. The second, 'I never eat meat, I'm Hindu'. And the third, 'I never eat meat on Fridays, I'm Catholic'. While not adding up to a joke, this anecdote is a dramatization of an actual incident. Moreover, this curious convergence of religious dietary restrictions became one of the inspirations that prompted Mary Douglas (1921–2007) to write what would become a classic text, *Purity and Danger* (1966). It happened sometime in the late 1940s or early 1950s after the Friday seminar of Oxford's Institute of Social Anthropology. The venue, the King's Arms, was a favourite pub of the Oxford anthropologists. Franz Steiner (1909–52) was the Jew, M. N. Srinivas (1916–99) was the Hindu, and Douglas herself was the Catholic. Half a century later, she recalled that Steiner's protest, 'Why should I be exposed to ham sandwiches when I come for a drink?', started her off 'on thinking about food taboos, pollution, and taboos in general'.[1] *Purity and Danger: An Analysis of Concepts of Pollution and Taboo* opened with a more general acknowledgement of this debt: 'I was first interested in pollution behaviour by Professor Srinivas and the late Franz Steiner who each, as Brahmin and Jew, tried in their daily lives to handle

---

[1] Mary Douglas, 'Franz Steiner: A Memoir', in Franz Baermann Steiner, *Taboo, Truth, and Religion: Selected Writings Volume 1*, eds. Jeremy Alder and Richard Fardon (Oxford: Berghahn Books, 1999), p. 4. Srinivas's daughter confirmed to me that her father believed that his Hinduism required him to be a complete vegetarian: Lakshmi Srinivas to Timothy Larsen, email, 1 February 2013.

problems of ritual cleanness'.[2] This scene from an English public house encapsulates several themes that would mark Douglas's work, including comparisons across different cultures, traditions, and religions; bringing an anthropological eye to daily life in modern, industrial societies; and the interaction between the personal religious beliefs and practices of an anthropologist and his or her professional insights and contributions.

The Lele people of the once and future Congo (among whom she did her fieldwork) held to a strict seniority system in which the highest position of authority went to the oldest. Douglas was honoured, not for mere longevity, but because of the outstanding merits of her work; nevertheless it is true that she did live long enough to rise to a pre-eminent place. In an interview published in the *Spectator* on 25 April 2007 (that is, less than a month before her death at the age of 86), Douglas was described unequivocally as 'Britain's foremost anthropologist'. The magazine did, however, employ a little equivocation in order to let the illustrious dead rest in peace: 'the greatest anthropologist, some say, that Britain has produced in the past half century'.[3] A fortnight later, Her Majesty the Queen invested Douglas a Dame Commander of the British Empire. At her death a week after that royal audience, the obituary in the *Guardian* acknowledged that Dame Mary Douglas was 'the most widely read British social anthropologist of her generation'.[4] In a typical tribute, the *Telegraph* pronounced that she was 'perhaps the leading British anthropologist of the second half of the 20th century'.[5] In the years since her death her reputation and fame have continued to hold up. Her books are kept in print in a Routledge Collected Works edition. The year this volume is being written—2013—has also witnessed the advent of two new posthumous volumes of her writings.[6] Her name is officially perpetuated

[2] Mary Douglas, *Purity and Danger: An Analysis of Concepts of Pollution and Taboo* (New York: Frederick A. Praeger, 1966), p. vii.

[3] Christopher Howse, 'The Pangolin and al'Qaèda' (an interview with Mary Douglas), *Spectator*, 25 April 2007, accessed online on 21 January 2013 at www.spectator.co.uk.

[4] Richard Fardon, 'Obituary: Dame Mary Douglas', *Guardian*, 18 May 2007. Accessed online on 3 December 2010 at www.guardian.co.uk.

[5] 'Dame Mary Douglas' (Obituary), *Telegraph*, 22 May 2007, accessed online on 1 April 2013 at www.telegraph.co.uk.

[6] Mary Douglas, *Cultures and Crises: Understanding Risk and Resolution* (London: Sage, 2013); Mary Douglas, *A Very Personal Method: Anthropological Writings Drawn from Life* (London: Sage, 2013). (Professor Richard Fardon, her literary executor, has been responsible for shepherding these pieces into print.) Although

in various ways, including Mary Douglas Awards of financial assistance at University College London and the Mary Douglas Prize for Best Book offered by the American Sociological Association. The first Mary Douglas Memorial Lecture—sponsored jointly by Oxford and UCL—is scheduled to be held in 2014. Or, to take a random example of her posthumous cultural cachet, the *Guardian Review*'s 'Money Issue' in December 2011 was illustrated by a fantasy British bank note, 'the Douglas', which in addition to having her portrait on it also contained a quotation from *Purity and Danger*: 'Money is only an extreme and specialised type of ritual'.[7]

Douglas herself felt that this ascent to the top tier was slow. The basic reasons for a brake on her acceleration were, firstly, the start of her professional life as a faculty member coinciding with the beginning of her life as a mother and, secondly, her decision to take a position with the Russell Sage Foundation in 1977 meant that she was dislocated both from a university post and from Britain—only with the passing of time would these changes in her career reap their own rewards. Still, climb she did. Douglas joined the faculty of University College London in 1951 and in 1970 was promoted to a personal chair, making her at that time a rare woman anthropologist who was also a full professor. To give just a few highlights of the recognition she went on to receive, in 1974 Douglas was elected to the American Academy of Arts and Sciences and, in 1989, to the British Academy. In 1992, she was awarded the Royal Anthropological Society's Huxley Medal and the Queen conferred upon her the first of her royal honours: Commander of the British Empire. In 1995 the *Times Literary Supplement* identified the hundred most influential books since the Second World War: Douglas was one of only four women to make the list.[8] To take once again a sounding on the more impressionistic side, in 2001 Douglas was interviewed for the Canadian Broadcasting Corporation's 'Original Minds'. This series aimed to present the greatest living public intellectuals, and its guests included figures such as Harold Bloom, Umberto Eco, Oliver Sacks, Jane Goodall, Jared

---

published after my research was completed, *A Very Personal Method* has now conveniently collected many of the occasional pieces cited in this chapter.

[7] *Guardian Review*, 17 December 2011, cover.

[8] 'The Hundred Most Influential Books Since the War', *Bulletin of the American Academy of Arts and Sciences*, 49, 8 (May 1996), pp. 12–13 (reprinted from the *Times Literary Supplement*, 6 October 1995).

Diamond, Amartya Sen, Susan Sontag, and Noam Chomsky. The introduction for Douglas included the fact that she was a genius.[9]

* * *

Margaret Mary Tew (to use her full maiden name) thought of herself as having been—to a large extent—raised by nuns. Her father worked in the India Civil Service and therefore the first few years of her life were spent in Burma.[10] At the age of five, while her parents stayed on, she was sent back to Britain to live in Devon with her maternal grand-parents, Sir Daniel and May Twomey. Mary and her only sibling, a younger sister called Pat, attended a French convent day school. Daniel, who was himself Catholic, took them to Mass, and May, although a Protestant, dutifully taught them the Catholic catechism and generally ensured that they were raised as Catholics as she had their mother, Phyllis. When Mary was 12 years old her mother died. Knowing she had terminal cancer, Phyllis had arranged for her daughters to become boarders at her own old Catholic school at Roehampton, the Convent of the Sacred Heart. The nuns understood that they were *in loco parentis* in an even more emphatic sense in the case of Mary and Pat. Their mother's alma mater would nurture them in her place.

Daily life at this school was put on display in a popular work of fiction, Antonia White's *Frost in May* (1933).[11] The main character is a girl who chafes against the exacting rules and restrictions at the 'Convent of the Five Wounds', and (spoiler alert) the plot culminates in her being expelled when the nuns discover that she has been secretly writing a novel that is deemed insufficiently imbued with piety. In other words, White was working mostly with the grain of a favourite life story of modern Westerners: a tale of coming to fulfilment and maturity by defying norms and authorities. Douglas, by contrast,

---

[9] Eleanor Wachtel (ed.), *Original Minds* (Toronto: HarperCollins Canada, 2003), p. 321.

[10] The unrivalled, scholarly authority on Douglas's life and work is Professor Richard Fardon. The major biographical sources have all been written by him, notably Douglas's entry in the *Oxford Dictionary of National Biography* and a substantive memoir in the *Proceedings of the British Academy*, as well as the only book-length life: Richard Fardon, *Mary Douglas: An Intellectual Biography* (London: Routledge, 1999). I shall not attempt to cite a source for each fact mentioned, but I do wish to acknowledge generally that I am extremely grateful for Fardon's perceptive and able work on Douglas and that I am usually in his debt when it comes to biographical specifics.

[11] Antonia White, *Frost in May* (London: Eyre & Spottiswoode [1933] 1948).

would war against the bias which made it impossible 'to establish the notion that institutional constraints could be beneficial to the individual'.[12] Indeed, she took lifelong delight in stubbornly defending what her contemporaries too complacently despised and dismissed. Douglas therefore always went out of her way to praise the Convent of the Sacred Heart. (Her own view of *Frost in May* was that it had made 'infamous' her beloved school.)[13]

Douglas's conscious refusal to let her own story be co-opted by the hackneyed tale of oppressive nuns who serve as foils in one's journey to a broad place might best be illustrated by a little bit of self-editing. One of the very few things she would say about her experience at Sacred Heart which might fuel a liberation-from-narrowness narrative was that the nuns disapproved of her idea of reading social sciences at the London School of Economics. (She had become interested in these kinds of questions because of a unit in doctrine class on Catholic social teaching.) How this LSE story functioned in her mind was to reassure anyone who might be worried that anthropology was somehow incompatible with Christianity: her own life testified that this suspicion was false. In a 1999 interview for a Catholic publication, she remarked: 'I'd really have liked to have gone to the LSE, but the nuns thought that was a dangerous place for one's faith!'[14] Likewise in 2006 she reminisced: 'the nuns also thought that sociology was anti-God and anti-religion. So they would never have sent me to the LSE, which is what I wanted to do, obviously'.[15] It is therefore curious that when an interviewer in 2003 prompted her to reflect on why the nuns thought this move would have been too radical, Douglas more or less denied the whole thing: 'I don't think really it was that. They just didn't know what the LSE was; they didn't know what sociology was. All they knew was Oxford. And all they really knew about Oxford was history'.[16] It would seem that she had become

[12] Mary Douglas, *How Institutions Think* (Syracuse: Syracuse University Press, 1986), p. 83.

[13] Mary Douglas, 'A Feeling for Hierarchy', in James L. Heft SM (ed.) *Believing Scholars: Ten Catholic Intellectuals* (New York: Fordham University Press, 2005), p. 99.

[14] Mary Douglas (interviewed by Deborah Jones), 'Can a scientist be objective about her faith?', *Priests & People*, October 1999, p. 383.

[15] Mary Douglas interviewed by Alan Macfarlane, 26 February 2006, Cambridge University Video & Audio Collections, Quick Time Video, 88:08, www.sms.cam.ac.uk/media/1115926 (accessed 3 September 2012).

[16] Wachtel, *Original Minds*, p. 326.

anxious that this anecdote might be reinforcing in people's minds the cliché of small-minded, thwarting nuns.

Douglas's main comments, therefore, were always calculated to upend that stereotype. She enthused:

> the nuns were very fine women and very highly educated. All the teachers had been to Oxford themselves…they believed in teaching us to be independent.… That's how we were brought up—committed and free…The nuns, for example, were all so open…they were very sophisticated…[17]

She emphasized that the nuns were 'all independent women' who inculcated the virtue of 'intellectual independence' (this last convent compliment recurs often).[18] In a 2002 address Douglas went so far as to assert that these 1930s nuns instilled in their girls 'a confident feminist bias'.[19] Moreover, Douglas's defence even extended to missionaries. *The Lele of the Kasai* (1963) included this testimonial to the Sisters of St Vincent de Paul: 'Their kindness and devotion were obvious to all, so that even in sticky situations when their efforts to save a mother's or child's life failed Lele never showed any serious mistrust'.[20]

The convent was a genuinely happy place for the girl Mary Tew. She thrived there, eventually winning the school prize in English and becoming head girl, and gushed sincerely in retrospect: 'I loved it!'[21] She never ceased to be grateful that the Church had given her an ordered, meaningful world. While the emotional response differed, it is striking how similar her recollections of life at Sacred Heart are to what is presented in *Frost in May*. Both speak again and again, for example, about studying the catechism and about wearing gloves. For Douglas, the gloves became a synecdoche of the richness of a ritualized, hierarchical culture, but White could see them as an oppressive imposition: '"Those dreadful gloves," wailed Mrs Grey'.[22] Then there is this passage from *Frost in May*: 'Nanda dropped her lily with awe. It stood, she knew, for some mysterious possession…her Purity. What Purity was she was still uncertain, being too shy to

[17] Douglas, 'Can a scientist be objective?', pp. 383–85.

[18] Wachtel, *Original Minds*, p. 325.

[19] Douglas, 'A Feeling for Hierarchy', p. 103.

[20] Mary Douglas, *The Lele of the Kasai* (London: Oxford University Press for the International African Institute, 1963), p. 265.

[21] Wachtel, *Original Minds*, p. 324. [22] White, *Frost in May*, p. 39.

ask, but she realised it was something very important'.[23] Purity and Danger indeed. Douglas kept up her contact with the school as an adult, even after it had moved from Roehampton to Woldingham. The acknowledgements in *Natural Symbols* include: 'I am grateful to the Woldingham Association Committee and especially, to Reverend Mother Eyre, Mary Don and Mona Macmillan. The research we hoped to promote on religious education has not yet been accomplished'.[24] (The Woldingham Association Committee was Sacred Heart's alumni organization.) Richard Fardon, the unrivalled authority on Douglas and her work, although not a co-religionist, came to the conviction that, if one wants to understand where her insights as an anthropologist came from, the Convent of the Sacred Heart 'seems to hold the key'.[25]

Upon graduation, Tew spent half a year studying at the Sorbonne in order to become better prepared for university. Although the education at Sacred Heart was patchy, it had just then hit a new stride and she matriculated at the University of Oxford along with three other girls from her year. Tew read 'Modern Greats'— Philosophy, Politics, and Economics—a course that allowed her to pursue her interest in social science in the reassuring solidity of Oxford. She was awarded her degree in 1943. While an undergraduate, Tew lived at a house the nuns had established in association with St Anne's—subsidized lodgings as a way of supporting Catholics that helped make her university education financially feasible. Despite this Catholic community, Tew found Oxford initially unsettling to her faith.[26] She did not discuss this thereafter. Once again, hers was the opposite of the expected, modern narrative—a non-story in its terms: not one of a loss of faith leading to a new kind of life but rather a period of crisis leading to a maturing and deepening of religious convictions—to continuity not discontinuity. A strange autobiographical comment of Douglas's seems incidentally to reveal her undergraduate unease:

> I first experienced hierarchy in a very modest form in my grandparents' home, and then in my convent schooling. So used to it was I that when

---

[23] White, *Frost in May*, p. 68. (The ellipsis is in the original.)

[24] Mary Douglas, *Natural Symbols: Explorations in Cosmology* (New York: Pantheon Books, 1970), p. xvi.

[25] Fardon, *Mary Douglas*, pp. 259–60.   [26] Fardon, *Mary Douglas*, p. 22.

I left school I was at a loss to understand what was happening around me. Only after the war, when I started anthropology in 1946, did I begin to understand it.[27]

As will be explored below, hierarchy for Douglas was a way of speaking about the Catholic Church in particular and, in general, the kind of culture that she liked best. As an anthropologist, she wrote repeatedly and at length about the category of hierarchy; yet she never spoke of the University of Oxford as being marked by it: an example that seems rather obvious, at least to this author. By contrast, she insisted that her grandparents' house was at least a proto-hierarchy, while being aware that this classification might seem a stretch to others. In other words, her undergraduate days were rather disorientating and therefore it somehow did not seem fitting to her to think of Oxford as hierarchical.

After being awarded her degree, Tew went to work in the Colonial Office as part of the war effort, staying there until 1946. In the course of her war work she encountered some first-rate anthropologists, including Audrey Richards, W. E. H. Stanner, and Raymond Firth, and thereby found her vocation: 'as soon as I met anthropologists I knew that I wanted to be one.'[28] And so back to Oxford. The university did not offer an undergraduate course in anthropology and expected its postgraduate students in anthropology to come to them with simply a bachelor's degree in another discipline, so she was not really behind. Her daughter Janet reported that part of the attraction of Oxford for her mother was that Evans-Pritchard was there: 'she had been told that you could not be an anthropologist and believe in God but she knew E. P. was a convert.'[29] Certainly, one of the things Tew came to appreciate about the Institute was an openness to faith. She later reflected on what Evans-Pritchard and Franz Steiner had in common:

> Both were interested in the place of religion in anthropology, and both lined up against the current rationalist consensus...They agreed with each other that religion was to be given a place in its own right, not to be treated as an emanation of something else.[30]

---

[27] Douglas, 'A Feeling for Hierarchy', p. 96.
[28] Wachtel, *Original Minds*, p. 327.
[29] Janet Farnsworth to Timothy Larsen, email, 9 August 2012.
[30] Douglas, 'Franz Steiner', pp. 6–7.

And there were others there who also took religious convictions seriously on their own terms, including the third member of the affair of the ham sandwiches, the Hindu anthropologist M. N. Srinivas, who became her official doctoral supervisor. This time, Oxford worked its charm. Douglas later reminisced about how thrilling it was to be at the Institute at that time: 'Everything about that post-war year was fresh and exciting: it is still famous'.[31] She was so struck by Evans-Pritchard's work that, after his death, she attempted to repay some of this debt by writing a book-length appreciation of this 'Modern Master'.[32] In 1948 Tew was awarded a BSc (which functioned for Oxford postgraduates in anthropology as the equivalent of a master's degree) for her thesis 'Bride wealth in Africa' (a term that Evans-Pritchard himself had championed to replace the inaccurate and pejorative 'bride price'). For her work on the Lele, she was awarded a DPhil in 1953. For the 1950–51 academic year she was also a lecturer. However mixed her undergraduate experience might have been, she now had a basketful of positive memories and associations with this ancient English university. To add one final glimpse from the surviving records, her undated handwritten notes on J. G. Bourke's *Scatalogic Rites of All Nations* (which tellingly focus on the Jewish material) are on the letterhead of the Oxford & Cambridge University Club, Ladies' Wing, 77, Pall Mall, S.W.1.[33]

* * *

An Oxford doctorate in social anthropology at that time was invariably based on fieldwork. Tew did hers among the Lele of the Kasai in what was then the Belgian Congo. It has repeatedly been remarked that it was unconventional of her not to go to a part of Africa under British control. Some have even speculated that this choice kept the resulting monograph from having as much influence as might have otherwise been expected. The explanation for this maverick decision has usually been that Tew wanted to study a matrilineal system. Another factor, however, was the cosmopolitanism of Catholicism. After all, Tew's very first school as a five-year-old had been run by French nuns. Sacred Heart had both French nuns and students, as well

---

[31] Sheila Hale, 'Closely Observed Brains', *Harper's Bazaar and Queen*, January 1977, p. 144.

[32] Mary Douglas, *Evans-Pritchard* (Brighton: Harvester Press, 1980).

[33] Mary Douglas Papers, Northwestern University archives, Evanston, Illinois: Box 5 (Leviticus).

as girls and teachers from elsewhere on the Continent. (To this should be added that Tew studied in Paris for six months before Oxford, all making a Francophone colonial context seem a perfectly comfortable option for her.) Uncannily, *Frost in May*—which was first published in 1933 while Tew's first period of fieldwork was not until 1949–50—has this passage: 'Mary Zulecca, an old child of the Five Wounds, who has been doing some splendid missionary work in Central Africa, has consented to give us three lantern lectures on the Congo'.[34] When Tew first arrived in the Congo, she was given a place to stay and other practical help and, in general, 'generously received' (as she was still gratefully acknowledging over a half a century later) by the missionary order of the Pères Oblats de Marie Immaculée at Basongo.[35] As she travelled closer to the Lele, this role was taken over by the Sisters of Vincent de Paul at Barbanta who 'energetically solved' her remaining practical problems (including finding her a cook) and 'kept an eye on my general well-being'.[36] In truth, the nuns were perhaps rather too solicitous for the ethnographer's own good. Tew missed her one chance to witness a pangolin ceremony as it happened to coincide with a day when some kind-hearted missionaries had made their way to her remote village in order to check up on her. (Far from being in need of rescue, she was sufficiently on top of things that some Lele even believed that she possessed a magical ability to control the weather!)[37]

Mary Tew finished her first period of fieldwork in 1950 and in that same year the economist James Douglas began working for the Research Department of the Conservative Party. He was also a devout Roman Catholic, and the sacrament of their marriage was solemnized on 31 March 1951 at Our Most Holy Redeemer, Cheyne Row, London.[38] The idea of English ladies in darkest Africa still had a Victorian frisson of the forbidden, and the betrothed couple had to endure a spate of tabloid articles with titles such as 'Tarzan Girl to

[34] White, *Frost in May*, p. 181.

[35] Wachtel, *Original Minds*, p. 332; Richard Fardon, 'Margaret Mary Douglas 1921–2007', *Proceedings of the British Academy*, 166 (2010), p. 149.

[36] Douglas, *Lele of the Kasai*, p. xiii.

[37] Mary Douglas, 'The Lele of the Congo', in Adrian Hastings (ed.), *The Church and the Nations: A study of minority Catholicism in England, India, Norway, America, Lebanon, Australia, Wales, Japan, the Netherlands, Vietnam, Brazil, Egypt, Southern Africa and among the Lele of the Congo* (London: Sheed and Ward, 1959), p. 86.

[38] Richard Fardon, 'Dame (Margaret) Mary Douglas [*née* Tew] (1921–2007)', *Oxford Dictionary of National Biography*, accessed online on 18 January 2013 at www.oxforddnb.com.

Wed'.[39] Mary Douglas promptly became pregnant and their daughter Janet was born before the year was out. Two sons followed, James and Philip, the youngest of their three children being born in 1956. Her husband James's career prospered as well and by 1970 he was the Director of the Research Department. Mary and James Douglas's lifelong companionship included their intellectual lives. He appears across her work—most often in the acknowledgements. *Risk and Blame* (1992) was dedicated to him: 'My husband has been tireless in efforts to make me relate the discourse of anthropology to the discourses in economics and political theory'.[40] The wife was eventually inspired by her husband's interests to pursue an interdisciplinary project with economics, *The World of Goods* (1979), in which she wittily reflected on this influence: 'The married state is a well-known forum for contesting different principles for the allocation of resources'.[41] She also playfully added an apology for professional duties eclipsing domestic ones: 'All our things have fallen into neglect while I have been writing, floors unpolished, curtains falling off hooks. I am grateful to my family for their patience'.[42] Once James and Mary Douglas even collaborated on research.[43] James's work, being in the service of national politics, naturally was orientated toward Westminster, and so in the year they wed Dr Mary Douglas left Oxford to become a lecturer at University College London.

Peoples of the Lake Nyasa Region (1950) was a volume that Mary Tew contributed to the series, Ethnographic Survey of Africa.[44] As Mary Douglas, she contributed the chapter, 'The Lele of Kasai', in *African Worlds* (1954), a volume edited by her senior colleague at UCL, Daryll Forde (1902–73).[45] (Speaking of hierarchy, Forde's position as the holder of the sole chair in anthropology was such that

[39] Fardon, 'Douglas', *Proceedings*, p. 149.

[40] Mary Douglas, *Risk and Blame: Essays in Cultural Theory* (London: Routledge, 1992), p. xii (and dedication page).

[41] Mary Douglas and Baron Isherwood, *The World of Goods* (New York: Basic Books, 1979), p. vii.

[42] Douglas, *World of Goods*, pp. vii, x.

[43] Douglas, *Risk and Blame*, p. 80.

[44] Mary Tew, *Peoples of the Lake Nyasa Region* (East Central Africa Part 1: Ethnographic Survey of Africa) (London: Oxford University Press for the International African Institute, 1950).

[45] Daryll Forde (ed.), *African Worlds: Studies in the Cosmological Ideas and Social Values of African Peoples* (London: Oxford University Press for the International African Institute [1954] 1970).

the department stationary supplied for Douglas's use had his name printed on it but not hers or that of any other member of the faculty.)[46] The full monograph, *The Lele of the Kasai*, finally appeared in 1963. Fardon reports that it 'became a minor anthropological classic' and Paul Richards that it 'was immediately recognized as a significant work among Africanists',[47] but it is not on her work as an Africa specialist that Douglas's fame chiefly rests. Her next two books, *Purity and Danger* and *Natural Symbols*, would mark a turn toward a comparative approach that would bring modern, industrial societies under her anthropological gaze. This shift was prompted by realities both at home and abroad. As to the latter, after independence came and the Republic of the Congo was founded in 1960, a period of violence and instability ensued which convinced Douglas that she needed to find a way for her career to develop that did not involve any more fieldwork there. Furthermore, she believed that Lele ways were Westernizing so fast that even in her book she was unwilling to use the ethnographic present: this made it seem less plausible to keep writing about the same people largely on the basis of past fieldwork in the way that anthropologists of the previous generation had done. Then there was home: as the wife of someone with his own successful career to pursue which was tied to London, and as the mother of three small children, she needed to find a way to do research that did not involve going away anywhere for months at a time. Motherhood makes invention a necessity, and her childcare duties helped to put Douglas on the path to becoming a major public intellectual.

* * *

Purity and Danger is one of the great classics of anthropology. At the height of its influence, it was probably the most widely assigned text in the discipline in Britain. Even undergraduate students reading anthropology were expected to know this seminal volume. In fact, as we have seen, it became a broadly read and referred-to book for the intelligent general reader, winding up being identified as one of

---

[46] Douglas Papers, Northwestern University archives: Box 5 (Leviticus). (Various notes of hers are on this stationery. To take just one example of her curious reading, on this letterhead are her notes on a 1960 article from the *Journal of Analytical Psychology* by Michael Rosenthall, '"Jesus-in-Reverse": Some notes on the Case of a Compulsive Jew'.)

[47] Fardon, 'Dame Mary Douglas', *Guardian*; Paul Richards, 'Obituary: Mary Tew Douglas (1921–2007)', *American Anthropologist*, 110, 3 (September 2008), p. 405.

the pre-eminent works of the second half of the twentieth century from across the entire range of genres and disciplines. By the time of Douglas's death, it had also been translated into some fifteen different languages.[48] In a prolific and often provocative oeuvre, it is standardly referred to as Douglas's best-known and most celebrated book. Frazerian in the wide sweep of its comparative method, Douglas later reflected that it was 'an attempt to generalize from Africa to our own condition'.[49] This was to sell its range short. Its magpie approach reached from Hinduism to Mary Baker Eddy and beyond. *Purity and Danger* repeatedly draws upon medieval Christianity—with illustrations from Catherine of Siena, Thomas Aquinas, Joan of Arc, and Teresa of Avila—and, most famously, offers an entire chapter on ancient Judaism as presented in the book of Leviticus.

This treatment of the Hebrew scriptures was widely anthologized and became the most discussed, memorable, and lauded chapter in the book. It is hard to know how far back this interest went for Douglas. The Bible was a common reference point among the Oxford anthropologists. Allusions to it would be made in their lectures and seminars; Steiner wrote pieces on scriptural passages and topics; and Evans-Pritchard made the Old Testament a running point of comparison in *Nuer Religion* (1956). As early as 1959, Douglas had composed a typescript on 'Leviticus XI' that included not only ideas but some specific prose that would eventually make its way into *Purity and Danger*.[50]

No less famous is the book's deployment of the definition of dirt as matter out of place: 'Where there is dirt there is a system. Dirt is the by-product of a systematic ordering and classification of matter'.[51] *Purity and Danger* was therefore an exposition of the basic human need to have order and the resulting necessity of classification. The Leviticus argument was that animals were deemed unclean because they transgressed classification boundaries and thereby sowed disorder and confusion. The unclean animals were rejected because they were indeterminate. Douglas's intellectual breakthrough can be

---

[48] 'Obituary: Professor Dame Mary Douglas', *The Times*, 18 May 2007, accessed online on 26 February 2010 at www.timesonline.co.uk

[49] Douglas, *How Institutions Think*, p. ix.

[50] Douglas Papers, Northwestern University archives: Box 5 (Leviticus). Another possible influence might have been the fact that pigs were also unclean for the Lele: Mary Douglas, 'The Lele of Kasai', in Forde, *African Worlds*, p. 5.

[51] Douglas, *Purity and Danger*, p. 35.

witnessed in her notes on Leviticus. In a moment of exuberance, she filled half a sheet of paper with her insight writ large: 'AMBIGUITY'.[52] Readers delighted: Douglas had taken biblical injunctions and Jewish taboos that hitherto had seemed arbitrary and had made them explicable. She believed that the logic behind Leviticus 11 was so coherent that it could even be extended to prediction: 'If penguins lived in the Near East I would expect them to be ruled unclean as wingless birds'.[53] How all this—on one (and not the only) level—might have also been in the service of her Christian faith would become much more explicit in *Natural Symbols*, but Douglas was already treading the narrow way that leads to the kingdom of God in her writings. Fardon observes that *Purity and Danger* seems to have been intended 'as a general defence of religion'.[54]

Natural Symbols (1970), although more controversial, is nevertheless Douglas's second-best-known work. Richards declares that it is 'sometimes regarded as her masterpiece', and Fardon that it is 'arguably her most significant' and, 'in terms of her intellectual career, undoubtedly Douglas's most important book'.[55] It was also explicitly Christian in origin. The first airing of the argument was her Thomas Aquinas Lecture for the Dominicans at New Blackfriars, Oxford, on 7 March 1968. Later that year it was published in two parts in the Dominicans' journal under the title, 'The Contempt of Ritual'. A lot of this material was transferred straight into the book, but the confessional context of this lecture freed Douglas to speak more explicitly as a committed churchwoman. The lecture began: 'The Church today is engaged in a great crisis of self-examination'.[56] This note of what direction the Church ought to take became a bit more muted in *Natural Symbols*, which, of course, was aimed at a more general audience. Here is a sample of what was lost: 'It will be well to consider, therefore, whether we are prepared for a doctrinal shift concerning the sacraments'. For a Catholic audience this was not merely analysis but rather a prophetic warning: 'It is part of my argument that people who have become unritualistic in every other way, for whatever reason, will eventually

---

[52] Douglas Papers, Northwestern University archives: Box 5 (Leviticus).

[53] Douglas, *Purity and Danger*, p. 56.

[54] Fardon, 'Douglas', *Proceedings*, p. 155.

[55] Richards, 'Obituary: Douglas', p. 405; Fardon, *Mary Douglas*, pp. xii, 103.

[56] Mary Douglas, 'The Contempt of Ritual' (Part 1), *New Blackfriars*, 49 (June 1968), p. 475.

lose their capacity for responding to condensed symbols such as that of the Blessed Sacrament'.[57]

In a paper given at the spring 1969 meeting of the American Ethnological Society, Douglas cited her next book as in press for later that same year and identified it as *Rite over Trace*.[58] This is clearly the same project (and with the same publisher, Barrie and Rockliffe), but she presumably decided it needed a bit more refining as it came out one year later and with a different title. For the purpose of this study what needs to be said about the name change is that 'natural symbol' is a category in Christian thought. In order to elucidate Dante's great medieval depiction of Christian cosmology, another British female Christian and public intellectual, Dorothy L. Sayers (1893–1957), defined it thus in 1948:

> A *natural* symbol is not an arbitrary sign, but a thing really existing which, by its very nature, stands for and images forth a greater reality of which it is itself an instance. Thus an arch, maintaining itself as it does by a balance of opposing strains, is a *natural symbol* of that stability in tension by which the whole universe maintains itself. Its significance is the same in all languages and in all circumstances, and may be applied indifferently to physical, psychical, or spiritual experience.[59]

In Catholic thought, this category is most often used to describe the sacred heart of Jesus.[60] Douglas's childhood school, the Convent of the Sacred Heart, seems to hold the key indeed. Douglas was far too good an anthropologist to imagine that there really were symbols that had the same significance across all cultures, so she was not using this term naively but, on the other hand, she was not merely using it in an 'ironic' manner either (to evoke one assessment);[61] rather she valued those forms of society and cultural practices which could

[57] Douglas, 'Contempt' (Part 1), pp. 476, 482.

[58] Mary Douglas, 'Social Preconditions of Enthusiasm and Heterodoxy', in Robert F. Spencer (ed.), *Forms of Symbolic Action: Proceedings of the 1969 Annual Spring Meeting of the American Ethnological Society* (Seattle: University of Washington Press, 1969), p. 79.

[59] Dorothy L. Sayers, 'Introduction', in Dante, *The Divine Comedy: Hell* (London: Penguin, 1949), p. 13.

[60] For example, see *Haurietis Aquas: On Devotion to the Sacred Heart*. Encyclical of Pope Pius XII, 15 May 1956, accessed online on 8 January 2012 at www.vatican.va.

[61] Sheldon R. Isenberg and Dennis E. Owen, 'Bodies, Natural and Contrived: The Work of Mary Douglas', *Religious Studies Review*, 3, 1 (January 1977), p. 3. The 1969 article makes it clear that she was not using it ironically: Douglas, 'Social Preconditions', p. 73.

allow common meanings to be widely recognized and shared. She even went so far as to claim that Catholic theology did capitalize on those symbols which came the closest to being natural ones in human experience.[62]

A goal of *Natural Symbols* was to call into question a whole nexus of contemporary assumptions about what is better. When it came to religion, Douglas wanted to challenge the view that what is better is what is more informal, personal, and extemporaneous rather than formal, structured, and scripted (hence the original title expressed her counterblast that prescribed rites are superior to spontaneous traces). In *Natural Symbols*, the equivalent of the abominations of Leviticus as the particularly captivating chapter was one on 'The Bog Irish'. By this term, Douglas primarily had in mind working-class Irish Catholics in London, and her case study is their seemingly exaggerated and therefore misguided attachment to the prohibition on eating meat on Friday. Modernizing Church leaders were embarrassed that something so external and apparently divorced from wider ethical impulses had become so elevated. Their solution was to revoke the rule of Friday abstinence in order to redirect the faithful towards weightier matters. Douglas responded that these reformers misunderstood the nature, importance, and function of symbolism and ritual. She boldly compares the Friday fast to the Jewish prohibition on eating pork. Friday abstinence was 'the only ritual which brought Christian symbols down into the kitchen and larder and on to the dinner table in the manner of Jewish rules of impurity'.[63] The ethical plea of the reformers was vacuous, as she witheringly observes: 'The problem of how to benefit the hungry by not abstaining from meat does not arise'. All they have managed to do is to evacuate spiritual meaning: 'Friday no longer rings the great cosmic symbols of expiation and atonement'. [64] The reformers know not what they do: 'It is as if the liturgical signal boxes were manned by colour-blind signalmen'.[65] Once again, the alarm is sounded: if you teach people to reject condensed symbols (even a humble one such as Friday abstinence), then you are leading them away from the greatest one of all, the Blessed

[62] Mary Douglas, 'Sacraments and Society: An Anthropologist Asks, What Women Could be Doing in the Church', *New Blackfriars*, 77, 900 (January 1996), p. 32.

[63] Douglas, *Natural Symbols*, p. 42. (My copy is the American edition: the British edition was published by Barrie & Rockliff.)

[64] Douglas, *Natural Symbols*, p. 44.   [65] Douglas, *Natural Symbols*, p. 42.

Sacrament. Douglas claims that these modernizing reforms will make the Eucharist 'hard for anyone to stomach'—a rather graphic image which suggests people's bodies physically rejecting the body of Christ.[66] To take the widest view, her polemic ran thus: so many of the traits that people in the late 1960s had come to assume were what was wrong with Catholicism—that it was ritualistic, symbolic, hier-archical, conformist, structured, formal, and ordered—were actually vital for the sustaining of the faith and therefore needed to be valued, defended, and preserved. Douglas's penchant for the comparative method fostered a tendency for her to line up all her enemies together. This meant that Protestantism and 1960s radicals were discerned to be from the same spirit—John Lennon is John Calvin *redux*; and Woodstock the new Wittenberg. Edmund Leach not only could not stomach the Eucharist, he was made queasy merely by an anthropolo-gist being openly Christian. In no less prestigious a forum than the *New York Review of Books*, he declared in a review of *Natural Symbols* that Douglas was no longer being a true professional but was wielding her erudition in 'the service of Roman Catholic propaganda.'[67]

In several subsequent publications Douglas claimed that she was just elaborating on the argument she had made in *Natural Symbols*. Notably, *Natural Symbols* had been the first book in which she had aired what would become a major recurring component of her work: grid-group analysis (or, as it was called in a later iteration, cul-tural theory). Grid refers to the extent to which one's behaviour and options in life are proscribed and confined on the basis of general, fixed categories of identity. A caste system would be an example of a particularly high grid context; another is the inflexible function of age seniority among the Lele of the Kasai. Group refers to the extent to which a collective commitment impinges on individualism. Living in a monastery as a religious under vows would be an example of an extremely high group context. The four possible combinations of high versus low grid and group therefore become an analytical tool. Definitions and labels would change over time, but the key point for our purpose is that one coordinate (high grid/high group) was hier-archy, and this was Douglas's own preferred place to be. The other possibilities were named and renamed with variations on overlapping

[66] Douglas, *Natural Symbols*, p. 47.
[67] Edmund R. Leach, 'Mythical Inequalities', *New York Review of Books*, 28 January 1971, accessed online on 21 January 2013 at www.nybooks.com.

terms such as sectarian, egalitarian, enclave, isolation, fatalist, individualist, and competitive.

Douglas commended grid-group analysis as a way to see one's own culture as just one possibility among others that are also valued by their champions: that is, as an aid to objectivity. Still, it is all too obvious that she was chiefly hoping that its despisers would learn to take a more objective view of hierarchy rather than worrying that her commitment to hierarchy was hampering her own objectivity. At the very least, however, Douglas sincerely believed grid-group analysis was a fair and fruitful way to create the possibility of a meaningful conversation about values among people from different perspectives. The sense of advocacy partially came from her assessment that hierarchy was currently under attack: 'Our civilization is convinced of the virtues of individualism and of the evils of hierarchy'.[68] Therefore 'being fair to hierarchists' was the lesson that now needed to be learned.[69] (The article of this title is a classic example of Douglas having it both ways. While she commends grid-group analysis as a neutral tool that does not teach that one culture is preferential to another, she simultaneously exposes an anti-hierarchical prejudice and thus the one thing needful is not to learn to be fair to individualists or egalitarians but hierarchists.)

Douglas's championing of hierarchy began with defining it. Here is a typical example: 'Hierarchy is the encompassing principle of order which systematizes any field of work, whether a library, a game, an alphabet, mathematics...'.[70] An implicit goal of such a definition was to de-emphasize the repellent notion of stratified ranks where those at the top have power and prestige and those at the bottom are fated to obey in humble obscurity. The fact that Philosophy is the 100s and History the 900s in the Dewey Decimal System does not tell us which one is more important: it simply tells us that there is a unified scheme that is giving order and coherence to the entire collection. Douglas was therefore apt to deprive institutions that might give hierarchy a bad name of the right to be considered ones—aristocracies and large corporations, for example, she insisted actually are marked

[68] Mary Douglas, *In the Wilderness: The Doctrine of Defilement in the Book of Numbers* (*Journal for the Study of the Old Testament* Supplement Series 158) (Sheffield: Sheffield Academic Press, 1993), p. 46.

[69] Mary Douglas, 'Being Fair to Hierarchists', *University of Pennsylvania Law Review*, 151, 4 (April 2003), pp. 1349–70.

[70] Mary Douglas, 'A Feeling for Hierarchy', p. 95.

by strong individualist impulses. Conversely, Douglas would bestow
the label of hierarchy upon more benign, if less obvious, alternatives
(most notably, her grandmother's house). She would candidly admit
her bias (to use one of her favourite words): 'My own preference has
emerged as an idealized form of hierarchy'.[71] Her writings are therefore littered with the alleged virtues of hierarchy: it allows the centre
to hold; it fosters deep meaning; it is the form of organization that is
strong enough to bear criticism; 'it is capable of being more aware
of minority interests';[72] it makes it 'easier to live at peace with one's
neighbours';[73] it better protects the interests of the weak; it is more tol-
erant; it better enables survival; it is more caring towards the sick and
accepting of those with physical defects; it fosters long-term planning
and great achievements; it is better at mobilizing people to respond
effectively in a crisis; it is more hopeful; it is 'a better place to grow
old in';[74] and it even reduces anxiety about sexual performance.[75] No
wonder Douglas conceded that her preferred version of hierarchy was
'an idealized form'!

Furthermore, when Douglas thought of a hierarchy she thought
first and foremost of her beloved Church. When asked to give an
address on how her faith had influenced her scholarship, Douglas
tellingly entitled it, 'A Feeling for Hierarchy', and averred: 'When
I say "hierarchy", I am remembering that the Roman Catholic Church
calls herself a hierarchy'.[76] She was always remembering this. In a
co-authored work, Douglas once illustrated what came under the
heading of hierarchy by saying that it included 'churches, industrial
corporations, and political hierarchies'.[77] This is a fascinating list,
not only because churches have pride of place, but also because she
would later pronounce that the second item did not belong in this category,[78] and the third one is tautological—leaving the Church as the
only concrete example. To come at it from the other direction, to fail

---

[71] Douglas, *Risk and Blame*, p. 266.   [72] Douglas, *Risk and Blame*, p. 35.

[73] Douglas, *Risk and Blame*, p. 144.

[74] Mary Douglas, *Cultural Bias* (RAI Occasional Paper 34) (London: Royal
Anthropological Institute of Great Britain and Ireland, 1978), p. 29.

[75] Douglas, *Cultural Bias*, p. 34.

[76] Douglas, 'A Feeling for Hierarchy', p. 94.

[77] Mary Douglas and Aaron Wildavsky, *Risk and Culture: An Essay on the Selection
of Technological and Environmental Dangers* (Berkeley: University of California Press,
1982), p. 90.

[78] Douglas, 'A Feeling for Hierarchy', p. 116.

to defend hierarchy would be to abandon one's spiritual mother, for 'the Catholic Church is inherently hierarchical'.[79] Echoing Marshall McLuhan (another Catholic public intellectual), Douglas argued that the form was also the content: 'When the Church holds on to a hierarchical conception, she might be saying that the organisation is the message'.[80]

Yet another Catholic public intellectual, the philosopher Charles Taylor (who received the Marianist Award a half a dozen years before Douglas), has critiqued a 'stadial consciousness' which views religion as part of primitive stage of development to be rejected in the name of progressing into modernity.[81] This study has shown how deeply E. B. Tylor and James Frazer were invested in that way of thinking. Douglas could turn Tylor's tools against him on this matter, pronouncing mischievously: 'The argument that modern science is incompatible with religion is a nineteenth-century relic'.[82] In fact—still enjoying herself—the assumption that 'moderns are utterly different from everyone else because of modernization' is itself evidence that we are strikingly similar to so-called primitive peoples: 'Every tribe that we study believes in its own uniqueness'.[83] Douglas countered the myth of secularity as a more advanced stage of human development with the biblical wisdom that there is nothing new under the sun. She did this by delighting in asserting that what we think of as distinctively modern can also be found in some primitive contexts and therefore these traits are actually part of a perennial range of ways of being human. The Yurok, though primitive, are an example of 'unfettered individualism'.[84] Youth in ancient Israel were like student protestors in Paris in 1968 or Beijing in 1989.[85] These conflations pleased her. At the end of her personal notes on the Bantu, Douglas scrawled the juxtaposition she had discerned triumphantly: '*Man-Centred Universe*

---

[79] Mary Douglas, 'The Gender of the Beloved', *Heythrop Journal*, 36 (1995), p. 405.

[80] Douglas, 'Sacraments and Society', p. 37.

[81] Charles Taylor, *A Secular Age* (Cambridge, Mass: Harvard University Press, 2007), especially p. 289.

[82] Mary Douglas, 'The Effects of Modernization on Religious Change', in Mary Douglas and Steven Tipton (eds.), *Religion and America: Spiritual Life in a Secular Age* (Boston: Beacon Press, 1983), p. 33.

[83] Douglas, 'Effects of Modernization', p. 26.

[84] Douglas, *World of Goods*, pp. 132–35.

[85] Mary Douglas, *Jacob's Tears: The Priestly Work of Reconciliation* (Oxford: Oxford University Press, 2004), p. 192.

Renaissance!!!!'[86] Whatever one might think of as a recent development, Douglas was inclined to present as merely a fixed point on
the same old compass. In the penultimate paragraph of *Purity and
Danger*, she informed readers that primitives also had their own exis-
tentialists.[87] When ostensibly new movements arose, she was ready
with this response, even going so far as to assert that 'postmodernism'
was an enduring option rather than a unique development, the stadial
structure built into its very name notwithstanding.[88] As it was in the
beginning, is now and ever shall be, world without end. Amen.

This move was repeatedly made in regard to religion. The
anti-ritualistic mood of her own day should not be mistaken as some
kind of advance—a rising above the mechanical, superstitious ways
of savages—it is a trait perfectly exemplified by pygmies. Likewise an
evangelical revivalist commitment to extemporaneous prayer may be
found among the peyotists.[89] Every contemporary religious option
has its primitive equivalent: 'They, too, will have their Protestant
ethic, their Shakers and Quakers and anti-sacerdotal movements'.[90]
Douglas came to wield this insight in order to reject the secularization
thesis. If we are becoming more secular, she averred, it simply means
that we have gravitated from one persistent way of life to another.
There are 'irreverent' tribes as well.[91] Doubt is not a new arrival 'along
with tramcars and electric light', but rather 'human history is studded
all the way from the beginning with nails driven into local coffins of
authority'.[92] The contrast between religious and secular distinguishes
between types of cultures not time periods or stages:

> When we look more closely at our information we find plenty of secular
> savages. Indeed, in certain tribal places there is a notable lack of interest
> in the supernatural. God is not suddenly dead with Western civilization.

---

[86] Douglas Papers, Northwestern University archives: Box 1. (These are her notes
on a study by Placide Tempels, whom she refers to as 'Rev. F. Tempels' or 'Father
Tempels'.)

[87] Douglas, *Purity and Danger*, p. 178.

[88] Mary Douglas, *Thinking in Circles: An Essay on Ring Composition* (New
Haven: Yale University Press, 2007), pp. 142–43.

[89] Douglas, *Natural Symbols*, pp. 12, 15.

[90] Mary Douglas, 'The Myth of Primitive Religion', *Commonweal*, 9 October
1970, p. 44.

[91] Douglas, *Natural Symbols*, p. 21.

[92] Douglas, *Thinking in Circles*, pp. 94–95. (She is perhaps alluding to Rudolf
Bultmann's famous dictum that we cannot use electric lights and still believe in the
spirit world of the New Testament.)

Science has not delivered the *coup de grace*. Anthropologists should really think twice before they subscribe to this particular fantasy about the difference between Us and Them.[93]

In short, 'there is a range of societies with a secular bias... We conclude that the secular world view is no modern development, but appears when group boundaries are weak and ego-focussed grid is strong.'[94] A lingering stadial consciousness among many intellectuals—far from proving that they are more enlightened—has actually blinded them to the world around them: religious revival and resurgence repeatedly catch them unawares.[95]

* * *

One of the habits that gave Douglas's writings an element of surprise was a tendency to travel down radical routes to reach conservative ends. She seemed to enjoy the disorientating effect of these twists. And she can sometimes be glimpsed smiling for the cameras as she strikes an unanticipated pose. To take a minor example, Douglas admitted that *Purity and Danger* was opposed to the 'flower children' impulses of the late 1960s,[96] and *Natural Symbols* was a full-blown polemic against such tendencies. The flower children are standardly referred to as a manifestation of the 'counterculture' which would presumably make someone opposed to their agenda something akin to a defender of the *ancien régime*. Douglas, however, delighted in referring to her own opposition to the spirit of the sixties radicals as 'countercultural'. Even *Natural Symbols* itself is dubbed 'counter-cultural' (by which is meant that it went against the grain of the counterculture!)[97] Likewise Douglas would refer to her support of hierarchy not as 'traditional' or 'conservative' (let alone 'old-fashioned'), but rather as countercultural.[98]

Perhaps the most substantive example of this approach is Douglas's stance toward relativism. Those who think that Christianity and anthropology are incompatible sometimes claim that the former is committed to absolutes while the latter to relativism. Douglas had

[93] Douglas, 'Myth', p. 41.   [94] Douglas, *Natural Symbols*, p. 139.

[95] Douglas, 'Effects of Modernization', pp. 25–26.

[96] Mary Douglas, *Purity and Danger* (London: Routledge Classics, 2002), pp. xvi–xvii (from a new preface dated February 2002).

[97] Mary Douglas, *Natural Symbols: Explorations in Cosmology* (London: Routledge, 1996), p. xiii (from a new introduction for this 1996 edition).

[98] Douglas, 'A Feeling for Hierarchy', p. 95.

no desire to be cast as a grumpy conservative raging against relativism. In *Implicit Meanings* (1975) she therefore rather breezily brushed aside 'the philosopher's bogy of relativism', arguing that new insights would emerge 'when relativism is feared less'.[99] The preface ends with a brave, full-body embrace of epistemological indeterminacy: 'Surely now it is an anachronism to believe that our world is more securely founded in knowledge than one that is driven by pangolin power'.[100] This was read by some as sounding like a denial that scientific findings uncovered objective reality, a suspicion that was raised again when her controversial *Risk and Culture: An Essay on the Selection of Technological and Environmental Dangers* (co-written with Aaron Wildavsky) appeared in 1982. *Risk and Culture* so emphasized that anxieties about environmental pollution correlated with grid-group positioning that for some readers it seemed to be dismissing the possibility that proven facts could ground and warrant such concerns. This antipathetic reading of *Risk and Culture* was undoubtedly reinforced by the book's willingness to mix and match examples from both scientific frames of analysis (such as illness through asbestos poisoning) with mystical ones (such as death by witchcraft).

In a 1999 interview Douglas reported: 'They call me a relativist'.[101] But that would not do either. She would therefore also include denials of this stance in her writings. Here is one from 1985:

> The logical difficulties start when we try to develop value-free ideas about the good society. And yet these difficulties must be met if we are not to leave the whole inquiry in a stew of philosophical relativism. It is not at all the purpose of this book to teach that because institutions do so much of our thinking there can be no comparisons between different versions of the world, still less to teach that all versions are equally right or wrong.[102]

Any attempt to present Douglas's philosophical position on relativism would be in danger of being more clear and consistent on this matter than her own thoughts were. In a personal letter written in 1978 she candidly confessed that she had not really formulated her own stance: 'Your remarks on relativism are very important for me. I shall try to avoid that

[99] Mary Douglas, *Implicit Meanings: Essays in Anthropology* (London: Routledge & Kegan Paul, 1975), pp. xvii–xviii.

[100] Douglas, *Implicit Meanings*, p. xxi.

[101] Douglas, 'Can a scientist be objective?', p. 385.

[102] Douglas, *How Institutions Think*, p. 109.

topic as much as possible in the Evans-Pritchard essay but I must confront it for myself'.[103] Her working approach to this whole issue seems to have been simply that relativism was a good servant but a bad master.[104] Douglas was thrilled with the sociologist Peter L. Berger's *A Rumor of Angels: Modern Society and the Rediscovery of the Supernatural* (1969). In a review of it, her cup overflowed at finding an intellectual who knew how to put relativism to work to do something useful: 'At last! A sociologist who uses the argument of the relativity of all experience to relativise the relativisers. This little book, vigorous and authoritative, could mark an important turning point in twentieth-century thought'.[105] Douglas did not seriously intend to allow relativism to become an inescapable final destination—although it was one of her radical routes.

Another of her winding paths to truth was Douglas's articulation of her position on women priests. Her stance was quite straightforward: she was opposed to admitting women into the Roman Catholic priesthood. In other words, she supported the traditional, official, current practice of the Church. In a 1987 article she argued that the Catholic Church was inherently hierarchical and that the exclusively male priesthood was an essential part of its interconnected web of symbols. It was already possible for women to be Christian priests or ministers in churches with a more egalitarian structure: if women want to pursue ordained ministry they should serve in one of them. To insist on doing so in the Catholic Church would be to destroy what they claim they want to join.[106] Again, bishops across the globe could have made the same point. In the mid-1990s, Douglas developed a compromise position in which women would find an official place in the hierarchy through a Women's Commission on Doctrine (or Catholic Commission of Women). The whole point of this proposal was to find a greater role for women without undercutting the existing theological and structural reasons that had been offered as a rationale for the male priesthood. In short, it was a suggested bit

[103] Mary Douglas to Thomas Luckmann, University of Wollongong, Australia, 11 September 1978: Douglas Papers, Northwestern University archives: Box 4 (Evans-Pritchard).

[104] This analysis accords with Fardon's assessment that it is not helpful to think of Douglas as a relativist even though she 'employs a rhetoric of relativity' and his pleasing, Douglas-like aphorism that she was 'dogmatic about her ends but open-minded about her means': Fardon, *Mary Douglas*, pp. 253, 251.

[105] Mary Douglas, 'Full turn of the secular wheel' (review of Peter L. Berger, *A Rumor of Angels*), *New Society*, 15 (April 1970), p. 610.

[106] Douglas, *Risk and Blame*, pp. 271–93.

of Burkean-style reform in the conservative-continuity mode. What is curious is her insistence that this idea of hers was actually 'more radical' than including women in the priesthood.[107] Moreover, the male priesthood was a sign of sacred marriage. This allowed Douglas to strike the counterintuitive pose that the modernist reformers are acting in a 'spirit of censorship' which is opposed to 'eroticism'—a classic Douglas manoeuvre to steal the clothes, as it were, of her opponents: it is the modernizers who are the prudes and the traditionalists who are the sensualists.[108] (Elsewhere she would argue that assuming that a faith which has lots of regulations regarding sex has a negative attitude toward it is like inferring that the high standards of gourmets reveal them to have a condemning rather than celebratory attitude toward food.)[109]

No less disconcerting was Douglas's tendency to redeem words and concepts that had become pejorative in general usage. We have already seen her efforts to do this with 'ritualistic' and 'hierarchical'. There was a mischievous defiance in this. Perhaps with the self-righteousness of the flower children still in view, *The World of Goods* (1979) was one long defence of the moral uprightness of conspicuous consumption and the acquisition of luxuries. While even Evans-Pritchard distinguished between erroneous magic and true religion, Douglas cheerfully insisted that she could see no advantage in trying to distinguish between magic and the sacraments. She even went so far as to label core doctrines of the Christian faith, the Incarnation and the Resurrection, as magical.[110]

Then there was her sympathy for the devil. Those who congratulated themselves on being so modern as to find belief in Satan risible she countered with an über-urbanity that found the prince of darkness a useful chap to have around. In 'The devil vanishes' she discerned that Satan had a 'benign role' in 'independent Protestant Churches in Africa'—he allowed a community to find reconciliation by acknowledging the wrong and harm that had been done while mitigating the culpability of the human agents and so allowing them to save face and be restored to good standing.[111] This diabolical

[107] Douglas, 'Sacraments and Society', p. 30. See also Douglas, 'Gender of the Beloved', p. 398.

[108] Douglas, 'Gender of the Beloved', p. 404.

[109] Mary Douglas, *Leviticus as Literature* (Oxford: Oxford University Press, 1999), p. 178.

[110] Douglas, *Natural Symbols*, 1970, pp. 190–91.

[111] Mary Douglas, 'The devil vanishes', *Tablet*, 28 April 1990, pp. 513–14.

insight frequently recurs. The forces of darkness were even elevated to an essential feature of the good life: 'The question is not why some peoples believe in demons, but why anyone can manage without demons'.[112] If only Robertson Smith had believed in demonic powers, she teasingly opined, he and the Free Church of Scotland could have found a way to resolve their conflict without the inexorable unfolding of events that led to his heresy trial and dismissal. Perhaps no scholar has ever lamented the disenchantment of the modern industrial world in quite so unflinching a way: 'If only we could believe in capricious demons and do exorcisms it might be easier'.[113] In one of her last books, Douglas was still insisting that interfering spirit ancestors and demons 'can make it a little easier for people to live together side by side in peace'.[114]

More substantively, 'bias' did not have the derogatory ring for Douglas that it typically does. For her, it meant something neutral, more akin to 'perspective' or 'point of view'. One presentation of grid-group analysis was entitled *Cultural Bias* (1978), and, as ever, the point was merely to make apparent the different waters people were swimming in rather than to label some of them as hazardous.[115] Far from being something shameful that one should seek to eradicate, she insisted, bias should be welcomed as both essential and valuable: 'Since an individual cannot look in all directions at once...People order their universe through social bias'.[116] Douglas's usage was so different from the common one which makes 'bias' and 'prejudice' synonymous that she could commend her own discipline thus: 'The special bias of anthropology is its bias against prejudice'.[117] (And Douglas's temptation to redeem words was so exuberant that she could use even that word innocently, as in her memorable reflection at the start of *Purity and Danger* that she had 'discovered in myself a prejudice against piecemeal explanations'.)[118] A young Jeffrey Stout, just beginning his distinguished career in the Department of Religion

[112] Mary Douglas, 'Demonology in William Robertson Smith's Theory of Religious Belief', in William Johnstone (ed.), *William Robertson Smith: Essays in Reassessment* (*Journal for the Study of the Old Testament* Supplement Series 189) (Sheffield: Sheffield Academic Press, 1995), p. 292.

[113] Douglas, *Risk and Blame*, p. 17.   [114] Douglas, *Jacob's Tears*, p. 179.

[115] Douglas, *Cultural Bias*.

[116] Douglas and Wildavsky, *Risk and Culture*, p. 9.

[117] Mary Douglas, *Thought Styles: Critical Essays on Good Taste* (London: SAGE publications, 1996), p. 202.

[118] Douglas, *Purity and Danger*, 1966, p. vii.

at Princeton University, wrote to Douglas in 1978: 'Your use of the word "bias", here and elsewhere, interests me greatly. It was on this point that, last January during our day long seminar, I compared you with H-G. Gadamer, who uses the term "prejudice" without its complete (pejorative) thrust'.[119]

The one that got away was 'primitive'. In *Purity and Danger* Douglas decried the trend toward avoiding or decommissioning this descriptor, not only using it herself but explicitly championing its retention. Douglas being Douglas she even playfully suggested that the desire to avoid the word—far from representing a new level of respect for others—was actually an indicator that one was protesting too much: 'I suspect that our professional delicacy in avoiding the term "Primitive" is the product of secret convictions of superiority'.[120] That was a tide, however, that either she could not swim against or came to wish not to do so. Increasingly, 'exotic' became her standard substitute—albeit one that somewhat tautologically just names the other as other. In *The World of Goods*, the 'them' in contrast to 'us' was 'distant, exotic places' and the expertise she had gained in her fieldwork was in 'the anthropology of exotic places'.[121] This usage recurred thereafter. By 1999, Douglas was openly expressing embarrassment about her past terminology:

> There are several obvious weaknesses of essays written thirty or forty years ago. One is due to the change in vocabulary, itself due to changes in public attitudes which anthropologists helped to bring about. I now get a shock to read of 'primitive peoples', 'primitive religion', 'primitive society', 'tribal religions', and 'tribes', terms which have practically disappeared. In those days anthropologists were struggling against a general assumption that moderns were different from 'primitives' and for that argument they needed contrasting terms in order to deny any difference.[122]

As right and wise as that is, it is also true that there are peoples once collectively identified as 'primitive' that scholars still wanted to refer to but now had no synonym that could encompass the same set. (A Detroit assembly line worker might well think of Edinburgh as distant

---

[119] Jeffrey Stout to Mary Douglas, 16 August 1978: Douglas Papers, Northwestern University archives: Box 4 (Evans-Pritchard).

[120] Douglas, *Purity and Danger*, p. 74 (see also p. 92).

[121] Douglas, *World of Goods*, pp. 11, 37.

[122] Mary Douglas, *Implicit Meanings* (London: Routledge, new ed., 1999), p. x.

and exotic, but that is not the other at which Douglas is trying to gesture.) One can feel the strain when Douglas contrasts 'exotic' with 'modern' even though neither is a logical antonym for the other.[123] In later decades she found herself unable to reflect upon the argument of *Purity and Danger* without finding some way to evoke a category that had since vanished like an extinct tribe—perhaps even like the extinction of the very notion of tribes. Thus Douglas was reduced to 'the so-called primitives' or even—forgetting to be shocked in her nostalgia—'primitives (as we were still allowed to call those others in those days)'.[124]

Coursing through Douglas's work was a lament and alarm about what was being lost as modern, industrial societies became more individualistic and less shaped by community, hierarchy, and common ritual. Again, while 'individualistic' and 'hierarchical' were officially just different points on the compass with their own strengths and weaknesses, a prophetic tone can sometimes be discerned in her pronouncements. *Natural Symbols* opened with a sense that we have lost something valuable: 'One of the gravest problems of our day is the lack of commitment to common symbols'. The solution offered towards the end was a call to action to the task of 'repairing the defences of grid and group'.[125] Over thirty years later, in one of her last books, Douglas was still letting a note of declension slip in: 'As community dissolves, so conventions come under challenge. In our generation, where this is happening, uncertainty is becoming the order of the day'.[126] Moreover, innumerable passages in which she is ostensibly describing a position or a change can be read—for those who have ears to hear—as indictments of the way we live now. These are the other side of the coin to the bountiful benefits of hierarchy. There are little cautionary tales sprinkled throughout. Poor little Jean-Paul Sartre (1905–80) was such an unhappy, anxious child because he was living in a patternless adult world.[127] Modernization deprived the Navaho of a generous, interconnected community and left them to eke out their existence stingy and alone.[128] The heroic figures of

---

[123] Douglas, *How Institutions Think*, p. 77.

[124] Douglas, *Risk and Blame*, p. 3; Douglas, 'A Feeling for Hierarchy', p. 111.

[125] Douglas, *Natural Symbols*, p. 1, p. 155.

[126] Douglas, *Jacob's Tears*, p. 155.

[127] Mary Douglas, 'The Contempt of Ritual' (Part 2), *New Blackfriars*, 49 (July 1968), p. 534.

[128] Douglas, *Natural Symbols*, p. 14.

individualism ought to be exposed for the unpleasant creatures they were: Henry David Thoreau (1817–62) was preachy, egotistical, and insufferably smug.[129] We are losing community, meaning, shared values, and the unity of knowledge. We are losing the ability to engage in metaphysical discussions and instead creating a fragmented world in which crackpot individualists believe in flying saucers and alien space invaders. The final triumph of the anti-ritualists would create a dystopia as bleak as Narnia under the tyranny of the White Witch: it would be always winter and never Christmas.[130]

* * *

While Margaret Thatcher was not the White Witch, the Douglases nevertheless found her brand of conservatism uncongenial, not least for its emphasis on individualism instead of community. As James was out of step with the direction of the political party that was employing him, it was time to look about for a change and, as the children were now grown, the Douglases were free to roam. They decided upon the land of opportunity. Meyer Fortes thoughtfully wrote Mary some kind words:

> I hope your stay in the US will be as fruitful as you expect—but that you may decide, in the end, not to deprive us, the British anthropological community, for too long of your presence. Peripheral as I now am, I still get enough 'feedback' to know that you will be much missed. You have been an innovator for so long that you are probably unaware of your influence on the development of ideas & explanations in our subject.[131]

Mary Douglas began a period of employment with the Russell Sage Foundation in New York City in 1977. She hoped to land a prestigious university appointment and came close to doing so—with the help of Victor Turner (1920–83) on the inside—at the University of Chicago. This fell apart at the last minute, apparently because Turner thought that an interview lecture was merely a perfunctory requirement, but some members of the Anthropology Department took offence when Douglas presented a paper that they had already heard at a conference. Douglas's consolation prize was to augment her primary position as

[129] Douglas, *Cultural Bias*, pp. 45–46.

[130] Douglas, *World of Goods*, p. 66. (The Narnia image is my own: Douglas invites us to imagine every meal being the same, even on Christmas.)

[131] Meyer Fortes to Mary Douglas, 31 August 1977, King's College, Cambridge: Douglas Papers, Northwestern University archives: Box 4 (Evans-Pritchard).

Director of Research on Culture at the foundation with a succession of appointments as a visiting professor: first at New York University, then Columbia, and lastly Yale. Finally there was a chair available for her in the Chicago metropolitan area, albeit at a different institution: in 1981 Douglas became Avalon Professor of the Humanities at Northwestern University. At some point during this period she had aspired to land a professorship back in Britain but, if the Conservative Party leader was to blame for her having to leave her native land, Douglas blamed Thatcher for her inability to return as well, attributing it to the cutbacks the prime minister had forced on the universities.[132] Douglas retired in 1985, but she spent two more academic years in America as a visiting professor at Princeton University. In 1988 the Douglases finally moved back to London. Mary Douglas, a professor emerita, made University College London her academic home once again, and UCL eventually strengthened this tie by appointing her a distinguished fellow.

The American years allowed Douglas to go in new directions. Her work became much more interdisciplinary and collaborative, beginning with her foray into economics with *The World of Goods* (1979), co-written with B. C. Isherwood, a researcher in the Department of Health and Social Security (a project begun in England). During this period she continued to emerge as a prominent public intellectual addressing issues confronting Western societies. Especially in terms of British scholars, Douglas is one of the pioneers of using anthropological methods to study 'us' rather than just 'them'.[133] Douglas always affirmed that people studied anthropology to understand themselves better—and she became convinced that as well as doing this through comparisons and contrasts with exotic cultures, it could be done directly by make one's own culture an object of study. Given her interdisciplinary proclivities and her own life story, it was almost inevitable that Douglas would become more engaged with the study of religion. This trajectory was reinforced by her appointment at Northwestern which was a joint one with Anthropology and the History and Literature of Religions (the rather ungainly name for what is now the Department of Religious Studies). One early result

---

[132] Douglas interviewed by Macfarlane.
[133] Another change in anthropology was that one could no longer assume that there was a 'them' that was not a part of the conversation. A volume edited by Douglas had a chapter on the Lele of the Kasai by the anthropologist Ndolamb Ngokwey (PhD, UCLA) who was himself Lele: Mary Douglas (ed.), *Constructive Drinking: Perspectives on Drink from Anthropology* (Cambridge: Cambridge University Press [1987] 1991).

of all these trends—the moves toward collaboration, towards studying the modern industrial West, and towards religious studies—was a
co-edited volume, *Religion and America: Spirituality in a Secular Age*
(1983).[134] What would change the course of her career most dramatically, however, was a turn towards biblical studies.

* * *

The Bible had always been apt to catch the eye of British anthropologists. We have seen how Frazer became preoccupied with it; and how
Douglas's mentor, Evans-Pritchard, made the Old Testament an illuminating conversation partner in his study of Nuer religion. At the
early date in her career of 1964, Douglas addressed the Association
of Social Anthropologists on 'What Anthropology Has to Offer'.
Making the argument that the discipline was useful not only at the
university level but even in the context of secondary education, she
listed a handful of 'school subjects on which anthropologists have
something to say' and one of these was 'Old and New Testament'.[135]
A couple of years later, an interest in the Bible was there in Douglas's
early work with the famed chapter on Leviticus in *Purity and Danger*.
Douglas identified several interconnected prompts for her later move
to intensive, sustained work in the field of biblical studies.[136] An earlier, indecisive one was when she was still at Northwestern. She had
been thrilled with a lecture by Wolfgang Roth on the 'pattern' in the
miracle accounts in Mark's Gospel.[137] This is revealing both because
her own approach to biblical studies would become one of finding
patterns and because it was a New Testament paper, underlining her
interest in the whole Christian canon. The first decisive nudge happened circa 1986 when Douglas was invited to give the Gifford lectures at the University of Edinburgh during the 1989–90 academic

---

[134] Douglas and Tipton, *Religion and America*.

[135] Archives, London School of Economics Library, London, Association of Social
Anthropologists, ASA/A/2/2, Mary Douglas, 'What Anthropology Has to Offer'
(Meeting of the Association of Social Anthropologists, 17th December, 1964). (I
learned of the existence of this source from a helpful study: David Mills, *Difficult Folk?
A Political History of Social Anthropology* [Oxford: Berghahn Books, 2008].)

[136] Curiously, her *Risk and Culture* collaborator had also gone on to raid the
Hebrew scriptures: Aaron Wildavsky, *The Nursing Father: Moses as a Political Leader*
(Tuscaloosa: University of Alabama Press, 1984).

[137] Douglas, *Thinking in Circles*, pp. xi–xii. Roth's work became a book which had
as its subtitle, 'Cracking the Code of Mark', and Douglas cited it: Douglas, *In the
Wilderness*, p. 137.

year. Accepting this prestigious offer committed her to a substantial piece of scholarship on religion. Douglas was a visiting fellow at Princeton University at that time, and Katharine Doob Sakenfeld, a professor of Old Testament at Princeton Seminary, invited her to be a guest in her class in order to provide anthropological insights on ancient Israel and purification from uncleanness as presented in Numbers 19 (a fairly obvious opportunity for Sakenfeld to seize as Douglas's Leviticus reading was so well known). But Douglas had never attended to this biblical material, and she found it both baffling and exciting. She now knew how she wanted to spend Lord Gifford's money. The resulting lectures were given the vague title, 'Claims on God', and the prospectus, at any rate, shows certain eclectic tendencies (ranging from Africa to the apostle Paul) and false starts ('Why do women in the Book of Numbers not come to each others' aid'?) that contrast with the resulting monograph; but the fourth book of the Pentateuch it was to be.[138]

Douglas brought a fresh mind to the subject. She cheerfully admitted that she had never even read Numbers until 1987. Her Gifford lectures were the product of a direct encounter with the scriptures—she had not even bothered to read a single commentary, let alone anything else from the vast body of biblical studies scholarship. And she did not know Hebrew. Yet she pressed on. The result was *In the Wilderness: The Doctrine of Defilement in the Book of Numbers* (1993). Moreover, it was published in a leading monograph series in the field of biblical studies, the *Journal for the Study of the Old Testament* Supplement Series. Douglas had enlisted David Goodman to be her Hebrew consultant, and several eminent Jewish biblical scholars came to her aid, most substantively, Jacob Milgrom (1923–2010). The subtitle signals a suitably anthropological theme—defilement—and when reading *In the Wilderness* one soon encounters other staples from her larder such as cultural theory (discussions of the nature of hierarchies and enclaves, in particular). Then something strange and wonderful happens. Douglas starts to unfold an original theory of the literary structure of this ancient sacred text. Biblical scholars had often been frustrated by the seemingly hodge podge nature of Numbers,

[138] Mary Douglas, 'Gifford Lectures 1989/90: Series A. Claims on God'. (Printed prospectus or précis in the National Library of Scotland, Edinburgh). I feel a little guilty about having dug this up as Douglas confessed that she was 'glad there's no record' of these lectures: Douglas interviewed by Macfarlane.

how bits of law on the same topic crop up here and there in isolated patches rather than a subject being addressed in a more orderly fashion. Douglas argued that millennia of scholars had been overlooking an intricate pattern of rungs which revealed the entire book to be an elaborately constructed whole. Missing this was akin to a reader complaining that a villanelle was too repetitive while being oblivious to the highly structured pattern to which it was so elegantly conforming. Indeed, Douglas refers to the redactor as 'the Numbers poet'.[139] Some biblical scholars have found her alleged discovery convincing or thought-provoking and others illusory or far-fetched, but one of the interesting things about it is that it is not in any obvious sense an anthropological insight or contribution. Douglas was simply doing biblical studies.

This led on to a return to Leviticus. She landed articles on this biblical book in non-anthropological peer-reviewed journals, *Jewish Studies Quarterly* and the *Journal for the Study of the Old Testament*. In 1995 a colloquium on Leviticus was arranged at Lancaster University which put Douglas and her work in dialogue with scholars from biblical and religious studies (as well as some other disciplines such as law). The papers presented there, and even a record of some of the impromptu exchanges, was published as *Reading Leviticus: A Conversation with Mary Douglas* (1996).[140] It included a chapter by Douglas on 'Sacred Contagion'. Her own monograph was published a few years later by Oxford University Press: *Leviticus as Literature* (1999).[141] It also contains anthropological insights, notably a stimulating discussion on divination as absent from the text even though it must have been present in practice. Still, the title accurately reflects Douglas's preoccupation with literary structure. Like lightning striking in the same place twice, she once again claimed to have found a sophisticated structural pattern that unified the whole book but which had been obscured throughout the entire known history of Jewish, Christian, and modern scholarly interpretation. This time the genre was a picture poem. The text, Douglas explains, is divided into three unequal parts which correspond to the three sections of the tabernacle.

---

[139] Douglas, *In the Wilderness*, pp. 116, 193, 207.

[140] John F. A. Sawyer (ed.), *Reading Leviticus: A Conversation with Mary Douglas* (*Journal for the Study of the Old Testament* Supplement Series 227) (Sheffield: Sheffield Academic Press, 1996).

[141] Douglas, *Leviticus as Literature*.

Douglas's biblical theories were academic and urbane, yet their tendency to champion a position that would be welcomed by traditional believers is also striking. Modern biblical criticism has often unsettled the faithful. Douglas rejected one of its central quests—to reveal that multiple authors and sources were behind individual biblical books—and instead focused on the unity of the texts in their final form. She frequently dismissed by name the work of the leading pioneer of the modern criticism of the Pentateuch, Julius Wellhausen (1844–1918). Instead, her stance closely resembled the canonical approach of Brevard Childs (1923–2007) (whom she cites). Douglas insisted: 'since the Pentateuch was treated in the 3rd century B.C. as a whole, as a single unit, it must be treated by us as such'.[142] She was emphatic that for anthropologists to engage in source criticism would somehow be a violation of one of their discipline's taboos: 'we are never allowed to chop a text about, cut off the ending, or drop out an awkward piece, liberties allowed to Bible scholars'.[143] Likewise, many scholars have attempted to undercut a naïve belief in scripture as a product of divine revelation by arguing that its contents were overwhelmingly similar to or even borrowed from the beliefs, practices, and writings of other ancient Near Eastern cultures. Douglas repeatedly took the exact opposite view, and even stated this conservative, faith-friendly position in the most robust terms: 'the gulf between the religion of the Bible and those of the surrounding peoples can hardly be exaggerated'.[144]

Most of all, there was Douglas's persistent attempts to find ways to recast seemingly offensive biblical passages in a more favourable light. The Old Testament scholar, John F. A. Sawyer, an admirer of Douglas's work on the Bible, reminisced that she was always sending him emails about specific scriptural texts which were 'searching for more benign meanings'.[145] As we have seen, she sought to vindicate entire books of the Bible—eventually championing Leviticus

---

[142] Mary Douglas, 'Critique and Commentary', in Jacob Neusner, *The Idea of Purity in Ancient Judaism* (Leiden: E. J. Brill, 1973), p. 137.

[143] Mary Douglas, 'Introduction' (Review Colloquium on *In the Wilderness*), *Religion*, 26 (1996), p. 69. For Childs, see Douglas, *In the Wilderness*, p. 83.

[144] Douglas, *Leviticus as Literature*, p. 4.

[145] John F. A. Sawyer, 'The Contribution of Social Anthropology to Biblical Scholarship: A Tribute to Mary Douglas', in John F. A. Sawyer, *Sacred Texts and Sacred Meanings: Studies in Biblical Language and Literature* (Sheffield: Sheffield Phoenix Press, 2011), p. 45.

as a 'great philosophical masterpiece' and writing an entire research article with the celebratory title, 'The Glorious Book of Numbers'.[146] Next, Douglas sought to counteract a prejudice against priests by revealing them—rather like the nuns at Sacred Heart—to have been both cosmopolitan intellectuals and compassionate human beings. This is most prominent in her final book on the Pentateuch, also published by Oxford University Press: *Jacob's Tears: The Priestly Work of Reconciliation* (2004). Here she is on the 'priestly editors' of Leviticus and Numbers:

> They obviously came from a high tradition of learning, both literary and scientific...many of the priests would have been the sages who were taken with the rich and noble families of Judah to exile in Babylon. They were up to the standard to talk with the famous Babylonian astronomers and mathematicians. They were unsurpassed masters of rhetorical techniques...able to draw on an international scientific tradition for astronomy, mathematics, poetry, and music.[147]

Moreover, these priests wrote to 'oppose racist policies' and to commend 'the Torah's message of God's love and forgiveness'.[148] Douglas's search for more winsome readings was relentless. The scapegoat had always been construed as a forlorn creature, weighed down with imputed sin and exiled into the wilderness to die as a substitutionary sacrifice. This standard interpretation can be seen, for example, in Holman Hunt's searing painting, *The Scapegoat*. Douglas felt sorry for the poor critter, however, and therefore decided that it was actually being pardoned and sent out in triumph as an ambassador of peace to the nations. It ought to be called 'the lucky goat'.[149] Closer to home was her increasing boldness in denying that passages in the Pentateuch were misogynist. In 1973, Douglas had conceded that some of the laws regarding impurity were designed to 'sustain male dominance'.[150] She later decided, however, that 'unclean' just made it sound pejorative to our ears and what was actually happening was that women were being placed in a 'set apart' state which was a kind of holiday from work and therefore should be thought of as a privilege rather

---

[146] Douglas, *Jacob's Tears*, p. 160; Mary Douglas, 'The Glorious Book of Numbers', *Jewish Studies Quarterly*, 1, 3 (1994), pp. 193–216.

[147] Douglas, *Jacob's Tears*, pp. 6, 122.

[148] Douglas, 'Introduction', *Religion*, p. 71; Douglas, *Jacob's Tears*, p. 80.

[149] Douglas, *Jacob's Tears*, pp. 41, 57–58.

[150] Douglas, 'Critique and Commentary', p. 141.

than a restriction. The pay-off is not left implicit: 'this reading would make a lot of difference to feminist complaints against sexist prejudice in the Bible'.[151]

A related issue is Douglas's approach to allegorical readings—a rich tradition in Catholic spirituality across the centuries. From the very beginning she ostensibly ruled them out on the grounds that such interpretations were 'a pious free-for-all' that has been 'now discredited' as a scholarly option.[152] Nevertheless, Douglas reintroduced them with gusto on the grounds that it was the biblical author or redactor who had done the allegorizing. This was at least partially a reflection of her deep instinct that everything must mean something if only one could discover what it is. One of her more far-fetched attempts to recover meaning was a theory that the long lobe of the liver which is named as a distinct part to be burnt as a sacrifice is intended to represent the holy remnant of Israel.[153] It is revealing that one of the key interpretative patterns she employed she credited to Jewish medieval mystic and kabbalist Ramban (Nahmanides 1194–1270).[154] To carry on the theme, many of Douglas's allegorical readings were ways of making a potentially odious text innocuous. One need not worry so much about lepers being treated harshly once it becomes clear that the disease is really being evoked as a metaphor for unfaithful Israel—and so it goes on. Once again, Douglas makes this move to evade the charge that a scriptural passage is sexist. References to a woman are generally to be read as statements about Israel and therefore are not being unfair toward actual women but merely making a spiritual point. There is no literal sense to the entire codified trial by ordeal of a wife accused of adultery. Once again the benefits of such a reading are spelt out: 'If these rites are to be read in the straight judicial sense, the Lord is terrible indeed, and the curse on the suspected woman would be a terrifying judgement. But if they are to be read allegorically, the implications are totally different'.[155] Douglas went so far as

---

[151] Mary Douglas, 'Why I Have to Learn Hebrew: The Doctrine of Sanctification', in Thomas Ryba, George D. Bond, and Herman Tull (eds.), *The Comity and Grace of Method: Essays in Honor of Edmund F. Perry* (Evanston, Illinois: Northwestern University Press, 2004), pp. 147–65 (esp. 157).

[152] Douglas Papers, Northwestern University archives: Box 5 (Leviticus). (From her 1959 notes.)

[153] Douglas, *Leviticus as Literature*, p. 85.

[154] Douglas, *Leviticus as Literature*, p. 59.

[155] Douglas, *In the Wilderness*, p. 169.

to judge entire female characters in the biblical narrative, Dinah, and even Miriam, as entirely allegorical.[156]

* * *

One of Douglas's great virtues was her unflinching quest for what was true. There is no better example than how willing she was to abandon *in toto* her thesis on 'The Abominations of the Leviticus' in *Purity and Danger*. It might be literally true to say that no one has been less reluctant to throw it out than her. Biblical scholars who value her later work on Leviticus tend to continue to appreciate this early effort as well, but Douglas herself insisted that she had been wrong the first time. She did this in print on multiple occasions. In a filmed interview, Douglas said simply that 'I've had to take it back', while literally laughing off the fact that it was this very material that made her most famous book famous.[157] In the end, she tried to stop it appearing in any more anthologies, like the sorcerer's apprentice desperately trying to recall a disconcertingly successful spell.[158] For the purpose at hand, what needs to be highlighted is that Douglas rejected her earlier reading of Leviticus 11 as insufficiently benign. The God of the Bible was just, rational, and compassionate, and the Creator would never deem some of his own creatures to be abominations.[159] As with women being judged to be 'unclean', so 'unclean animals' were now rehabilitated as in a privileged, protected state—like those in a game preserve.[160]

Both her early and revised interpretations of Leviticus 11 involved reading this chapter through the book of Genesis. The abominations thesis evoked the three categories of animals created according to Genesis 1—those that belong to the water, to the sky, and to the land—and argued that those identified as unclean had been rejected because they are, as it were, neither fish nor fowl.[161] Initially Douglas had gone so far as to think of these animals as 'ambiguous monsters'.[162] Her later view countered her first one with the knowledge that Genesis 1 also records that the Almighty created all the animals and

---

[156] Douglas, *In the Wilderness*, pp. 197, 206.
[157] Douglas interviewed by Macfarlane.
[158] Fardon, *Mary Douglas*, p. 100.
[159] Mary Douglas, *Purity and Danger*, 2002, p. xv.
[160] Douglas, *Leviticus as Literature*, p. 158.
[161] Douglas, *Purity and Danger*, 1966, p. 55.
[162] Douglas Papers, Northwestern University archives: Box 5 (Leviticus). (From her 1959 notes.)

pronounced them to be good—theologically, there can be no species that are monsters.[163]

This, in turn, raises the question of Douglas's view of the nature of the Bible and its canon. To say that the beliefs expressed in Leviticus 11 cannot be in fundamental conflict with those articulated in Genesis 1 is to betray an assumption about how the content of these two books relate to one another. Douglas rejected the charge that she believed that 'the Bible is a seamless web'.[164] She rightly pointed out that a key part of her argument was based on exposing a tension between Ezra/Nehemiah and Leviticus. Ezra, in particular, is a foil throughout Douglas's biblical studies—he is a 'slippery customer', and even 'xenophobic'.[165] She also emphasizes the differences between Leviticus and Deuteronomy.[166] Nevertheless, one suspects that—as with structural opposition among the Nuer—these differing segments are meant to unite at a higher level. Her apparent slights to other parts of the canon are always in the context of Douglas championing the merits of the book of the Bible she is currently expounding. It would be easy to imagine that if Ezra or Deuteronomy became her primary focus she would suddenly find that she was dealing with a masterpiece edited by a genius, the contents of which are less offensive than a cursory reading might indicate. In *Jacob's Tears*, Douglas contrasts the compassionate deity revealed in Leviticus with the 'ferocious God' of Numbers.[167] Curiously, she had already written an entire monograph on Numbers without conceding that its deity seems rather sinister. Moreover, this view is only acknowledged now as she had found a way to mitigate it. Numbers, it turns out, is also in the genre of an epic and the conventions of this literary form necessitate grandiose horror for effect: 'It is the epic style of Numbers that requires the pitiless slaughter, not God's character'.[168] Some wider canonical unity is indicated by the freedom in which she includes other books of the Bible in her discussions, sometimes even quoting them as epigraphs. Douglas goes so far as to bring in passages from the New Testament which conform to a pattern she is presenting in the Hebrew scriptures.

---

[163] Douglas, *Thought Styles*, p. 195. Genesis 1 probably also informed Douglas's persistent thinking in terms of form and order being given to what is formless and chaotic.

[164] Douglas, 'A Response', p. 85.

[165] Sawyer, *Reading Leviticus*, p. 175; Douglas, *Thinking in Circles*, p. 66.

[166] For example, see Douglas, *Leviticus as Literature*, pp. 94, 107, 137, 155.

[167] Douglas, *Jacob's Tears*, p. 17. [168] Douglas, *Jacob's Tears*, p. 18.

Structural oppositions unite at a higher level: Douglas often referred to the Pentateuch as a whole as teaching certain things. Numbers may have a ferocious God and Leviticus a compassionate God, but one can also think of these two books as 'complementing each other' like 'a duet'.[169] Douglas repeatedly made claims regarding what is taught in the biblical tradition as a whole, or in biblical theology, or throughout the Bible. Over and over again, Douglas asserted that her new view of Leviticus was the right one because it brought the teaching of this text into line with the rest of the Pentateuch and with the psalms and prophets. She even explicitly named this goal as the very purpose of *Leviticus as Literature*: 'This study's aim is to reintegrate the book with the rest of the Bible'.[170] Even this particularly puzzling biblical book need not be viewed as comprised of irreconcilable bits as had been done in source criticism: 'the Wellhausen project can be challenged and the unity of the theological teaching justified'.[171]

Mary Douglas was herself an Old Testament seer—and what she saw were patterns. Sartre's nightmarish childhood was finding oneself in a patternless world. (During her own childhood, Mary drove her grandmother to distraction by searching for reasons for absolutely everything. Why is Monday laundry day and not Tuesday? and so on.) Douglas read G. K. Chesterson's fiction.[172] His Catholic detective, Father Brown, once remarked: 'What we all dread most is a maze with *no* centre. That is why atheism is only a nightmare'.[173] Douglas was always determined to keep hunting until she had made sense of what was initially bewildering. Some critics believed that she occasionally thought she had found something when it was not actually there. Her study of Evans-Pritchard was sometimes faulted for over-systematizing his oeuvre, overlooking discontinuity in it, and asserting a hidden key to the whole that did not exist.[174] Douglas's obituary of Godfrey Lienhardt is almost comic in her dutifully acknowledging that he was well known for disliking overarching systems, theories, and structures before she goes on compulsively to

---

[169] Douglas, *Jacob's Tears*, p. 82.

[170] Douglas, *Leviticus as Literature*, p. 1.

[171] Mary Douglas, 'Sacred Contagion', in Sawyer, *Reading Leviticus*, p. 106.

[172] Douglas, *Thought Styles*, p. 156.

[173] G. K. Chesterton, *The Wisdom of Father Brown* (London: Cassell and Company, 1914), p. 140.

[174] Mary Douglas, 'Evans-Pritchard' (letter to the editor), *New Society*, 24 July 1980, p. 187.

insist that she has nevertheless discerned the unifying coherence in his work.[175]

I must confess that I am sceptical about some of the patterns that Douglas claimed to find in the Pentateuch. Numbers is said to be a ring composition in which the key meaning is at the centre and parts on each side of it are arranged in corresponding rungs. Douglas enthused: 'For the reader or listener who keeps track of the ingeniously contrived lateral reading it gives intense pleasure... The enjoyment is of the same order as the pleasure of a sonnet or a play'.[176] Like a joke so subtle no one can get it, I find it hard to imagine ancient Hebrews delightedly holding these rungs in their minds and listening expectedly for their parallels. And, as Douglas herself admits, no one apparently ever did so after the generation in which these biblical books were first created. When told that her interpretation of the long liver lobe was too fanciful, Douglas retorted that there were no rival theories to explain its significance and she was reluctant to leave it uninterpreted.[177] Things must mean something! Douglas was also reluctant to entertain the possibility that sometimes there might not be a pattern. No doubt she would counter my scepticism with grid-group analysis demonstrating that I have a cultural bias against formal structures and unifying systems. (On the other hand, Douglas herself could baulk at the attempts of others. She accused Lévi-Strauss of imposing a structure rather than finding it, dismissing his alleged achievement with delicious condescension: 'He thus claims to have answered the sphinx, unscrewed the inscrutable, and effed the ineffable'.)[178]

What is clear is that the Bible provided Douglas with a final, grand intellectual passion. Again and again she recalled the thrill that she had when she first started reading Numbers in 1987 and the ongoing delight of finding meaning in the scriptures. She claimed that her

---

[175] Mary Douglas, 'Obituary: Godfrey Lienhardt', *Anthropology Today*, 10, 1 (February 1994), pp. 15–17.

[176] Douglas, *Jacob's Tears*, p. 95.　　　　[177] Douglas, *Jacob's Tears*, p. 152.

[178] Mary Douglas, 'A Savage Thought on Structuralism as Used by Levi-Strauss', undated typescript. Douglas Papers, Northwestern University archives: Box 5 (Leviticus). This piece would seem to have been written in the late 1960s and, as far as I can tell, was never published. It is definitely not an early draft of her book review of *The Raw and the Cooked* even though she preserved the playful idea for the title: Mary Douglas, 'Smothering the Differences—Mary Douglas in a savage mind about Lévi-Strauss', *Listener*, 3 September 1970, pp. 313–14. (On the other hand, Douglas was more favourable toward Lévi-Strauss's work later on.)

biblical studies were more exciting for her 'than anything I had ever done before'.[179] When she worked out her theory of the literary structure of Numbers she thought it was so important that she went about for a couple years worrying that she might be hit by a bus and the world would thereby be deprived of this momentous discovery. When asked in 2001, 'What do you feel is your own greatest contribution to the field [of scholarship]?', she replied, 'Probably Leviticus'.[180] She was like King Josiah finding the lost book of the law. For millennia it would seem that only the Son of God incarnate and Professor Mary Douglas had grasped the full meaning of the third book of the Pentateuch: 'I'm quite tempted to go out on a limb and say that this is the book that Jesus was thinking of when he told the Pharisees and the scribes that they had it all wrong'.[181] Mary *contra mundum*. While it is certainly not what she is most remembered for, there was at least one amen regarding her biblical studies work from her own guild: Douglas's obituary in the *American Anthropologist* claimed that *In the Wilderness* was perhaps her greatest book.[182] Douglas herself reported in 2004: 'For fifteen years the Bible has been my main interest and the central focus of all my work'.[183] Just a month before her death a journalist interviewed Douglas in her study and found that she had filing cabinet drawers labelled to reflect those interests of hers that were still active: one was 'Family', another 'Reviews', and the third was 'Leviticus'.[184]

* * *

For her entire career Mary Douglas was a Catholic intellectual, using her training and gifts to serve her co-religionists. A full four years before *The Lele of the Kasai* (1963) Douglas contributed to a volume published by Sheed and Ward (a Catholic press that specialized in works of apologetics), and edited by scholar-priest Adrian Hastings: *The Church and the Nations: A study of minority Catholicism in England, India, Norway, America, Lebanon, Australia, Wales, Japan, the Netherlands, Vietnam, Brazil, Egypt, Southern Africa and among the Lele of the Congo* (1959).[185] The subtitle should make it clear that Douglas was not included because she was qualified to write on the

---

[179] Douglas, 'A Feeling for Hierarchy', p. 169 (endnote 16).
[180] Wachtel, *Original Minds*, p. 349.
[181] Wachtel, *Original Minds*, p. 344.
[182] Richards, 'Obituary: Douglas', p. 406.
[183] Douglas, *Jacob's Tears*, p. 3.   [184] Howse, 'Pangolin and al'Qaeda'.
[185] Hastings, *Church and the Nations*.

Lele, but rather the Lele were included because Douglas was a Catholic scholar. The volume as a whole offered an appeal for Catholic academics to no longer hide their light under a bushel but rather learn to give compelling, thoughtful appeals to 'the non-Catholic intellectual'.[186] The chapter on England written by John Lynch (then a Lecturer in Modern History, University of Liverpool), called for Catholic scholars to not just do good, obscure, technical work in their disciplines but also to dare to speak to issues of 'general as well as specialist interest and significance'; to learn to communicate 'with the secular world on religious subjects in intelligible language'; and 'to apply their religious principles to the facts of the modern world'.[187] One could read Douglas's career as an answer to this call.

Douglas's oeuvre is littered with explicitly Catholic contexts. The acknowledgements for *Purity and Danger* include a word of thanks for insights provided by the Bellarmine Society of Heythrop College.[188] *Natural Symbols* grew out of her St Thomas Aquinas Lecture for the Dominicans at Blackfriars, Oxford, on 7 March 1968. Delightfully, Douglas insisted that monks were not allowed to include a woman at their common table and therefore her wrong-footed hosts were forced to set up a place for her to take her evening meal in the parlour while they dutifully ate in the refectory.[189] As with championing Friday abstinence in *Natural Symbols*, here Douglas is again insisting that a small practice from the past cannot be abandoned without weakening an entire web of meaning and the culture that preserves it. Her Aquinas lecture was published in *New Blackfriars* and, in the decades that followed, Douglas contributed to a range of Catholic periodicals, including *Commonweal*, the *Tablet*, and *Priests & People*. It is a tribute to her ability to win a wide and varied audience by speaking in such unexpected, compelling ways that a piece of hers reprinted in the Catholic *Commonweal* originally appeared in the 'unashamedly rationalist' *New Society*.[190] At UCL, Douglas organized a party in 1966 for the incoming Catholic chaplain and invited the Catholic members of the faculty from across the departments.[191] In 1988, Douglas was awarded an honorary Doctor of Laws degree from a leading

[186] Hastings, *Church and the Nations*, p. xix.
[187] John Lynch, 'England' in Hastings, *Church and the Nations*, pp. 7, 9, 16.
[188] Douglas, *Purity and Danger*, p. viii.
[189] Fergus Kerr to Timothy Larsen, email, 27 April 2012.
[190] Douglas, 'Myth', pp. 41–44; Fardon, *Mary Douglas*, p. 77.
[191] John Lynch to Timothy Larsen, email, 27 May 2013.

Catholic institution of higher education in America, the University of Notre Dame (in Indiana). In 2002, another Catholic institution, the University of Dayton (in Ohio), presented her with its Marianist Award: an honour bestowed upon 'a Catholic intellectual who has made a major contribution to the intellectual life'.[192]

What is perhaps more striking than her writings for Catholics is the habitual—if not compulsive—way that Douglas brought explicitly Christian material into her general anthropological writings. This went well beyond the famous ones of Leviticus in *Purity and Danger* and the Friday fast in *Natural Symbols*. It would appear that Douglas never wrote a single book—whatever the subject matter—that did not include Christian examples. Her mind was continually thinking of the Church and she tended to allow it to roam there unchecked. In her very first publication, *Peoples of the Lake Nyasa Region* (1950), Mary Tew wrote: 'Sometimes the whole group is referred to by the name of one of its dominant members, such as the *Cewa* (*c* pronounced as *ch* in English 'church')'.[193] 'Church' was always the example that came readily to mind. An extreme case is her entry on 'Taboo and Sin' in the *Encyclopedia of Africa South of the Sahara* (1997). The clear geographical focus of this reference work notwithstanding, Douglas is already discussing medieval Christianity by the second paragraph. The bibliography includes seven works, none of which are focused on Africa, and most of which are centred on (European) Christianity, including a book on purgatory, another on seventeenth-century discussions of eternal torment, as well as *The Stripping of the Altars: Traditional Religion in England, 1400–1580*, the Catholic historian Eamon Duffy's lament regarding the effects of the Protestant Reformation.[194] Following Evans-Pritchard's lead, here is Douglas on the Lele: 'In their descriptions of the pangolin's behaviour and in their attitude to its cult, Lele say things which uncannily recall passages of the Old Testament, interpreted in the Christian tradition. Like Abraham's ram in the thicket and like Christ, the pangolin is spoken of as a voluntary victim'.[195] Likewise in her studies of ancient Israel, Christianity was ready to hand. This is a line from *In the Wilderness*: 'To give a contemporary example, the Catholic church in our day is upholding an

---

[192] Heft, *Believing Scholars*, p. 1.   [193] Tew, *Peoples*, p. 30.
[194] Mary Douglas, 'Taboo and Sin', in John Middleton (ed.), *Encyclopedia of Africa South of the Sahara* (New York: Charles Scribner's Sons, 1997), pp. 205–208.
[195] Douglas, *Purity and Danger*, p. 169.

anti-birth-control and anti-abortion doctrine'[196] Describing the relationship between priests in ancient Jerusalem and Samaria in *Jacob's Tears*, Douglas confesses: 'It reminds me of the political implications of the Catholic priests' allegiance to Rome in post-Reformation England'[197] This monograph on the Hebrew scriptures also has whole sections on the Gospels and on the teaching of the apostle Paul. Out of the abundance of the heart, the mouth speaks.

Moreover, Douglas wrote entire scholarly articles which were structured as sustained analogies with themes from Christian thought (often in ways that seem too clever by half). Her address to the European Association of Social Anthropologists in 1994 used doctrines of God to explore contemporary understandings of the concept of personhood.[198] Her essay on 'Credibility' is framed around Pascal's argument for the existence of God.[199] 'The Hotel Kwilu' is an elaborate analogy between anthropological theory and Gospel studies: Clifford Geertz is a small-scale version of Albert Schweitzer; Lévy-Bruhl is like Reimarus; Raymond Firth corresponds to Ernst Renan; and so on.[200] For non-Christian readers, these analogies must sometimes have been just as obscure as the point they were meant to illuminate. To wit, 'Rather as the synoptic gospels need the structural analyses of John and the Pauline epistles for their exegesis, so the miracles of the pangolin...'[201] Douglas also frequently evoked the category of morals. Fardon attended her UCL course, 'Religion, morals, and symbols'[202] Douglas's work was interdisciplinary on multiple fronts and one of these was decidedly theological. She recalled that doctrine was her best subject at school; she was disappointed at being unable to demonstrate her mastery of this material because the school board did not offer an examination in it.[203] A wide variety of theologians appear across her work ranging from figures from the historic Christian tradition such as St Augustine of Hippo, St Thomas Aquinas, and John Henry Newman, to an impressive array of contemporary theologians

---

[196] Douglas, *In the Wilderness*, p. 44.   [197] Douglas, *Jacob's Tears*, p. 15.

[198] Mary Douglas, 'The cloud god and the shadow self', *Social Anthropology*, 3, 2 (1995), pp. 83–94.

[199] Douglas, *Risk and Blame*, pp. 235–54. (The original title was 'Pascal's Great Wager'.)

[200] Douglas, *Risk and Blame*, pp. 295–313.

[201] Douglas, *Implicit Meanings*, 1975, p. x.

[202] Fardon, *Mary Douglas*, pp. xiv–xv.

[203] Douglas, 'A Feeling for Hierarchy', p. 102.

of varied stripes, including Pierre Teilhard de Chardin, Mary Daly, Rowan Williams, Janet Soskice, Richard Niebuhr, Anders Nygren, Harvey Cox, Rosemary Radford Ruether, and Sarah Coakley. Even figures that others might think of as philosophers often interested Douglas because of their theological reflections. One thinks of Søren Kierkegaard, Martin Buber, Simone Weil, and Paul Ricoeur. This tendency is made explicit, for example, in a reference to 'the theologian, Heidegger'.[204] *Religion and America* had contributors from a variety of disciplines and it is telling that theologians were included. The introduction commends the chapter by Richard McBrien, a professor of theology at the University of Notre Dame, for putting on display 'a contemporary Catholic theologian calmly confident that his tradition has much to say to our present situation'.[205] Sometimes theologians were even preferable to the ostensible experts: her source for a sociology of schism was the priest and theologian Ronald Knox and she judged Richard Niebuhr to be more insightful on the matter than the Oxford sociologist Bryan Wilson.[206]

If some have been able to reassure themselves with the thought that, although Evans-Pritchard was a Catholic, at least he was a bad one, there is no such consolation to be had in the case of Mary Douglas. When I asked Douglas's daughter, Janet Farnsworth, to comment on her mother 'as a practising Catholic' (the category I offered), her response began: 'I would describe her as a good Catholic'. In a follow-up—again without prompting—Farnsworth remarked: 'I forgot to say that my Father was also a "good Catholic"'.[207] As an octogenarian, Douglas was mugged in Waterlow Park, North London, on her way back from attending church.[208] This incident is indicative of her tenacious commitment to corporate worship. Her son Philip Douglas recalled that she made the effort to attend even when she was quite weak: 'I remember her going there when she had little physical stamina for any other physical exercise'.[209] The last Christmas before her death she had the priest arrange an escort for her so she could still come to Midnight Mass. Repeatedly when I asked scholars who had

---

[204] Douglas, *Risk and Blame*, p. 301.

[205] Douglas and Tipton, *Religion and America*, p. x (from the introduction by Robert N. Bellah).

[206] Douglas and Wildavsky, *Risk and Culture*, pp. 111–14.

[207] Janet Farnsworth to Timothy Larsen, emails, 9 August 2012 and 10 August 2012.

[208] 'Obituary: Douglas', *The Times*.

[209] Philip Douglas to Timothy Larsen, email, 14 August 2012.

known Douglas to talk about her religious life I was surprised when they volunteered that they had attended church with her. Such was the case, for example, with the eminent scholar of Hinduism, Wendy Doniger.[210] Edith Turner recalled that when Douglas visited her in Chicago they both went to confession before Mass and that Douglas was so earnestly engaged with this sacrament that she was moved to tears.[211] None of us think of the James Bond films as realistic depictions of modern life, but Douglas is probably the only one ever to cite as a case in point the fact that they do show people going to church.[212] Douglas lived her insight that the liturgical year is recapitulated in the liturgical week. Attending Mass is merely a particularly public manifestation of a life of devotion. Befitting the author of *Natural Symbols*, Farnsworth also recalls that they would keep the fasts of the Church. All three children were sent to Catholic schools. When Janet was a teenager, her mother gave her a book on Christ's crucifixion to augment her religious education which she still remembers as 'very gory'.[213] She also recalls that her parents were disappointed with what they saw as a watered-down spiritual formation being given to children in the post-Vatican II era and they wished that she had received the old dogmatic emphasis on understanding why certain views are heretical. Douglas took great comfort in knowing that a priest had been able to administer the last rites to James before he died. Upon her own death, Dame Mary Douglas duly received a funeral Mass in a Catholic church, St Patrick's, Soho Square, London.[214]

Part of being Catholic for Douglas was exposing a Protestant bias. Protestantism had unleashed an anti-clericalism which meant that priests were not treated fairly; it promoted an individualism which worked against social unity; it was behind the contempt for ritual; and so on. The very first paragraph of the first chapter of *Natural Symbols* was already outing what was behind these pernicious trends: 'Shades of Luther!'[215] Corralling her heterogeneous foes, Douglas's writings are replete with moves that ostensibly show that some group that she dislikes—radical environmentalists, for example—are infected

---

[210] Wendy Doniger interviewed by Timothy Larsen, University of Chicago, 30 November 2012.

[211] Edith Turner interviewed by Timothy Larsen, phone, 12 May 2009.

[212] Douglas, *Jacob's Tears*, p. 160.

[213] Janet Farnsworth to Timothy Larsen, email, 10 August 2012.

[214] Fardon, 'Mary Douglas', *Oxford Dictionary of National Biography*.

[215] Douglas, *Natural Symbols*, p. 1.

with the spirit of Protestantism. When defending her academic discipline against the blind spots of others, she tends to present it as
if anthropology is from Rome and psychology or economics from
Geneva. At her most polemically tinged, this devolved into hinting
that Protestantism is prone to heresy: it fosters Gnostic or Manichean
impulses and so on. Also pejoratively tinged is her insistence that 'low
church' Protestants are like pygmies. One might argue that an anthropologist could evoke such connections with no disrespect, but for
Douglas the putdown was palpable: 'Like the pygmies (I say it again,
lest it seems they have reached some high peak of intellectual development)'.[216] If E. B. Tylor's anti-Catholic anthropology had left a score to
settle, Douglas did her bit to help redress it. Nevertheless, in her case,
there was no irreconcilable animosity. Catholic versus Protestant,
once again, was a structural opposition in which the segments united
at a higher level. 'The body of Christian churches' were an example of
a situation in which different cultures actually need one another and
each would be worse off if the other was not there. The institution of
the feud accords with a higher good that serves the whole.[217]

* * *

A more fundamental conflict was with secularists, agnostics, free-
thinkers, rationalists, and atheists. In this struggle, she was more often
attacked than on the offensive herself. It is not always clear to what
extent her being specifically Roman Catholic got up the noses of these
critics or if any orthodox Christian might have been treated in a similar way. When she first met anthropologists during her war work she
was irritated by their insisting: 'No anthropologist can be a sincere
Catholic'.[218] Once established in the profession, Douglas discovered
that, as a general rule, ethnographers were willing to view traditional
African religions with a level of sympathy and respect that they would
never accord to Catholicism. Her own boss at the UCL, Daryll Forde
(1902–73), was not at ease with the very idea of an anthropologist being
a Catholic.[219] A feature on women anthropologists in *Harper's Bazaar
and Queen* profiled Douglas and several others, including Jean La
Fontaine, Lecturer in Social Anthropology at the LSE, who explained

---

[216] Douglas, *Natural Symbols*, pp. 49–50.
[217] Douglas, 'A Feeling for Hierarchy', p. 115.
[218] Douglas, 'A Feeling for Hierarchy', p. 105.
[219] Fardon, *Mary Douglas*, p. 52.

that their discipline was designed to fill the gap left by the death of God: 'Once you stop religious thought, you start thinking anthropologically'.[220] Edmund Leach, as we have seen, could not resist lashing out at Christian anthropologists. One of the more bizarre passages from his hostile review of *Natural Symbols* ridicules a spiritual reading of the Song of Songs—something he imagines Douglas would approve of even though she does not say so and, moreover, the whole discussion has no obvious connection to the contents of the book he is ostensibly reviewing but seems to be just gratuitous Christian-bashing.[221] Douglas herself most often exemplified such hostility by telling an anecdote about a colleague at UCL, the biologist Helen Spurway. Spurway was working on parthenogenesis and decided to consult Douglas as an anthropologist regarding theories of virgin births in traditional cultures. Having given her ethnographic answer, Douglas then volunteered that she was a Catholic and offered to explain to Spurway why she personally believed in the orthodox Christian doctrine of the Virgin Birth.[222] Spurway, an atheist, was openly shocked, blurting out that she had hitherto been utterly confident that it would be impossible at this late date in history to be both a member of the faculty of University College London and a Catholic. They then had a long discussion in which Douglas expounded upon the nature and reality of miracles and the role of authority in personal beliefs. Douglas would occasionally give as good as she got, however, insisting that it was actually this kind of Tylorian view that faith was a thing of the past which was out of date: 'You will meet the occasional old-fashioned anthropologist who takes all religion for mumbo-jumbo'.[223]

Douglas sincerely believed that anthropological theory and findings were compatible with the Christian faith. In arguing for the use of anthropology in schools, she dismissed as wrongheaded the assumption that this material was inherently 'harmful to faith and morals'.[224] One of her Northwestern students complained that the material Douglas was exposing them to was causing him to lose his religion. The anthropologist's uncowed response was that a faith which needs sheltering is of no use in the real world and therefore

---

[220] Hale, 'Closely Observed Brains', p. 71.
[221] Leach, 'Mythical Inequalities'.
[222] Douglas, 'Can a scientist be objective?', p. 384.
[223] Douglas, *Thought Styles*, p. 194.
[224] Douglas, 'What Anthropology Has to Offer'.

not worth preserving.[225] Moreover, arguably the burden of proof is on the person who claims that anthropology (or modern thought elsewhere or more generally) has somehow discredited faith. What are the grounds for such a claim? By the time of Douglas's career, secular anthropologists no less than Christian ones generally found the theories of Tylor and Frazer to be flatly erroneous, if not downright embarrassing, so the case against Christianity could not be secured in that quarter. More widely, Evans-Pritchard and Steiner had already modelled a rejection of reductionistic theories of religion. An analysis of religion in other terms such as social, psychological, or economic could be accepted as true as far as it went, but must be rejected when it made the overreaching claim that it not only explained but exhaustively explained away. Douglas followed this line:

> It is naturally annoying for believers to find the professionals endlessly prepared to reduce religion to something else. (I am referring to anthropology, sociology, Freudian styles of psychoanalysis and philosophy.) However, when believers feel irked in this way, they can remember that there is this thing about religion that escapes reductionist analysis.[226]

Or even more forcefully: 'Beyond an intellectual account of doctrine lie the evils of reductionism. Religions can be described but not further explained; reductionism leads to shallow and false conclusions and must be avoided'.[227] Once again, such theories could be valid and illuminating as long as they did not try to play king of the hill: 'There is no objection to this approach unless it excludes other interpretations'.[228] Reductionistic thinkers offer flat, prosaic readings which blind them to richer levels of meaning.[229] The tendency toward unbelief among anthropologists—far from being hard-won insights—should rather be viewed as a kind of occupational hazard to be pitied. In fact, modern scepticism in general should not be seen as a product of the advance of knowledge but merely as a cultural bias resulting from a shift to a low grid position.[230]

---

[225] Douglas, *Thought Styles*, pp. 196–97.

[226] Douglas, *Thought Styles*, p. 194.

[227] Douglas, 'Sacred Contagion', p. 92.

[228] Douglas, *Purity and Danger*, p. 32.

[229] Mary Douglas, 'The Meaning of Myth: with special reference to "La Geste d'Asdiwal"', in Edmund Leach (ed.), *The Structural Study of Myth and Totemism* (London: Tavistock Publications, 1967), pp. 49–69.

[230] Douglas, *Cultural Bias*, p. 10.

Nevertheless, Douglas did have a modern secular master to wrestle with in order to integrate her anthropological ideas with her Christian faith: Émile Durkheim (1858–1917). Once established as an anthropologist, Douglas was always quite willing to self-identify as an intellectual disciple of the French social scientist. She sometimes did this defiantly in the knowledge that younger or more self-consciously trendy anthropologists considered him passé, referring to herself, for example, as 'a humble practitioner of the Durkheimian art derided by Geertz'.[231] Douglas's obituary in the *American Anthropologist* argued that her later work had been less widely discussed in the guild because of 'her unyielding commitment to the realism of the Durkheim-Mauss school'.[232] Douglas, of course, was well aware that Durkheim was generally considered to be not only an avowed but a formidable enemy of faith: 'Durkheim caused scandal among Christians by teaching that religion is a projection of society...Durkheim was bound to attract hostility of pious Christians by announcing his sociological theory of religion from an atheist platform'.[233] When Douglas was interviewed by Alan Macfarlane in 2006 he pointed out to her that people have wondered how she could be both an anthropologist and a Catholic, confessing frankly: 'it has always puzzled me too'. To which she replied: 'Does it really? Seriously? [laughs] I think it's a terrible ignorance on their part'. Macfarlane then sharpened the point:

> For some people there is a puzzle. If you take the Durkheimian view and if you are culturally relativist and you look at other religions, some people say that that logically, shouldn't that undermine your belief in your Catholicism?

Douglas likewise doubled down on her initial reaction: 'I can only think of that as an extraordinarily ignorant question, if you'll excuse me'. [laughs again][234]

Douglas went on to give some elucidation in that interview, but rather than continuing to track with it we will instead return to her writings in order to try to dissipate any lingering ignorance

---

[231] Mary Douglas, review of Victor W. Turner and Edward M. Bruner (eds.), *The Anthropology of Experience, American Anthropologist*, n.s. 92, 1 (March 1990), p. 253.

[232] Richards, 'Obituary: Douglas', p. 404.

[233] Douglas, 'A Feeling for Hierarchy', p. 107.

[234] Douglas interviewed Macfarlane. Fardon rightly cautions against assuming that there can be no such thing as a 'Catholic Durkheimian Oxford Anthropology': Fardon, *Mary Douglas*, p. 246.

on this matter. As the reader has been primed to expect, Douglas deals with Durkheim by asserting that he was not radical enough. Moreover, this is not a mere rhetorical move: Douglas really does apply Durkheim's theories much more comprehensively and daringly than he was willing to do himself. Durkheim taught that knowledge is socially constructed. He was willing to apply this insight only selectively, however—most notably to religion. He piously protected his own god: one can see 'the sacred which in Durkheim's universe is not to be profaned: it is scientific truth'.[235] Douglas then sics Foucault on him. Actually, *all* human knowledge is socially constructed. This radicalized, thoroughgoing form of Durkheimian thought presents no particular challenge to Christianity: religious beliefs are just as warranted as scientific ones. In short, 'It is no more easy to defend non-context-dependent, non-culture-dependent beliefs in things or objective scientific truth than belief in gods and demons'.[236] This epistemological quandary is the human condition and no more an argument against the existence of God than against the existence of germs.

* * *

At this point the theologian must take over from the anthropologist. Douglas was well aware that she was first and foremost an anthropologist: part of the valuable contribution that she and her guild had to make was facilitated precisely by their ability to bracket a direct interrogation of truth claims and come at a discussion of religion from a different direction.[237] Douglas told a delightful tale of admitting to an American taxi driver that she taught religious studies, and him seizing the moment to ask the question that had been perturbing him: 'Who came first, Adam and Eve, or the Dinosaur'?[238] She had no wish to become a jukebox theologian. Nevertheless, she was deeply interested in theology and thought about it a great deal. She also believed it was difficult to exclude it altogether from any substantive discussion: 'Debates which originate in quite mundane issues tend to become religious if they go on long enough'.[239] Her works are therefore replete with statements that can be read as theological— at the very least in their drift. She commended *Natural Symbols* to

---

[235] Douglas, *Implicit Meanings*, p. xvi.
[236] Douglas, *Implicit Meanings*, p. xv.
[237] Douglas, *Evans-Pritchard*, p. 104; Douglas, 'The devil vanishes', p. 513.
[238] Douglas, *Risk and Blame*, p. 3.   [239] Douglas, *Risk and Blame*, p. 271.

'anyone interested in theology'.[240] Moreover, this tendency, if anything, increased as her career progressed. One of the differences between her early and late interpretations of Leviticus 11 is that the second one was significantly more theological: it was less about the nature of pigs and more about the nature of God. Douglas valued her work on both Numbers and Leviticus for revealing the central theological meaning of these texts. There are times when one can glimpse her shading into treating the Bible as Holy Scripture given to instruct believers. For example:

> When the Lord told Moses that his people should love the stranger as themselves (Leviticus 19:34), who was the stranger?
> The question fits with our contemporary concerns for refugees and immigrants. We face the moral issue in our own times. Strangers are here, refugees, exiles seeking political asylum, and immigrants, legal and illegal, some rich, some poor, some working, some on public assistance. How should we treat them? What should they expect from us? What did the Bible mean by enjoining kindness to strangers? Was it a universal moral percept, or did it have local overtones.[241]

Even though that was written for social scientists, the implication is that the teaching of the Bible might guide us in our response to contemporary issues.

Douglas continued to mature in her religious thinking throughout her entire life. She thought it would be a sad thing—not least for her study of anthropology—if her faith had been 'fixed in childhood'.[242] John Henry Newman's teaching on the development of doctrine aided her: 'The universal Church is old, but not a fossil, she must develop; truth is revealed gradually, the doctrines have to be unfolded. I understand that the work of the Holy Spirit is to safeguard doctrine and practice'.[243] Still, she always longed to get the lion to lie down with the lamb and therefore was on something of a quest to integrate traditional Catholic doctrine and practice with the modern insights of anthropology. Her appreciation of the ideas of others

---

[240] Douglas, *Natural Symbols*, 1996, p. xi. Theologians have found her work useful. See, for example, Paul Bradshaw and John Melloh (eds.), *Foundations in Ritual Studies: A reader for students of Christian Worship* (Grand Rapids: Baker Academic, 2007).

[241] Mary Douglas, 'The Stranger in the Bible', *Archives européennes de sociologie*, 35, 2 (1994), pp. 283–98.

[242] Douglas, *Thought Styles*, p. 197.

[243] Douglas, 'Sacraments and Society', p. 29.

should not be over-read as her rejecting historic Christian teaching: in a private letter she was quick to dispel decisively a confusion
in the mind of a fellow anthropologist that she might not be standing
by the doctrine of salvation as articulated by Augustine and Thomas
Aquinas.[244] She had been taught in childhood that the two central
mysteries of the Christian faith were the doctrines of the Trinity and
the Incarnation. The second one—Christ being both fully God and
fully human—became a theological keynote in her mind for this task
of integration.[245] There are two ways that she deployed this doctrine
in her thought. First, on the assumption that Christians generally
recognized the centrality of the doctrine of the Incarnation, Douglas
championed hierarchy (and therefore the Roman Catholic Church) as
the culture which was capable of sustaining and defending the faith
once and for all delivered unto the saints: 'And it was Rome, alive to
the need for mediation and reconciliation which tried to protect the
doctrine of the mediating Second Person of the Trinity, the official
doctrine of the Incarnation.'[246]

Secondly, and more importantly, the Incarnation demonstrates that
God works from within this world and therefore the Durkheimian
insight that doctrines arise from social conditions—far from undercutting the possibility of the results being a divine revelation—
accords precisely with orthodox dogma on the process of God's
self-disclosure. By becoming a real human being, the Almighty demonstrated that the divine way is to influence history and culture from
the inside. The contingent is the ordained vessel of the eternal. Jesus
of Nazareth was both fully human and fully God. Just as one cannot
disprove the divinity of Christ by emphasizing how human he was
(as if this would be some kind of discrediting exposé when it is actually further proof of orthodox doctrine), so one cannot disprove that
the Christian faith is a divine revelation by showing that it is fully
socially constructed. It all depends on which end of the telescope

---

[244]   Douglas to Luckmann, 11 September 1978.
[245]   Others have noticed the importance of this doctrine in Douglas's thought. Most
notably, see Lucien Richard OMI, 'Anthropology and Theology: The Emergence of
Incarnational Faith According to Mary Douglas', *Église et Théologie*, 15 (1984), pp.
131–54. Douglas would mention that the nuns taught that these were the chief mysteries of the faith. This was straight from the catechism: *A Catechism of Christian
Doctrine, as Approved by the Archbishops and Bishops of England and Wales, and
directed by them to be used in all their dioceses* (Ditchling, Sussex: St Dominic's Press,
1931), question 315 (no pagination).
[246]   Douglas, 'Social Preconditions', p. 70. See also, Douglas, *Cultural Bias*, p. 23.

one is looking through: 'What appears as a human projection in one may appear as a reflection of divine realities in another. The logic of the first perspective does not preclude the possibility of the latter'.[247] Douglas believed that God had so arranged social conditions to produce the very revelation that came through the Hebrew prophets and priests and then the apostles and evangelists. Here she is wielding this point of view in order to do apologetics:

> Many students of religion display a bias against the idea that an individual human being receives and sustains his religious beliefs in a social medium. But can they seriously discount the possibility that God, having made man a social being, allows His Face to be seen only through a distorted lens, through the medium of the society which men themselves create?[248]

And again more forcefully elsewhere:

> When social correlates of a religious response are revealed, the rationalists chalk up a point against the devout. The believers usually agree the score, sharing the doubtful assumption that a sacred doctrine must sprout in thin air and never be the product of social experience. In that debate, my particular thesis about mediators, though radically sociological, is neutral. If anything, it puts the thumb upon the other nose. If these connexions hold good and if this is how classification systems are shaped to social ends, how could the extraordinary destiny of the Jewish people have been otherwise achieved? If you were God, could you devise a better plan? If you wanted to choose a people for yourself, reveal to them a monotheistic vision and give them a concept of holiness that they will know in their very bones, what would you do?[249]

Douglas had travelled intellectually a long way from the faith of her childhood, yet she never despised her spiritual birthright. Instead, she was always finding more sophisticated and mature ways to defend and value it. Jesus of Nazareth was both fully God and fully human, so the Church proclaims and she profoundly believed; and Dame Mary Douglas was both fully a Christian and fully an anthropologist.

---

[247] Douglas, 'Full turn of the secular wheel', p. 610.
[248] Doulas, *Risk and Blame*, p. 237.
[249] Douglas, *Implicit Meanings*, pp. 309–10.

5

Victor Turner and Edith Turner

On 30 January 1943, Edith Lucy Brocklesby Davis married Victor Witter Turner at a registry office in Oxford. The choice of a secular ceremony was at least partially motivated by their defiant unwillingness to let the faithful even charitably surmise that they might be Christians. It certainly rattled her devout Anglican parents—which, again, was probably part of the plan.[1] Having joined their lives together while still in their early twenties, Edie was Vic's intellectual as well as personal partner before they ever became interested in anthropology, and was by his side throughout his rise and reign as one of the leading scholars in the discipline.[2] In the thirty years since his death in 1983, Edith Turner has become recognized as a prominent anthropologist in her own right and has developed new theories, convictions, and practices. In particular, shamanism has become a cherished feature of her own spirituality. Her longevity and evolving beliefs therefore create a challenge for the historian as many of the biographical details that are available about Vic's own childhood and adult life (let alone hers) are ones for which Edie's memories are the only source and which she has narrated precisely because they reinforce ways of thinking she has

---

[1] Matthew Engelke, '"The Endless Conversation": Fieldwork, Writing, and the Marriage of Victor and Edith Turner', in Richard Handler (ed.), *Significant Others: Interpersonal and Professional Commitments in Anthropology* (History of Anthropology 10) (Madison: University of Wisconsin Press, 2004), pp. 12–13.

[2] It is my standard practice to refer to my subjects primarily by their surname. This is not practicable in this chapter, however, as it is about two figures with the same last name. In my correspondence with her, I addressed her as 'Professor Turner' until I received the exasperated reply, 'Please please call me Edie I don't know who this professor is!' (Edith Turner to Timothy Larsen, email, 8 August 2013). I will therefore exercise this privilege, and will also use its well-established parallel, 'Vic,' for the purpose of equality and symmetry.

developed since his death. To take an extreme example, Edie recounts how at a party in Chicago her husband once raised a man from the dead by 'the old technique of laying on of hands' even though, firstly, neither Vic nor any other witnesses ever went on record with this story and, secondly, Edie herself would presumably concede if asked that Vic was not intending to engage in a practice of spiritual healing, but rather was merely responding to a crisis with natural gestures of care that she can now discern had spiritual efficacy.[3] As she reflected in her autobiography, 'I necessarily write from the viewpoint of my "now" in 2005'.[4] The historian's task (and the reader's as well) must involve attending to such eye-catching reminiscences in a manner that is neither dismissive of them nor overbalanced by them.

Victor Turner (1920–83) had a Glaswegian childhood until his parents divorced. Then, at the age of 11, he moved with his mother to Bournemouth, and was estranged from his father thereafter. When, as an adult, Vic pleaded for his grant for fieldwork to include the expense of his family accompanying him, he wrote poignantly: 'the absence of a father is no good for kids, as I know from experience'.[5] His mother Violet had been a founding member of the Scottish National Players, and she instilled in him an appreciation of drama. Vic had been baptized as an infant in a Congregational church.[6] As a 12-year-old boy without a father in his life, he was befriended by a local Anglican clergyman. This discipleship took the form of an impressive and ambitious reading programme in the Christian mystics. Then the 'Padre' suddenly died. Although Vic was unaware of what was happening to his mentor at the time, while in his own bedroom he simultaneously experienced a vision of the Shekinah glory of Almighty God.[7] Despite this resonant interlude, unsurprisingly, in 1930s Britain it was unlikely that a divorcée actress was going to create a life for herself and her son in which the church had a significant part. Instead,

---

[3] Edith Turner, with William Blodgett, Singleton Kahona, and Fideli Benwa, *Experiencing Ritual: A New Interpretation of African Healing* (Philadelphia: University of Pennsylvania Press, 1992), p. 179; Edith Turner, *The Hands Feel It: Healing and Spirit Presence among a Northern Alaskan People* (DeKalb: Northern Illinois University Press, 1996), p. 71.

[4] Edith Turner, *Heart of Lightness: The Life Story of an Anthropologist* (Oxford: Berghahn, 2005), p. 4.

[5] Engelke, 'Endless Conversation', p. 22.

[6] Richard Fardon, 'Turner, Victor Witter (1920–1983)', *Oxford Dictionary of National Biography*, www.oxforddnb.com, accessed 10 March 2009.

[7] Turner, *Heart*, pp. 40–41, 136.

Violet dabbled in Spiritualism. In short, the spiritual foreshadowing entailed in the story of his vision notwithstanding, Vic was not raised religious. Instead, he would join the Young Communist League. In 1939, he began reading literature at University College London. With the outbreak of war, he declared himself to be a conscientious objector but not, of course, on religious grounds. His war work was therefore in a non-combatant position with a bomb disposal squad on the home front. In this band of brothers, his best friend was John Bate. Vic wrote to him in May 1942 musing self-reflectively that he was not 'a Christian', but rather knew himself to be 'sceptical' and 'pagan' and 'uncompromisingly opposed to authorities and institutions'.[8]

Edith Davis was born on 17 June 1921 in Ely. Her father, a Cambridge University man, was a medical doctor as well as an ordained Anglican clergyman and her mother was a trained teacher. Both parents had served as Church Missionary Society (CMS) missionaries in India and married and began their family there before returning to England in 1919. The Revd Dr George Brocklesby Davis, MA, MD, then set up a medical practice, while her mother Lucy continued to work for the CMS and would become a town councillor. Edie was the seventh of their eight children. When she was 8 years old she was sent away to boarding school. She cried for her mother for three months and was bullied. Edie's teen years were marked by defiance and rebellion against her parents. She admits in retrospect to a 'bad attitude' and being a 'bitchy daughter'.[9] She even thinks of herself as having been unwittingly a teen witch, casting malicious spells with her anger and hatred. Edie's writings as an adult are punctuated with the concept of 'unconditional love'. In describing why a course in spiritual direction she attended at the age of 76 meant so much to her, she used this term four times in just three pages.[10] Her understanding of the Virgin Mary became that she is also the mother of us all who 'forgives her children and loves them unconditionally'.[11] In short, one suspects that Edie deliberately tried to make herself unlovable as a teenager to find out whether or not she was loved unconditionally. For their part, her parents ran an oppressive

---

[8] Victor Turner to John Bate, 27 May 1942. Victor Turner Papers, typescript of poems and letters from the 1940s and 1950s, in the private collection of Edith Turner.

[9] Engelke, 'Endless Conversation', p. 9; Turner, *Heart*, p. 47.

[10] Turner, *Heart*, pp. 235–37.

[11] Edith L. Turner, 'Our Lady of Knock: Reflections of a Believing Anthropology', *New Hibernia Review*, 15, 2 (Summer 2011), p. 125.

regime of 'thought control' and were expecting a high degree of conformity.[12] The result was alienation and estrangement. When Edie attended the Perse School, Cambridge, she was so 'impossible' at home that her parents eventually sent her there as a boarder as well.[13] As she grew more openly hostile toward them, her mother retaliated by informing her that, unlike her brothers and sisters, she was not going to be enrolled in the sixth form, the course for university preparation: Edie's formal education thus came to an abrupt and premature end at the age of 16. She would go on to embrace communism for the thorough way that it had been 'wrung clean of religion', and Nietzsche for his forthright rejection of the Holy Spirit.[14] And she, too, joined the Young Communist League.

The parents-daughter relationship never really healed, although Edie was impressed (at least as she reflected upon it later in life) by her mother's sacrificial kindness when she let Edie stay in her house for a time during the war when she was a young mother with no home and a husband away on service. Still, Edie was cut out of her mother's will—as were the other children who had become apostate—while the ones who had remained Christians received thousands of pounds each. As with 'unconditional love', in her adult life Edie has always been finding 'home' elsewhere. Her real home is in Africa. Or among the Iñupiat in the North Slope of Alaska. And so on. One suspects that this too is an expression of the fact that she does not remember her childhood house fondly as a home. Among the Ndembu of Zambia, 'the mother's spirit is thought frequently to afflict her daughter'.[15] Having suffered long enough, at the age of 76 Edie had 'a kind of dream' in which some closure was achieved. Her spectral parent was still as Anglican as ever: 'giving a vague sense that she was wearing a black hat and carrying a Bible'.[16] Still, 'Mummy' was able to communicate that she had really loved her seventh child—and indeed loves her still—and they managed to forgive one another. 'This woman was my

---

[12] George Mentore, 'Interview with Edith Turner', *AIBR* (*Journal of Iberoamerican Anthropology*), 4, 3 (2009), p. iv.

[13] Turner, *Heart*, p. 28. [14] Turner, *Heart*, p. 31.

[15] V. W. Turner, *Schism and Continuity in an African Society: A Study of Ndembu Village Life* (Manchester: Manchester University Press [for the Rhodes-Livingstone Institute], 1957), p. 243.

[16] Edith Turner, *The Ancient and the Holy: The Spirituality of Modern Ireland*, unpublished book-length manuscript, n.d. [c.2001–2004], ch. 2, pp. 13–15 (the pagination restarts with each chapter).

ancestor spirit', Edie pondered. One hopes that henceforth she was an assisting rather than afflicting one.

* * *

Edie and Vic met on 12 June 1942, when she was just a few days shy of her twenty-first birthday. He wrote a report to John Bate three days later that described her as 'vivacious and buxom, full of ideas, energetically expressed, with all the intellectual's contempt for the intellectuals'.[17] They had a sweet romance and were married six months later. Violet pegged her daughter-in-law as a 'bohemian' and Edie came to glory in this description of their young married life, making much of the fact that their first home was a gypsy caravan. Moreover, as pacifists, religious sceptics, and communists—they even joined a Marxist reading group and sold the *Daily Worker*—their defiance of respectable conventionality was more than merely superficial. Here is part of an unpublished poem of Vic's, 'To the Insurgent Peoples of the World', which he wrote sometime during the 1940s or 1950s:

> The humble have become the proud,
> The red flower buds from dust,
> But we have no word for the way it comes
> In English,
> Comerado, Kamerad.
> Wistfully we watch the changing maps,
> Inhale a gust of gunsmoke like the memory of a rose,
> Hold out our hands for happiness
> But we have no living word
> For comrade or for comradeship,
> Comerado, Kamerad.[18]

Their son, Frederick, was born before the war was over, and two other children, Robert and Irene, followed in this period of their lives.

Before the advent of their daughter, the Turners were in the habit of pushing the two boys in a pram the four miles from their caravan to the nearest public library (which was in Rugby). It was there that Vic discovered Margaret Mead's *Coming of Age in Samoa* (1928). This led on to the British anthropologist A. R. Radcliffe-Brown. It was while

---

[17] Victor Turner to John Bate, 15 June 1942. (Edith Turner private collection.)
[18] Victor Turner, 'To the Insurgent Peoples of the World', n.d. (Edith Turner private collection.)

reading *The Andaman Islanders* (1922) that Vic found his vocation, announcing simply: 'I'm going to be an anthropologist'.[19] He returned to University College London, but gained permission to shift from the comparative literature course to Daryll Forde's Department of Anthropology. During this period of their lives, the Turners became Communist Party members. Max Gluckman (1911–75) was seeking to build up the new Department of Anthropology at Manchester. When he made a visit to London, Gluckman saw Vic's potential and he promised him a grant if he would come to the northwest of England to do his postgraduate work there—an offer the Turners were happy to accept. Gluckman also had Marxist sympathies (as well as being non-religious), and the original plan had been for Vic to do fieldwork focused on the economic life of the Mambwe in what is now Zambia. In a momentous last-minute reconsideration, however, Gluckman somehow divined Vic's fascination with ritual and telegraphed: 'Suggest you change to Ndembu tribe Northwestern Providence much malaria yellow fever plenty of ritual'.[20] Vic did secure funding for their entire family of five to share in the experience. The Turners undertook fieldwork among the Ndembu of what was then Northern Rhodesia from December 1950 through February 1952 and then for another year from mid-1953 to mid-1954. They brought Marxist literature with them into the field, frantically hiding it when white visitors stopped in unannounced lest they should be exposed as communists and thereby lose the cooperation of colonial authorities. In terms of anthropological method and theory, Vic endeavoured to follow the prescribed structuralist path: 'I filled my notebooks with genealogies; I made village hut-plans and collected census material; I prowled around to catch the rare and unwary kinship term'.[21] Yet a time of questioning was looming ahead.

And so back to the department at Manchester. Vic would participate in the seminar as a postgraduate student, be awarded his PhD in 1955, and then remain as a faculty member—securing the position of lecturer in 1958 and promoted to senior lecturer in 1960—before finally leaving for a professorship at Cornell in 1963. There

---

[19] Edith Turner, 'Prologue: From the Ndembu to Broadway' in Victor Turner, *On the Edge of the Bush: Anthropology as Experience*, ed. Edith L. B. Turner (Tucson, Arizona: University of Arizona Press, 1985), p. 2.

[20] Turner, 'Prologue', p. 2.

[21] Victor W. Turner, *The Ritual Process: Structure and Anti-Structure* (Chicago: Aldine Publishing Company, 1969), p. 7.

was a pulsing desire in the department to do something distinctive that would set them apart from more established centres for the study of anthropology in Britain such as Oxford and Cambridge. It was therefore gratifying when Mary Douglas (an Oxford-trained member of the faculty at University College London) announced in a 1959 review of a book by William Watson that 'it is evidently time to salute a "school" of anthropology'.[22] The anthropologists gathered around Gluckman have therefore gone down in the literature as 'the Manchester School'.[23] Cohesion was self-consciously fostered through shared social activities, including obligatory outings to Manchester United matches. A leftish political perspective added a common outlook on life. Several members of the department were communists and the Turners would eventually become card-carrying members of the Communist party in Manchester in whom party officials saw growing potential as speakers and organizers. As to the actual anthropology, the Manchester School's greatest distinctive was its use of the extended case study method. Another was an emphasis on process, which served as a corrective to the static assumptions of structuralism.

It seems fair to say that Dr Victor Turner became the star exemplar of the Manchester School. Both Turners would later express dissatisfaction with his PhD thesis, 'Social system of the Lunda-Ndembu of Mwinilunga District' (1955), and the resulting monograph, *Schism and Continuity in an African Society: A Study of Ndembu Village Life* (1957), seeing it as straitjacketed by the conventions of structuralism and as failing to let ritual breathe on its own terms. Gluckman told his protégé to include material that Vic thought was unimportant and to leave out or take out material about which he was passionate. However, this seems to have been the kindly advice of someone on Vic's side who wanted to make sure that his work was widely acknowledged to be successful rather than a reflection of the narrowness of Gluckman's own views. Even Edie—who is particularly scathing about such restrictions—concedes that as the sole provider for a family of five it was essential that Vic play it safe at this early stage of his career. Vic himself reflected on the pressures placed on young

[22] Mary Douglas, review of William Watson, *Tribal Cohesion in a Money Economy*, *Man*, 59 (1959), p. 168.

[23] T. M. S. Evens and Don Handelman (eds.), *The Manchester School: Practice and Ethnographic Praxis in Anthropology* (Oxford: Berghahn Books, 2008); Richard P. Werbner, 'The Manchester School in South-Central Africa', *Annual Review of Anthropology*, 13 (1984), pp. 157–85.

anthropologists in a way that was surely a refracted comment on his own experience:

> Their best thoughts may be tabooed and their integrity undermined by 'city state' shibboleths in the way of concepts and styles to which they must render at least lip service to obtain support from nationally and locally prestigious departmental faculty. Students often seem to suffer from the guilt of 'self-betrayal'—which pursues them even into their fieldwork in far places. I am sure this is not an optimal condition for fieldwork. For they have to process their fieldwork into Ph.D. dissertations acceptable by their sponsoring departments.[24]

Still, if the goal was to win approbation, it worked. Few would be so purist as Edie, who takes the PhD thesis being described by its examiners as 'brilliantly orthodox' as shameful proof that it was a fundamentally compromised piece of work.[25] In a pioneering study of the Manchester School, Richard P. Werbner described *Schism and Continuity in an African Society* as Turner's 'outstanding classic within the mainstream of these studies', as the 'one book' that 'could be regarded as a centrepiece for understanding the Manchester School's principal current of ideas, orientations, and empirical concerns', and as the Manchester mainstream's 'high-water mark'.[26] Likewise Adam Kuper, when assessing the work of the Manchester School, found *Schism and Continuity* to be 'the most satisfying of these studies' and 'in a class of its own'.[27] The Manchester-style advance that it made beyond Oxford-style structuralism was in the introduction of what Turner called 'social dramas', his own dashing iteration on the extended case study method. A social drama was a conflict that had a processional form: breach, crisis, redressive action, and, finally, reintegration or recognition of schism. This insight arose naturally from his birthright as the son of an actress. One can also glimpse him during the war suddenly becoming intoxicated by drama:

> What has filled me with joy beyond measure in the past few weeks has been the conception and partial realisation of a three-act play... Philosophy itself is too barren a field to suit my sensuous sowing.

[24] Turner, *On the Edge*, pp. 152–53.

[25] Edith Turner, 'Advances in the Study of Spirit Experience: Drawing Together Many Threads', *Anthropology of Consciousness*, 17, 2 (2006), pp. 37, 55 n.1.

[26] Werbner, 'Manchester School', pp. 157, 176.

[27] Adam Kuper, *Anthropology and Anthropologists: The Modern British School* (London: Routledge & Kegan Paul, 1983), pp. 151, 153.

But the drama! Absurd that I hadn't tried it out before, not for nine years at any rate. This play is pouring out in a way that makes mockery of my theories of deliberate construction…What matters is that I am certain I have found my medium.[28]

In the end, however, it turned out that the anthropological social drama was his true medium. Turner would also go on to model and champion yet more thoroughly the Manchester emphasis on process. In the year that Vic was awarded his PhD, Gluckman himself published *The Judicial Process* (1955), and tellingly, Turner would go on to establish his reputation as one of the leading anthropologists of the second half of the twentieth century with a volume entitled *The Ritual Process* (1969).[29]

* * *

In May 1958 all five Turners were received into the communion of the Roman Catholic Church.[30] Members of the department responded with open opposition. Bill Watson and his wife Pamela were also card-carrying members of the Communist party and atheists. Edie remembers them both ranting at her and Vic, with Bill pronouncing bluntly: 'You're betraying us'.[31] Fellow Manchester School anthropologist Ronald Frankenberg recalls that the Turners were 'bitterly blamed and criticised' and subjected to 'hostile semi-isolation'.[32] This reaction was no doubt partially grounded in the disdain felt for religious convictions in general—and for Catholicism in particular—by people who were personally Marxists and agnostics. To this was added, however, a sense that they had been painstakingly crafting a common, cohesive identity that had now been shattered. It is not too much to say there was at least a fear that the conversion of the Turners might have destroyed the Manchester School. Ian Cunnison, an anthropologist who had joined the team in 1955, seemed to sense that the vehemence of the department's reaction looked odd in retrospect and attempted to explain it:

Max Gluckman was so intent on the idea of Manchester as a unified school with one general mood of thought, and one general way of analyzing society, that this change in Vic's position really brought that to

---

[28] Victor Turner to John Bate, 14 October 1942. (Edith Turner private collection.)
[29] Turner, *Ritual Process*.   [30] Fardon, 'Turner, Victor', *Oxford DNB*.
[31] Turner, *Heart*, p. 89.
[32] Ronald Frankenberg, 'Foreword', in Turner, *Heart*, p. xx.

an end. And this is why we all viewed it with such consternation at the time.[33]

It is emblematic that Bill Watson serves in this story both as the anthropologist whose work prompted the coining of the term 'Manchester School' and as the one who was most outspoken in his attacks on the Turners for finding faith (and thereby breaching their solidarity). Edie indicates that the cleavage over Catholicism was what prompted them ultimately to look for a new academic home:

> It would be hard to fully explain—or understand—the reaction we got in the Manchester department. A lot of our friends were card-carrying members of the CP [Communist Party], and almost everyone in anthropology was a left-leaning atheist. Joining the Catholic Church was probably the worst thing we could have done. It didn't end friendship, but it did cause tensions with some people. In any case, we wanted to get out.[34]

But why did they do it? Edie's reflections decades later provide a prominent source for answering this question. These recollections are very much shaped by her position at that time in which a tangible, spiritual realm which envelops different religious traditions looms large. Both Turners agree that what happened in Africa refused to stay in Africa. Witnessing and participating in Ndembu rituals changed them, even if the full impact was delayed. They make this point both in terms of theory and methodology (structuralism and Marxism did not adequately account for these rituals) and in terms of their own religious beliefs. Therefore, while 'primitive' beliefs and practices made it impossible for E. B. Tylor to accept Christian claims, in a complete reversal, traditional African religion made it possible for the Turners to take Christianity seriously once again. Vic testified that when he witnessed a Catholic priest presiding at Mass: 'I felt in the texture of his performance something of the same deep contact with the human condition tinged with transcendence that I had experienced in central Africa when I attended rituals presided over by dedicated ritual specialists.'[35] Or, as he reflected back some eighteen years after his Catholic turn:

---

[33] Engelke, 'Endless Conversation', p. 29.

[34] Matthew Engelke, 'An Interview with Edith Turner', *Current Anthropology*, 41, 5 (December 2000), p. 847.

[35] Victor W. Turner, 'Ritual, Tribal and Catholic', *Worship*, 50, 6 (1976), p. 516.

I have not been immune to the symbolic powers I have invoked in field investigation. After many years as an agnostic and monistic materialist I learned from the Ndembu that ritual and its symbolism are not merely epiphenomena or disguises of deeper social and psychological processes, but have ontological value...I became convinced that religion is not merely a toy of the race's childhood, to be discarded at a nodal point of scientific and technological development, but is really at the heart of the human matter.[36]

Edie, however, has spoken much more often about the connection with Africa and made it central to her explanation. Here is a typical account: 'After we came back home, with the drums still echoing in our heads and making us long for Africa, both of us suddenly joined the Catholic Church, a religion full of ritual.'[37]

In Edith Turner's retelling of the specific sequence of events that led up to their conversion, she and Vic decided to attend various churches as a bit of local fieldwork. They worked their way through a range of denominations. For example, one Sunday they joined the Quakers but, Edie quips laughingly, 'It was a bad day and nobody got the Spirit.'[38] Then one Advent Sunday in 1957 they had decided to attend a Unitarian chapel. This plan was thwarted by a confusion about the meeting time, and they found themselves in the flow of others heading for another congregation (which would turn out to be a Roman Catholic church): 'They passed, and then in the empty street I felt a hand take my shoulder and propel me down the alley toward the church. Vic felt this too. I looked around, but there was no one doing any shoving.'[39] When the words of consecration were pronounced over the cup, Edie shivered with the realization that she had found the Holy Grail.

There are other clues, however, which set this decision in a different light. Another way of explaining this change would involve Vic embarking on an intellectual quest which involved a programme of reading and a concerted examination of the claims of Christianity in general and of Catholicism in particular. This version can be glimpsed

---

[36] Victor Turner, *Revelation and Divination in Ndembu Ritual* (Ithaca: Cornell University Press, 1975), p. 31.

[37] Edith Turner, *Among the Healers: Stories of Spiritual and Ritual Healing from around the World* (Westport, Connecticut: Praeger, 2006), p. xiii.

[38] Edith Turner, phone interview with Timothy Larsen, 12 May 2009.

[39] Turner, *Heart*, p. 88. One thinks of the long history of Catholic reflection on the scriptural text, 'Compel them to come in.'(Luke 14:23).

even in a comment by Edie herself, 'I went the way of Vic being a Catholic. He got the sense of it first and I did afterwards, although when I was given the original sense it was very strong to me'.[40] Here Edie is not portraying a moment when they both, without premeditation, stumbled upon the faith and found themselves simultaneously nudged into it, but rather a journey that Vic went on first. This also aligns with Ronald Frankenberg's recollection that already by 1956, he and Vic were studying the Bible together in the Catholic Ronald Knox's new translation of the Vulgate.[41]

Most of all, the research for this study has led to the discovery of a major new primary source with regard to this question: Victor Turner's own statement of his reasons for converting in a letter to Max Gluckman, dated 7 July 1959.[42] From a historian's perspective, this source has the advantage of being a contemporary one. Nevertheless, it should not be handled uncritically either—not least because it is an *apologia pro vita sua* for a very important audience of one. For example, Turner offers a convoluted and unconvincing reflection on how he thinks that the Catholics at the Oxford Institute 'lean to the heresy of Gnosticism' which is clearly calculated to reassure Gluckman that he is still a Manchester School man and has 'been totally uninfluenced by Oxford anthropology or anthropologists'. Nevertheless, the letter is striking for the way that it offers exclusively intellectual reasons: its thesis from first to last is that Turner has reasoned his way to the Catholic faith. This begins with the general question of the existence of God:

> I became a theist because I could see no rational grounds for making an act of faith in the *non*-existence of God. It seemed more reasonable to hypothecate a purposive somebody behind the structure of the universe than a purposeless something. In fact, even in my Communist days I could not meet the argument I posed to myself that if materialism were true, our thoughts are the mere by-product of material processes uninfluenced by reason. Hence, if materialism be right, our thoughts are determined by irrational processes and therefore the thoughts which lead to the conclusion that materialism is right have no relation to reason.

---

[40] Engelke, 'Interview', p. 850.   [41] Frankenberg, 'Foreword', p. xiv.
[42] Victor Turner to Max Gluckman, 7 July 1959, Max Gluckman Papers, Royal Anthropological Institute, London.

Then came the case for Christianity in particular (and Catholicism with its historic claim to be the authentic Church of Christ in the world):

> I became a Christian (and *hence* as Ronnie Frankenberg said a Catholic) by reading the New Testament as a series of social dramas. In the course of this reading it came home to me that unless Jesus of Nazareth was what he claimed to be, i.e. God, he was either a lunatic, a criminal or a simpleton. The manner of his life and teaching, and especially the manner of his death, convinced me that he was none of these. Once I believed in the divinity of Jesus the rest followed. In a perfectly rational way. Catholicism is a rationalistic religion, and the Catholic claims to demonstrate by reason the existence of God, the deity of Christ and the authority of the church, I find perfectly valid.

This passage is fascinating for multiple reasons. Firstly, it cites the Bible as the prompt for his Christian conversion. Secondly, it neatly puts his dazzling contribution to Manchester School anthropology, the social drama, in the service of this cause. Thirdly, it rests on the so-called 'trilemmia' (liar, lunatic, or lord?), an apologetic argument that the Anglican literary critic C. S. Lewis (1898–1963) had made famous in a wartime radio broadcast which became part of his popular classic *Mere Christianity* (1952). Turner addresses a variety of other issues in this letter that he anticipated Gluckman might raise as objections, including the question of the authority of the Church, but for each in turn his defence of the faith always runs along the same lines: 'I think it's important to use our reason about such matters'.

The Turners took to their adopted faith wholeheartedly, with the zeal of new converts. An obvious outward and visible sign of this was that they conformed to the Church's teaching on birth control. Edie recalls: 'Vic and I complied—we obeyed all the commandments. We threw away the condoms'.[43] Ironically, as atheists, they had adhered to such restrictions in reverse: Gluckman had made it a condition of allowing the family to accompany Vic to Africa that no children were to be conceived in the field.[44] The first fruits of this now-Catholic couple was a daughter named Lucy who was born in 1959. She had Down's syndrome and only lived for a few months. (As will be seen, however, in this author's view, Lucy had her part to play in the development of the anthropology of the Turners.) Over the course of time,

---

[43] Turner, *Heart*, p. 95.   [44] Engelke, 'Endless Conversation', p. 17.

two more boys followed, Alex and Rory, making them from mid-April 1963 onwards a family of seven.

As the decades rolled by, neither Turner felt a need to maintain every enthusiastic notion of what it might mean to be a dutiful Catholic which initially occurred to them in these early years. While abandoning Marxism for good, Vic would nevertheless find his way back to more left-of-centre politics, although for a time 'he was something of an ultramontane G. K. Chesterton conservative'.[45] Still, for the rest of his life Victor Turner would be a fairly conservative Catholic in ecclesial and theological terms. Edie's testimony is that he remained 'obstinately Catholic'.[46] (This would appear to be a word of approbation in the lexicon of this lifelong rebel as she also praises the Irish for remaining 'obstinately Catholic' in the face of persecution under Protestant British rule.)[47] In more traditional language, Edith Turner and their son Frederick have also described Vic as a 'pious Catholic'.[48] A tangible manifestation of his conservative ecclesial outlook was that for all the decades which followed between his conversion and his death, Vic would receive communion only in a Roman Catholic Church. He had tremendous respect and affection for the Anglican clergyman, the Revd Brian Dupré, but he still refused on principle to receive the Eucharist when Dupré was presiding even when it was at the Turners' own son Robert's wedding service—and Dupré was the father of the bride.[49] Likewise one can see this theological vigilance as late as 1981 (just two years before his death) when their interest in the anthropology of performance led the Turners to have their students stage a contemporary Virginian wedding. Vic was aware that, as a true marriage is a sacrament, one could end up playing 'with fire', and therefore he carefully established a 'frame' of make-believe so as to avoid any spiritual impropriety 'in terms at least of Catholic theology'.[50]

Perhaps most notably, Victor Turner also became a public champion of 'the traditional Latin ritual' in opposition to the modernizing

---

[45] Edith Turner and Frederick Turner, 'Victor Turner as We Remember Him', *Anthropologica*, n.s., 27 (1985), p. 14.

[46] Edith Turner to Timothy Larsen, email, 8 August 2013.

[47] Turner, *Ancient*, ch. 1, p. 9.

[48] Turner and Turner, 'Victor Turner', p. 12.

[49] Edith Turner, phone interview with Timothy Larsen, 12 May 2009.

[50] Victor Turner, *The Anthropology of Performance* (New York: PAJ Publications, 1987), pp. 141–42.

of the Mass initiated by Vatican II.[51] In an article in the Benedictine
journal *Worship* in 1972 he practically preached a crusade against
the reformers: 'the Philistines are upon us!'[52] Instead, he passionately
defended the old forms: 'It is a mistake to think that the archaic is the
fossilized or surpassed. The archaic can be as contemporary as nuclear
physics'.[53] Returning to this same confessional venue four years later,
he was even more forceful:

> Rituals which represent the *fine fleur* of generic human experience
> understood in the light of the gospel have been jettisoned in favour of
> sometimes jaunty verbal formulations which are thought to be 'rele-
> vant' to the experience of 'contemporary man'...[54]

Hilariously, the work of the council meant that he can no longer use
the ethnographic present, but rather was reduced to constructions
such as 'on which the celebrant stands while he says Mass—or did
until recently'.[55] This article ends by more or less sounding the alarm
against ecclesial treason: 'We must not dynamite the liturgical rock
of Peter'.[56] In the 1970s and beyond, both Turners would commend
the spirituality of Catholic pilgrims precisely because it was an area
where the old faith continued on without being marred by modernizing efforts. It should also be noted that—beginning in 1957 if not earlier—Vic became a voracious reader of Christian authors and serious
theological literature. He was fond of the Catholic novelists and intellectuals of the twentieth century (Waugh, Greene, Chesterton, Knox,
and so on), but also read leading Christian intellectuals beyond the
confines of his new communion such as the Methodist-Anglican historian Herbert Butterfield (1900–79). Moreover, his reading ranged
across the centuries of Christian thought, not only the great mystics,
but also weighty theologians such as Augustine and Thomas Aquinas.
And he continued to read the Bible, with the Gospel of St John and
the Sermon on the Mount in Matthew's Gospel being particular
favourites.

[51] Turner, 'Ritual, Tribal and Catholic', p. 525.
[52] Victor Turner, 'Passages, Margins and Poverty: Religious Symbols of
Communitas', *Worship*, 46, 7 (1972), p. 392.
[53] Turner, 'Passages', p. 391.
[54] Turner, 'Ritual, Tribal and Catholic', p. 524.
[55] Turner, 'Ritual, Tribal and Catholic', p. 513.
[56] Turner, 'Ritual, Tribal and Catholic', p. 525.

Henceforth Victor Turner's anthropology would be profoundly influenced by his Christian faith, albeit in some publications more than others. The first fruits of this new spiritually infused perspective was a contribution to the Rhodes-Livingstone Papers, *Chihamba, The White Spirit: A Ritual Drama of the Ndembu* (1962).[57] It is an astonishing document. *Chihamba* was a ritual of initiation into secret knowledge for those seeking healing. What was revealed in the rite was, in Frazerian fashion, the 'mystical death and rebirth' of a god, *Kavula*.[58] Turner had discussed *Chihamba* in *Schism and Continuity* but, as a Christian, he now found that treatment reductionistic and publicly repented for it:

> At one time I employed a method of analysis derived essentially from Durkheim via Radcliffe-Brown...But I found that ritual action tended thereby to be reduced to a mere species of social action, and the qualitative distinctions between religious and secular custom and behaviour came to be obliterated. The ritual symbol, I found, had its own formal principle. It could be no more reduced to, or explained by any particular category of secular behaviour or be regarded as the resultant of many kinds of secular behaviour, than an amino-acid molecular chain could be explained by the properties of the atoms interlinked by it.[59]

Now Turner ferociously denounced Frazer and Durkheim by name for their efforts 'to explain away religious phenomena in naturalistic terms': 'Like Captain Ahab, such scholars seek to destroy that which centrally menaces and wounds their self-sufficiency, i.e. the belief in a Deity, and like Ahab they suffer shipwreck without transfixing the quick of their intended victim'. Instead, he insisted: 'Religion is not *determined* by anything other than itself'.[60] Moreover, he repeatedly spoke of nature versus grace and natural religion versus revealed religion in ways that make it clear, for those who have ears to hear, that he is claiming for the Ndembu authentic spiritual insights of the former category. In fact, he later republished *Chihamba, The White Spirit* as half of a book entitled *Revelation and Divination in Ndembu Ritual* (1975).[61] Writing for a Catholic audience in the Benedictine journal *Worship*, Turner confided that he had chosen this title in order to proclaim his own spiritual convictions:

---

[57] V. W. Turner, *Chihamba, The White Spirit: A Ritual Drama of the Ndembu*, (Rhodes-Livingstone Papers 33) (Manchester: Manchester University Press, 1962).
[58] Turner, *Chihamba*, p. 83. [59] Turner, *Chihamba*, p. 86.
[60] Turner, *Chihamba*, p. 92. [61] Turner, *Revelation*.

Theologians have long used the term 'natural revelation' to signify the manifestation of divine truths obtained by the use of human natural faculties alone. I am personally convinced from my experience of Chihamba in its social setting, where it made for reconciliation among former rivals and induced a pervasive mood of mild happiness, that the ritual and symbolism of Chihamba was just such a natural revelation—hence the title of my book about it.[62]

This affirmation is why Edith Turner has come to value *Chihamba* the most highly of all of Vic's books.[63]

Nevertheless, *Chihamba, The White Spirit* does not reflect her generous religious egalitarianism, but rather Vic leavened it with orthodox proclamations of the superiority of the true faith. For example, when drawing a comparison between this traditional African ritual and the story of Moses and the burning bush as recorded in Exodus 3, he cautions reverently: 'The difference, of course, is great. The historical Jahveh cannot be compared with the woodland demi-god'.[64] And again: 'Of course the killing of Kavula is hardly cognate with Jesus Christ's sacrifice'.[65] Even more explicit is this affirmation of the historicity of Christ's resurrection: 'But if there are many points of resemblance, there is a crucial difference between the Christian and pagan examples. For the Christian, the Resurrection is a historical event; fact and symbol are one'.[66] His faith is typographically emphasized with even pronouns about Jesus being capitalized (for example, 'Himself' repeatedly), while *Kavula* must be content with being a 'god' of the lower-case variety. Then there is the exuberant overflowing of Vic's Christian reading. A leading Catholic intellectual of the twentieth century, Étienne Gilson (1884–1978), is deployed to explain the philosophical theology of Thomas Aquinas (1225–74) which is in turn meant to illuminate the religious thought of the Ndembu. The Bible is repeatedly quoted at length—and from the official English translation for Catholics, the Douay Version. Butterfield's *Christianity and History* (1959) is put to work even though it had only been published a few years earlier. And the entire monograph ends with an aphorism from G. K. Chesterton's *The Everlasting Man*, the import of which is that the Ndembu are closer to spiritual truth and reality than secular moderns in the West. Moreover, Turner's life of worship is now a point

---

[62] Turner, 'Ritual, Tribal and Catholic', p. 519.
[63] Engelke, 'Endless Conversation', p. 28.   [64] Turner, *Chihamba*, p. 83.
[65] Turner, *Chihamba*, p. 91.   [66] Turner, *Chihamba*, p. 93.

of reference that seems so obvious to him as to be almost inevitable or irreplaceable: 'Subjectively, the nearest one can get to it is to say that the feeling tone resembled that among a group of Catholics just after the Easter Vigil service which ends the tragic drama of Passiontide'.[67] Perhaps most substantively of all for the purpose at hand, this monograph on traditional African ritual also provides a close reading of the canonical Gospels and a profound meditation on the theological meaning of Christ's resurrection.

* * *

In the year following the publication of *Chihamba, the White Spirit*, Victor Turner was offered and accepted a professorship at Cornell University. He resigned from Manchester and the whole family left the area, taking up temporary accommodation in Hastings. But then there was uncertainty regarding their United States visas as the Turners had been members of the Communist Party in good standing before renouncing that affiliation in 1957. In short, they were betwixt and between, no longer on the faculty of Manchester but not yet established on that of Cornell, having said their goodbyes to their British colleagues, but not yet any hellos to American ones. It was in this context that Victor Turner developed his celebrated theory of liminality. Back in 1909 Arnold van Gennep (1873–1957) had published a seminal work on *rites de passage* which had identified a three-phase process: separation, margin (or *limen*), and aggregation. Turner came to see that this middle liminal period had portentous power for illuminating human experience. It is a time outside the standard structures. For example, a traditional rite of initiation into adulthood might have a period of seclusion in the middle that could last for a month or longer. During that liminal phase one is neither a boy nor a man, neither a girl nor a woman. Turner published an article heralding this theory in 1964 which then became a chapter in his *The Forest of Symbols: Aspects of Ndembu Ritual* (1967).[68] The books were coming fast apace now; in the following year appeared *The Drums of Affliction: A Study of Religious Processes among the Ndembu of Zambia* (1968).[69] One of its main subjects was the *Ihamba*

---

[67] Turner, *Chihamba*, p. 86.

[68] Victor Turner, *The Forest of Symbols: Aspects of Ndembu Ritual* (Ithaca, NY: Cornell University Press, 1967).

[69] V. W. Turner, *The Drums of Affliction: A Study of Religious Processes among the Ndembu of Zambia* (Oxford: Clarendon Press, 1968).

healing ritual. Turner did not resonate with it as a natural revelation of spiritual truths as he had *Chihamba*, not least because it involved the claim that a human tooth, wandering in the patient's body, is then mystically extracted by the doctor. Turner dismissed this as a conjuring trick. His analysis therefore proceeded on the assumption that what really mattered was happening on the social rather than spiritual plane: 'I felt at the time that what was being drawn out of this man was, in fact, the hidden animosities of the village'.[70]

The Ritual Process: Structure and Anti-Structure was published in 1969, making it the third year in a row to welcome a single-authored book by Victor Turner. This one was destined to become not only the most well-received and influential work in his entire oeuvre but also a classic of the discipline and an inspiration beyond it. Once again, Turner denounced the atheistically underpinned reductionism of so many influential theorists, naming again both Tylor and Frazer, as well as others such as Freud and Durkheim: 'Most of these thinkers have taken up the implicitly theological position of trying to explain, or explain away, religious phenomena as the product of psychological or sociological causes of the most diverse and even conflicting types, denying to them any preterhuman origin'.[71]

A key concept developed in *The Ritual Process* was *communitas*: a spontaneously arising phenomenon where a group of people begin to relate to one another just as fellow human beings without regard to any differences of status, and experience mutual love and interconnectedness. Liminality fosters this. Ndembu males in the seclusion lodge, for example, by enduring together a common experience which places them on an egalitarian plane, forge deep bonds of affection with one another. A related concept, given in the subtitle, was anti-structure. Indeed, the Turners could use *communitas* as synonymous with 'social anti-structure'.[72] There is a mischievousness to Vic's development of the notion of anti-structure. He had been persistently attempting to break out of the confines of the traditional British anthropology of structuralism, and discovering something dubbed 'anti-structure' was a playful way for him to declare that there are more things in heaven and earth, Radcliffe-Brown, than are dreamt of in your anthropology. Liminality, to reiterate, is a time

---

[70] Turner, *Drums*, p. 172.   [71] Turner, *Ritual Process*, p. 4.
[72] Victor Turner and Edith Turner, *Image and Pilgrimage in Christian Culture* (New York: Columbia University Press, 1978), p. 250.

outside structures when status, roles, and hierarchies are set aside. A section in *The Ritual Process* was entitled, 'Hippies, Communitas, and the Powers of the Weak'.[73] It argued that hippies give up status and position in the social structure (they dress like outcasts, eschew careerism, and so on) to experience the spontaneous love and connectedness of *communitas*. This celebration of anti-structure was so with the *zeitgeist* that the book became enormously popular with students in the early 1970s and developed something of a cult status in the more bookish wing of the counterculture.

Still, while some of Vic's anthropological insights were indeed code for the counterculture, they were also code for Christianity. In a theological frame, the difference between structure and anti-structure was the difference in Augustinian thought between the City of Man and the City of God. Turner repeatedly made this connection explicitly.[74] The Christian categories piled up. *Communitas* was Eden; it was the millennial reign of Christ; it was the *unio mystica* so emphasized in medieval spirituality. It was Pentecost. Edith Turner especially came to see the outpouring of the Holy Spirit on the Day of Pentecost as recorded in the Book of Acts as a root paradigm for *communitas*.[75] Most of all, it was what Jesus Christ referred to as the kingdom of God. The Turners, like John the Baptist, were continually announcing that the kingdom of heaven is at hand. Here, for example, is a biblically saturated meditation which Vic published in a work on aesthetics, theatre, and play in the last full year of his life: 'Thy Kingdom' (which being *caritas, agape,* 'love,' is an anti-kingdom, a *communitas*) 'come.'[76] Victor Turner was sometimes willing to spell out how his anthropology could be transposed into a Catholic key:

A Catholic must think here of the hyperliminal moment of the Eucharist elevation when bread is transubstantiated into Host whose consumption converts parishioners of diverse social structural attributes into the

[73] Turner, *Ritual Process*, pp. 112–13.

[74] See, for example, Victor Turner, *Blazing the Trail: Way Marks in the Exploration of Symbols*, ed. Edith Turner (Tucson: University of Arizona Press, 1992), pp. 109–10.

[75] Edith Turner, *Communitas: The Anthropology of Collective Joy* (Contemporary Anthropology of Religion series) (New York: Palgrave Macmillan, 2012), pp. 93, 131, 156–58.

[76] Victor Turner, *From Ritual to Theatre: The Human Seriousness of Play* (New York: PAJ Publications, 1982), p. 49.

single Mystical Body of the Church, and a moment of pure existential *communitas* is realised.[77]

Even when they were not made explicit, however, these analogues were nevertheless alive in Turner's own mind. It seems reasonable to postulate that just as for Mary Douglas 'hierarchy' became a category of wider anthropological utility which she nevertheless cherished because it captured something of what she valued in her Catholic faith, so *communitas* served in a similar way for Victor Turner.

* * *

In 1968, Vic left Cornell for the University of Chicago, taking a position in its famed Committee on Social Thought. During the Chicago years, the Turners became pioneers in the field of pilgrimage studies. This is where their baby Lucy helps to shape the story. A few months after her death in 1960, the Turners went on a pilgrimage to Aylesford Priory, a place made holy by its association with St Simon Stock. It would appear to have been a response to their grief. At least in hindsight, Edie became convinced that a wonder-worker there, Father Malachy, performed a miracle that enabled them to have healthy children again.[78] As a result, in the fullness of time, Alex was born. The point to emphasize here, however, is that the Turners were going to sacred sites as a spiritual practice before it ever occurred to them to do research on this phenomenon. Eventually, Vic would decide that Catholic pilgrimage was a way for his anthropology to move 'from tribal to world religions, and more generally, from small-scale to mass societies'.[79] (This, of course, reflected a wider trend and turn in anthropology during the second half of the twentieth century, as we have already seen in Douglas's career.) Moreover, he had been searching for a site of liminality in Catholicism: its rites of passage did not offer a significant amount of time in a betwixt and between stage. A pilgrimage, however, was a form of spirituality that was outside the normal structures and that could produce *communitas*. Once again,

---

[77] Victor Turner, 'Religion in Current Cultural Anthropology', in Mircea Eliade and David Tracy (eds.), *What Is Religion? An Inquiry for Christian Theology* (*Concilium* 136) (New York: Seabury Press, 1980), p. 70.

[78] Turner, *Heart*, p. 91.

[79] Frank E. Manning, 'Victor Turner's Career and Publications', in Kathleen M. Ashley (ed.), *Victor Turner and the Construction of Cultural Criticism Between Literature and Anthropology* (Bloomington: Indiana University Press, 1990), p. 171.

it is crucial to understand that the Turners were Christian believers undertaking a spiritual discipline for their own personal edification. Edie hints that in some ways the scholarly project was respectable cover in intellectual circles for an unfashionably traditional form of piety: 'it was almost embarrassing to say one had gone to Lourdes unless one was doing research'.[80] She is emphatic that they were going to these holy places to worship.[81] Vic's sly way of admitting this was to reflect that perhaps it would be more accurate to say that he was an 'observing participant' rather than the standard anthropologist's identity as a participant observer.[82] Long after Vic's death, when Edie went to the Shrine of Our Lady of Knock again in May 2000 she stressed that she went 'as a pilgrim, pure and simple'.[83] As it happens, she did write about that fieldwork as well, but the point she was emphasizing is, once again, that she was there to participate and could not help but also observe rather than merely participating the better to observe as anthropologists usually did.

In 1974 Victor Turner's *Dramas, Fields, and Metaphors: Symbolic Action in Human Society* was published.[84] It demonstrated how he was learning to blend this devotional practice into his anthropological theory by including a chapter on 'Pilgrimage as Social Processes'. Then there are two remarkable chapters which revel in ecclesiastical history. One is on Father Miguel Hildalgo (1753–1811) and the Mexican revolution in 1810. Turner reads these events as a social drama, recapitulating the life of Christ. In terms of pilgrimage, he uncovers the way that Hildalgo harnessed the people's devotion to Our Lady of Guadalupe. The other such chapter is a brilliant exposition of the social drama between Henry II (1133–89) and Thomas Becket (c.1120–70). Vic freely confesses that he first became interested in Becket's violent death because his shrine was an important site of pilgrimage in the late medieval period. Once again, Becket is shown to have lived the *via crucis* and to have consciously brought his life story into conformity with the Christian root paradigm of martyrdom. The book was as fierce as ever when pushing back at

---

[80]   Edith Turner, Preface to the paperback edition [1995], in Victor Turner and Edith Turner, *Image and Pilgrimage in Christian Culture* (New York: Columbia University Press, 2011), p. xix.

[81]   Engelke, 'Interview', pp. 848–49.   [82]   Turner, *Blazing*, p. 35.

[83]   Turner, *Heart*, pp. 201–11.

[84]   Victor Turner, *Dramas, Fields, and Metaphors: Symbolic Action in Human Society* (Ithaca: Cornell University Press, 1974).

anti-Christian theorists, going so far as to accuse Durkheim and Comte of 'a curious egolatry'.[85]

The full flowering of this new area of interest, however, was *Image and Pilgrimage in Christian Culture* (1978): the first and only book where Victor Turner and Edith Turner were named as co-authors.[86] Although it also delves into ecclesiastical history, much of the book is informed by their fieldwork as observing participants at shrines such as Lourdes, Knock, and Guadalupe. For the purpose at hand, one of the arresting things about this book is how deeply engaged it is with Christian theology. In that sense, it is one long confession of faith. The Turners state in the preface that they are Catholics and then the rest of the book is written in a 'Catholics believe…' mode, creating a kind of syllogism in which the reader is invited to deduce that the theological claims being presented are ones which the authors themselves affirm. The text continually traces practices and beliefs back to biblical warrant, to the life of Christ, to theological formulations from the early ecumenical councils, and to catechismal teaching. While the Turners were surely right to claim that the faithful are more theologically literate than scholars probably imagine, the reader would nevertheless be forgiven for assuming that the Turners are moving beyond the articulated knowledge of their ordinary informants when they start referring to the doctrine of the hypostatic union, the Council of Ephesus (AD 431), and the like. It is apparent that Vic revelled in such careful doctrinal formulations because they interested him personally as an intellectually curious, thoughtful Christian. (Edie would later dismiss at least some parts of *Image and Pilgrimage* as 'theological hairsplitting', which makes it hard to discern to what degree she herself was enthusiastic about this material at the time.)[87] Theologically infused though it was, *Image and Pilgrimage* made its mark in the discipline of anthropology. The secular Jewish anthropologist, Alan Morinis, observed in 1992: 'The only significant theory of pilgrimage that has been put forward to date is that of Victor Turner. He is owed credit for bringing pilgrimage to the forefront of anthropological consideration.'[88] (It is to be regretted, however, that Morinis neglected to give Edith Turner co-authorship credit.)

---

[85] Turner, *Dramas*, p. 57.   [86] Turner and Turner, *Image* (1978).

[87] Turner, Preface, Turner and Turner, *Image* (2011), p. xx.

[88] Alan Morinis (ed.), *Sacred Journeys: The Anthropology of Pilgrimage* (Westport, Conn: Greenwood Press, 1992), p. 8.

To move to some cumulative comments on Victor Turner's oeuvre, biblical and theological themes pulse through his writings from his conversion right to his death. One text of scripture, from his beloved Gospel of John, became a kind of proof text for his post-structuralist anthropology: the wind of the Spirit 'bloweth where it listeth' (John 3:8). This insight often recurs in the writings of both Turners.[89] Likewise, Vic would often counter materialistic tendencies with Christ's words: 'Man shall not live by bread alone' (Matthew 4:4). Here, for example, is an impassioned case:

> Positivism and rationalism have reduced ritual and its symbolism to scarcely more than the reflection or expression of aspects of social structure, direct or 'veiled' or 'projected.' The liminal, and the ritual which guards it, are proofs of the existence of powers antithetical to those generating and maintaining 'profane' structures of all types, proofs that man does not live by bread alone.[90]

Vic's writings are also marbled with references to theological thinkers. Even writers that many scholars might use for other aspects of their work—such as perennial favourites Blake, Kierkegaard, Dante, and Buber—are clearly often being drawn upon as spiritual voices. (Vic literally never wrote a book in which he did not quote William Blake.) This was true long before his conversion. When he started reading Kierkegaard during the war, even though he was a religious sceptic, his letters began to be filled with Christian concepts such as the Holy Ghost, Messiah, Sin, and Forgiveness (all with capital letters), and he attributed this new religious turn in his thinking to the Danish philosopher.[91] Turner took advantage of the interdisciplinary nature of the Committee on Social Thought to teach seminars at the University of Chicago on Dante, Blake, and Kierkegaard.[92] The mystic Jacob Boehme also reappears across Turner's writings, as do a great cloud of witnesses from St Benedict to St Frances de Sales and beyond. Augustine and Aquinas are the more formal theologians from ages past most drawn upon (and Pascal belongs in this account somewhere, perhaps as a kind of d'Artagnan alongside the Three Musketeers of Blake, Dante, and Kierkegaard).

---

[89] See, for example, Turner and Turner, *Image* (1978), pp. 32, 222.

[90] Victor Turner, 'Passages', p. 391.

[91] Victor Turner to John Bate, 10 June 1942. (Edith Turner private collection.)

[92] Turner, *Blazing*, p. 78.

There are also, of course, references to twentieth-century theologians such as Pierre Teilhard de Chardin. Most striking, however, was Vic's use of the Roman Catholic intellectual, theologian, mystic, and apologist Friedrich Von Hügel (1852–1925). In an article published in the last few years of Turner's life, tellingly in the *Harvard Theological Review* (1981), he ended with a long passage from Von Hügel's theological treatise, *Eternal Life: A Study of Its Implications and Applications* (1913). Turner sheepishly admits that this sudden turn to the explicitly doctrinal at the end of his essay was a kind of 'leap of faith' that some might find a 'non sequitur', but that those who have ears to hear might discern it to be 'a capstone of my argument'.[93] The import of this concluding spiritual meditation is that the timeless quality of ritual allows human beings to apprehend what is truly Eternal. Turner also wrote for confessional publications, not only the Benedictine journal, *Worship*, but also for a special 'inquiry for Christian theology' on religion in the international Roman Catholic theological journal, *Concilium*.[94] Indeed, Victor Turner was so comfortable with advanced theological reflection that, like Mary Douglas, he can endearingly deploy it in the naïve assumption that it can serve as a clarifying analogy. To take an extreme case, he imagines that his readers will understand the neurology of the human brain better once he has referenced the double procession of the Holy Spirit as articulated in the *filioque* clause of the Western creed.[95] Fascinatingly, the scholar and theatre director Richard Schechner, who collaborated with the Turners on the anthropology of performance, has been highly perceptive on the theological underpinnings of Vic's work.[96] Naturally, theologians have returned the favour by often engaging with Turner's ideas; an article in *Theology Today* can serve as just one of many such examples.[97] In fact, the only single-authored book on Victor Turner's thought was written by a scholar with a PhD in Systematic Theology from Union Theological Seminary.[98]

[93] Turner, *On the Edge*, p. 246. (The article was reprinted in this collection.)

[94] Turner, 'Religion in Current Cultural Anthropology', pp. 69–71.

[95] Turner, *On the Edge*, p. 272.

[96] Richard Schechner, 'Victor Turner's Last Adventure' (Preface), in Turner, *Anthropology of Performance*, pp. 7–20.

[97] J. Randall Nichols, 'Worship as Anti-Structure: The Contribution of Victor Turner', *Theology Today*, 41, 4 (January 1985), pp. 401–409.

[98] Bobby C. Alexander, *Victor Turner Revisited: Ritual as Social Change* (American Academy of Religion Series) (Atlanta: Scholars Press, 1991). Alexander also has a PhD in Religious Studies from Columbia University.

We have not thus far belaboured just how eminent Victor Turner became. Still, that has been apparent already in what has gone before. He was the star of the Manchester School. By 1965 he had been awarded the Royal Anthropological Institute's coveted Rivers Memorial Medal. Then he was headhunted by the Ivy League with a professorship at Cornell University. Next came the still more prestigious Committee on Social Thought at the University of Chicago, where his department chair, Saul Bellow (1915–2005), won the Nobel Prize for Literature during Vic's tenure, and where his colleagues included Hannah Arendt (1906–75) and Mircea Eliade (1907–86). By that time, Vic had a world reputation as a leading anthropologist and a celebrity intellectual. He became the kind of figure whose name added cachet to even the most elite institutions, serving, for example, on the board of the Smithsonian. While it is typical to complain that one has been under-appreciated, the Turners' complaint is a peculiar one: 'Vic did not like the "high-up" positions into which people pushed him'.[99] All of this led to the University of Virginia making Vic an offer he could not refuse: in 1977 he took up an appointment there as William R. Kenan Professor of Anthropology and Religion. Virginia was intent on being able to boast that it had this famous, world-class scholar on its faculty and was therefore willing to offer him whatever he wanted. Not only was he excused from all committee and administrative work, but his path was made exceedingly smooth in many crafty ways: 'He had the uncanny ability, for example, to teach two courses at the same time— always on a Thursday night'.[100]

Much has happened since Vic's death to confirm his enduring place as a major contributor to the field of anthropology. A tribute to him in *Anthropologica* observed: 'The caliber of his work was so outstanding that his name was eventually entered into dictionaries and encyclopedias as a standard reference'.[101] Lest his status as a public intellectual might cause people to forget what his reputation was built upon, Mary Douglas reiterated in an obituary: 'It is important to record that he was an unrivalled ethnographer'.[102] The Society for Humanistic Anthropology perpetuates his memory through the Victor Turner Prize in Ethnographic Writing. His

---

[99] Turner, *Heart*, p. 125.   [100] Engelke, 'Endless Conversation', p. 39.
[101] Peter L. McLaren, 'A Tribute to Victor Turner (1920–1983)', *Anthropologica*, n.s. 27 (1985), pp. 17–22 (here 18).
[102] Mary Douglas, 'Obituary: Victor Turner', *RAIN*, 61 (1984), p. 11.

own books continue to be in print—to be read, cited, discussed, and to serve as a starting point for new studies—and some of his work has been translated into a variety of languages. Moreover, a whole stream of scholarship continues that focuses on Turner's anthropology: notably, *By Means of Performance: Intercultural studies of theatre and ritual* (1990)—a volume dedicated to him; *Victor Turner and the Construction of Cultural Criticism Between Literature and Anthropology* (1990); *Victor Turner Revisited: Ritual as Social Change* (1991); and *Victor Turner and Contemporary Cultural Performance* (2008).[103] A volume celebrating the founding of the Anthropology Department at the University of Notre Dame is also dedicated to him as an 'exemplar'.[104]

Victor Turner had a heart attack in October 1983 and was hospitalized for a week. He was at home on 18 December 1983 when a second one killed him. During his period in hospital that autumn, the comforting ministry of 'the pastor of our church', Father Carl Naro, meant a great deal to both Turners.[105] Vic had been a practising Catholic and regular communicant from 1958 onwards. Edie emphasized that Vic lived his whole spiritual life in the Roman Catholic Church from conversion to the very end, 'last rites and everything'.[106] His solemn requiem Mass was held in the local congregation where the Turners were faithful members, Holy Comforter Church, Charlottesville, Virginia. The readings included the great English poet and Jesuit priest, Gerard Manley Hopkins, as well as selections of Holy Scripture from both Testaments: Ezekiel, St Matthew's Gospel (Vic's beloved Sermon on the Mount), and Paul's First Epistle to the Corinthians (the famous chapter 13 on true love).[107] Fittingly, natural revelation was also allowed to have its due. There was a gathering at the Turners' home that same evening—as if Vic's storied 'midnight seminar' were to meet one last time—and they mourned in traditional African ways such as ritual dance. Some students had even made a Ndembu funeral mask.[108]

---

[103] Richard Schechner and Willa Appel (eds.), *By Means of Performance: Intercultural studies of theatre and ritual* (Cambridge: Cambridge University Press, 1990); Ashley, *Victor Turner*; Alexander, *Victor Turner Revisited*; Graham St John (ed.), *Victor Turner and Contemporary Cultural Performance* (Oxford: Berghahn Books, 2008).

[104] Kenneth Moore (ed.), *Waymarks: The Notre Dame Inaugural Lectures in Anthropology* (Notre Dame: University of Notre Dame Press, 1987). (Vic himself gave one of these lectures and it is also included in this collection.)

[105] Turner, *Heart*, p. 140.

[106] Edith Turner, phone interview with Timothy Larsen, 12 May 2009.

[107] Turner and Turner, 'Victor Turner', p. 16.

[108] Turner, *Heart*, pp. 144–45.

Unlike such reenactments in the past, however, the loss this time was painfully real: there was no need to create a frame of make-believe.

* * *

And so we move towards the anthropology of Edith Turner since 1983: among the Ndembu, the present belongs to the men, but the future is dominated by the mothers.[109] One must first backtrack, however, to underline that it always had been Vic and Edie together.[110] It was collaboration all along: they discovered anthropology together in Rugby Library; they read aloud together works in the discipline; Vic shared with Edie what he learned attending lectures and seminars; they did the fieldwork together; and she was always there shaping the ideas in Vic's publications as well as helping with the writing and man-uscript production. This is how Edie experienced it. Nevertheless, this was presumably not always readily apparent even to those who knew them personally, let alone the wider guild. For example, Edie can refer to Gluckman as her 'old mentor', but it is not likely that he thought of himself in that way.[111] Likewise, while others would not have per-ceived this, the doctoral thesis, although the degree was awarded to Vic, was her work too. Thus she can write: 'We were in England writing a thesis for a PhD'.[112] Not that Vic was trying to disguise or downplay her contribution. Indeed, one of his earliest anthropological publi-cations—an article written before the doctoral thesis—was explicitly presented as co-authored by the Turners: 'Money Economy among the Mwinilunga Ndembu: A study of some individual cash budgets' (1955). Moreover, her name—presented as 'E. L. B. Turner'—is even given before his, a decision apparently based on alphabetical order.[113] While this was only what justice would accord, it was not every aspir-ing professional man in the 1950s who would have acknowledged a

---

[109] Turner, *Schism*, pp. 59–60.

[110] While it has already been cited, I should emphasize here that an entire chapter-length study has been published on their collaboration: Engelke, 'Endless Conversation'. For an account that locates Edie in a wider context, see Lyn Schumaker, 'Women in the Field in the Twentieth Century: Revolution, Involution, Devolution?' in Henrika Kuklick (ed.), *A New History of Anthropology* (Oxford: Blackwell, 2009), pp. 277–92.

[111] Turner, *Communitas*, p. 52.   [112] Turner, *Heart*, p. 2.

[113] E. L. B. Turner and V. W. Turner, 'Money Economy among the Mwinilunga Ndembu: A study of some individual cash budgets', *Rhodes-Livingstone Journal*, xviii (1955), pp. 19–37. (This article was written in 1953: Graham St John, 'Victor Turner and Contemporary Cultural Performance: An Introduction', in St John, *Victor Turner*, p. 25.)

wife without so much as a bachelor's degree as his academic collaborator in this unstinting manner.

And now one greater than William Blake has arrived, for there is certainly no Victor Turner book where Edie is not visibly present. This is most obvious in the acknowledgements. In *Schism and Continuity*, they conclude with a separate paragraph just on her (just part of which is cited here), before going on to a summary statement: 'My wife collaborated actively in all aspects of my field-work...Her comments on the argument have helped to shape its form...In short, this book is in a very real sense the product of collective authorship'.[114]

Hearty recognition continued steadily. This is from *The Forest of Symbols* (1967): 'My wife has worked with me from the beginning of this venture, in the field, until its completion in book form'.[115] A year later in *The Drums of Affliction* (1968) he again insisted that she was the alpha and omega in his work: 'My wife, Edie, from first to last, from fieldwork to index, has given me her careful and insightful help'.[116] Eventually, even Vic began to anticipate that his loyal readers had seen such affirmations before. *Dramas, Fields and Metaphors* (1974) reiterates: 'Finally, I would like once more to acknowledge my debt to my wife, Edie, for her incomparable help with this book as with all my other publications'.[117] Moreover, Edith Turner did not disappear once one had waded into the main content of these books. Nothing is more common in a Victor Turner book than the refrain 'my wife and I': she had been there in the field as well, and out of the mouths of two witnesses let the matter be established. Likewise, numerous bits of evidence are stated in the main body of the text to have been gathered or reported exclusively by 'my wife'. In *The Drums of Affliction*—which, incidentally was also dedicated to Edie—a major recurring source is 'my wife's best informant'.[118] This trend culminated in 1978 when Edie was once again named as co-author, and now it was on a book: *Image and Pilgrimage in Christian Culture*. Although this time around his name came first, given Vic's eminence this order might have been a marketing decision.

---

[114] Turner, *Schism*, p. xvi. (As that last sentence was a fresh paragraph concluding the acknowledgements it would seem that Turner was including others already mentioned in this collective authorship as well.)

[115] Turner, *Forest*, p. vii.   [116] Turner, *Drums*, p. [vii].

[117] Turner, *Dramas*, p. 19.

[118] Turner, *Dramas*, pp. 206, 216, 219, 220, 242, 254.

In a beautiful mirror image of this pattern, Edie, in her turn, has been unfailingly careful to acknowledge Vic in her books. In *The Spirit and the Drum* (1987)—which is also dedicated to 'the Loving Memory of Victor Turner 1920–1983'—she wrote: 'Vic was the exemplar of the anthropology of experience, and thus I can say that without him this book would never have been written'.[119] In a 1992 volume she observed: 'Finally, I acknowledge the intellectual legacy of Victor Turner, which is beyond price'.[120] In her most recent book, *Communitas* (2012), she declares: 'My greatest thanks are due to Victor Turner whose book this ought to have been'.[121] It is also clear that Edie wishes other people had been more willing to credit her contributions to her husband's work—and perhaps even that this debt had been expressed in formal co-authorship more often. Her own life history is therefore no doubt partially the prompt for her tendency to name her key informants as co-authors or to explain that they had been offered this recognition but declined it. Most notably, *Experiencing Ritual* names three other people on the title page as additional authors, an undergraduate student who accompanied Edie in the field as an assistant (William Blodgett) and two African informants (Singleton Kahona and Fideli Benwa).

Edith Turner's rise to prominence as an anthropologist in her own right was facilitated by her fortuitous decision to earn a master's degree. The University of Virginia was willing to accept her on to a postgraduate programme (despite her never having taken an undergraduate degree) in light of her life experience (including editing a feminist literary journal arising out of the University of Chicago community, *Primavera*) and out of a sense that flexibility was needed to meet the needs of a generation of talented women who had been expected to become stay-at-home mothers in the postwar years. Edie enrolled in the English Department. She seems to have felt that studying anthropology would put Vic's colleagues in an awkward position by requiring them to mark her work. She wrote a thesis on Shakespeare's *Measure for Measure*—the utility for anthropology of which she would emphasize by noting that it was about symbolism—and was awarded her MA in 1980.[122] Thus her anthropological

[119] Edith Turner, *The Spirit and the Drum: A Memoir of Africa* (Tucson: University of Arizona Press, 1987), p. xii.

[120] Turner, *Experiencing Ritual*, p. xiii.   [121] Turner, *Communitas*, p. xiii.

[122] Turner, *Heart*, p. 125.

education has been an informal one and her work is shaped by the autodidact's tendency to think outside and beyond the established answers and conventions.

After Vic's first heart attack she stepped in to lead his seminar, and a colleague in the department kindly arranged for Edith Turner to be granted a position as a lecturer in the Department of Anthropology at Virginia in 1984 (a position which she still holds at the age of 92 at the time this volume is being written). Thus at the age of 63 an astonishing professional career with a formal status within the academy began. Her first single-authored book appeared in 1987 (it was a reworking of a manuscript she had prepared in the mid-1950s): *The Spirit and the Drum: A Memoir of Africa*. Since then she has gone on to publish more works than most scholars who obtain a permanent, full-time faculty appointment while still in their twenties do in their entire careers. In 1992, Edie became editor of the journal *Anthropology and Humanism*, fulfilling this responsibility until 2010 (and she is still serving at the time of writing as one of two Associate Editors). In 2000, the College of Wooster conferred upon Edith Lucy Brocklesby Turner a Doctor of Humanities degree, *honoris causa*, in recognition of her 'extraordinary achievements as an anthropologist'.[123] Kenyon College followed suit in 2003 with the Doctor of Humane Letters.[124] The twenty-first century was the time for Edie to be the eminent one. By 2006, she was being referred to as 'a renowned anthropologist'.[125] In 2009 she was heralded as 'one of the legends of anthropology of our times'.[126]

After almost thirty years had gone by, in 1985 Edith Turner returned to the Ndembu in Zambia. What happened to her there was one of a handful of key turning points in her entire, long life: during further fieldwork she took part in the Ihamba healing ritual as an assisting doctor. Releasing the patient from an afflicting spirit is correlated with removing a human tooth which is believed to be wandering inside their body. At the climax of the ritual:

---

[123] R. Stanton Hale (President, The College of Wooster) to Edith Turner, 18 February 2000. (A copy of this letter was provided to me by Denise D. Monbarren, Special Collections Librarian, College of Wooster, Wooster, Ohio.)

[124] Information provided by Lydia Shanan, Gleenslade Special Collections and Archives, Kenyon College, Gambier, Ohio.

[125] From the publisher's statement about the author: Turner, *Among the Healers*, p. [185].

[126] Mentore, 'Interview', p. i.

Suddenly Meru raised her arm, stretched it in liberation, and I *saw* with my own eyes a giant thing emerging out of the flesh of her back. This thing was a large gray blob about six inches across, a deep gray opaque thing emerging as a sphere. I was amazed—delighted I still laugh with glee at the realization of having seen it, the ihamba, and so big![127]

This event was so significant for Edie because she knew that she had physically seen a spirit. Thereafter, in publication after publication she would recount this story. Its import was far-reaching: namely, that Western anthropologists could discern the existence of spirits and therefore do academic work based on that premise.

Edith Turner's advocacy for such an ethnography was potently presented in a 1993 article in *Anthropology of Consciousness*: 'The Reality of Spirits: A Tabooed or Permitted Field of Study?'[128] This manifesto was so welcomed by like-minded scholars that it has been reprinted in at least a half dozen different venues. Tellingly, the subtitle was dropped and it became thereby an even more straightforward assertion of 'The Reality of Spirits'. This is how it was titled, for example, when presented in the journal *Shamanism*.[129] Edie has steadfastly insisted that what she means by 'reality' in this context ought to meet the approval of even those most loyal to the standards of the Enlightenment: 'The spirit is "out there," real, and not a subjective construction of the mind'.[130] As her son Rory Turner, who is himself a cultural anthropologist on the faculty of Goucher College, has explained: 'Edie is not saying that there are psychological forces that act as spirits, or that beliefs in spirits have real consequences in social action, or something careful like that. She is saying that there really are spirits'.[131] She co-coined the term 'actuality' to refer to something that is discerned to be a spiritual reality in itself rather than being merely a metaphorical reference to a spiritual reality. In Catholic theology, the Eucharist is not merely a symbol of the body of Christ, it *is*

---

[127] Turner, *Experiencing Ritual*, p. 149.

[128] Edith Turner, 'The Reality of Spirits: A Tabooed or Permitted Field of Study?', *Anthropology of Consciousness*, 4, 1 (March 1993), pp. 9–12.

[129] Accessed online at www.shamanism.org on 28 June 2013.

[130] Edith Turner, 'The Anthropology of Experience: The Way to Teach Religion and Healing', in Linda L. Barnes and Inés Talamantez (eds.), *Teaching Religion and Healing* (New York: Oxford University Press, 2006), p. 202.

[131] Rory P. B. Turner, 'A Sense of Presence', *Anthropology and Humanism*, 26, 2 (2002), p. 188.

the body of Christ, and an actuality is Turner's way of applying this spiritual insight in any religious or cultural context.[132]

Ihamba is a healing ritual, and Edith Turner thereafter became deeply motivated to seek out rites and techniques of healing in other forms, contexts, and cultures. The corollary to spirits being real is that spiritual healing is real. As seeing with her own eyes is the warrant she gives over and over again for believing in spirits, so finding relief in her own body is the evidence that she gives for believing in spiritual healing. One oft-told incident occurred during the annual meeting of the American Anthropological Association in San Francisco in November 1996. Turner was so ill (her symptoms included dizziness and vomiting) that she stayed in her Hilton hotel room unable to attend sessions, but she was then instantly healed through the laying on of hands. 'The healer' (her term) was another scholar at the conference who had been on the same panel with her.[133] She later developed a taxonomy of spiritual healing and recognized this one as of the spirit-energy variety. Turner frequently includes this account in her academic writings as evidence. Here is a typical specimen: 'The most dramatic healing I ever experienced was performed by a sociology professor.'[134]

Edith Turner has steadily insisted that these realities can be empirically validated, although (evoking William James) it must be a 'radical empiricism' that does not rule out the possibility of the realm of spirit: scholars must accept 'the truth that a consistent body of empirical data falls outside the purview of currently established scientific methodology.'[135] Nevertheless, this is something akin to an Enlightenment claim, and it is certainly not a kind of postmodern refusal to privilege positivistic pronouncements that certain things are true and others false. Vic had gone along with the postmodern turn quite cheerfully, declaring in 1980 that it was 'having a liberating effect on anthropology, as on many other disciplines', and even suggesting that he had anticipated it: 'My own work for many years had inclined me in a similar theoretical direction. This direction is towards

---

[132] See, for example, Edith Turner, 'Psychology, Metaphor, or Actuality? A Probe into Inupiaq Eskimo Healing', *Anthropology of Consciousness*, 3 (1992), pp. 1–8.

[133] Turner, *Among the Healers*, p. 28.

[134] Turner, 'Anthropology of Experience', p. 201.

[135] Turner, *Hands Feel It*, p. 137; Edith L. B. Turner, 'The Soul and Communication between Souls', in Helmut Wautischer (ed.), *Ontology of Consciousness: Percipient Action* (Cambridge, Massachusetts: MIT Press, 2008), p. 79.

postmodern ways of thinking'.[136] Edie, however, came to see the post-modern emphasis on the social construction of reality as threatening to evacuate meaning from her claim that spirits are real. She has gone so far as to say that anthropology needs to be saved from the 'death' that would be inflicted on it if postmodernism triumphed.[137] (It is therefore ironic that her *The Spirit and the Drum* was praised as an 'exemplary post-modern text', the reviewer apparently mistaking a true believer in traditional African spirituality for an urbane practitioner of epistemological relativism.)[138] Instead, Turner frequently insists that including spirits in one's ethnographies is merely a matter of reporting 'the facts'.[139] This is exactly equivalent to the work of scientists—and indeed those scientists whose task is the discovery of material realities. Do you wish that she would not insist that she saw a spirit? 'But supposing the astronomers had failed to believe the evidence of their senses when they found Pluto'.[140] She has repeatedly remarked that a social or cultural anthropologist doing this kind of work should be thought of as like a 'natural historian': the latter tells us they have seen a hitherto unknown animal species, and the former that they have seen a spirit.[141] Edie claims that traditional African healers were more effective when she visited in the 1980s than they had been when she was there in 1950s because they have been proceeding in an empirical way, 'gradually improving their treatments'.[142]

For some years Edie ran a monthly meeting from her home in which practitioners of a wider variety of different traditions of spiritual healing were invited to demonstrate them. Her instinct was a kind of the-more-the-merrier approach to these varied paths as she sought to accept each one in turn. Not only has Edith Turner witnessed spiritual healing, and even experienced herself being cured, but she has gone on to learn some of the techniques and then to heal others, and even to incorporate practicum sessions into some of her anthropology courses during which students are trained to heal. Edie's own remarkable longevity no doubt inspires confidence that she does indeed know something about warding off sickness and death. Vic was criticized for ignoring the dark side of *communitas*: was it not

---

[136] Turner, *On the Edge*, pp. 177, 185.
[137] Turner, 'Anthropology of Experience', p. 193.
[138] This review is referred to in Engelke, 'Endless Conversation', p. 26.
[139] Turner, *Hands Feel It*, p. 201.   [140] Turner, *Experiencing Ritual*, p. 4.
[141] Turner, *Hands Feel It*, p. 231.   [142] Turner, *Hands Feel It*, p. 229.

manifestly present at Hitler's rallies? Likewise, Edie has not been very interested in the sinister possibilities of spiritual practices. When among the Iñupiat she was often told that the shamans had been evil people doing wicked things with their power, but she would just brush such reports off quickly and instead focus on the potential of shamanistic power to do good. This helps to explain her focus on spiritual healing. One of Edith Turner's profound insights is that, of all the religious activities people engage in, 'healing is the most innocent'.[143] Where one finds the ministry of healing, there one is most likely to find a wholesome desire for human flourishing.

* * *

This is not the place to engage in a normative evaluation of these claims, but it is perhaps proper to notice that the foundational narratives that Edie uses to give warrant to these beliefs are not unassailable. First, her sighting of a spirit during the Ihamba: as an assisting doctor, she was given traditional medicines with hallucinogenic qualities to drink. As the main doctor explained about another ritual, 'You can only see musalu [a ghost], which comes in smoke or mist, when you drink pounded leaf medicine'.[144] When Edie drank it at the Ihamba it made her head swim. Still, while not denying that it was a hallucinogenic, her view seems to be that these medicines are perception-enhancing rather than perception-impairing. Nevertheless, she concedes of the notes she took during the ritual: 'Here my writing showed some sleepiness, for I noted, "stridulator with the cat," but can't remember what I meant'.[145] It seems reasonable to hypothesize that it might have been the medicine rather than tiredness that caused this impairment. Finally, she did not even ask the presiding doctor what he did or did not see (let alone whether he had actually brought the human tooth he showed off triumphantly with him or whether it really had been recovered from inside the patient's body as the rite asserted): 'I was in no mood to become analytical, so I did not push the matter further'.[146] In short, one does not have to rule out the existence of spirits a priori to wonder whether when Turner thought she saw a spirit she was actually experiencing a drug-induced hallucination.

---

[143] Turner, 'Anthropology of Experience', p. 196.

[144] Turner, *Experiencing Ritual*, p. 219.

[145] Turner, *Experiencing Ritual*, p. 135.

[146] Edith Turner, 'Drumming, Divination, and Healing: The Community at Work', in Michael Winkelman and Philip M. Peek (eds.), *Divination and Healing: Potent Vision* (Tucson: University of Arizona Press, 2004), p. 73.

Her most dramatic experience of personal spiritual healing is a problematic story in its own way. While she never names the man she credits with her cure, she gives so many details that he is easily identifiable as Dr Tom Arcaro, Professor of Sociology, Elon University. Arcaro does not in any way see himself as a spiritual healer, but rather self-identifies as 'a lifelong sceptic'. He remembers the incident and even more so because of Edie's subsequent expressions of gratitude, but his own story is that he was not consciously engaging in any healing practice at all, but merely offering sympathy.[147] This, of course, does not undermine the fact that Edie was healed in a sudden and unexpected manner, nor even that some agency such as spirit-energy was how it happened, but it does demonstrate that the account sometimes becomes more ambiguous if one gets into an analytical mood and pushes the matter further.

Edith Turner also began to do fieldwork in other parts of the world. Especially important was her work with the Iñupiat of the North Slope, Alaska, beginning in 1987, fresh work in Ireland in the mid-1990s on traditional healers, as well as continuing her work with Vic on Catholic pilgrimages. All this, together with other influences such as her monthly group on varieties of spiritual healing, has prompted her to continue to collect new beliefs and techniques until she has acquired an overflowing cornucopia of alternative practices. Sometimes these seem, at least partially, to be merely an effort to think along with her informants, for example, when she defends belief in Bigfoot or the Abominable Snowman. Nevertheless, she has deeply incorporated shamanism, reincarnation, and clairvoyance into her own view of the world, and quite happily and sincerely accepts acupuncture, divination (including a hilarious story of divining rods finding a waterpipe leak in her front garden!), ghosts, ley lines, and much more. Stumbling upon some of this material unprepared, one might be tempted to exclaim: 'Come back Tylor, all is forgiven!'

Vic could be an 'observing participant' on a pilgrimage to Lourdes because he happened also to be a worshipping Catholic, but Edie has expanded this concept to become the normative way to do fieldwork in all contexts. She has sought for phrases such as 'ultimate and real participation' to express that something more is meant than the old participant-observer model. The anthropology of experience means for

---

[147] Tom Arcaro, phone interview with Timothy Larsen, 16 August 2013.

her 'an anthropologist being fully inside the experience of the people she studies'.[148] Full fieldwork can only be done by believing along with the people one is studying: 'theoretical Marxists do not conduct *participatory* studies of magic'.[149] Along these same lines, Edie has emphasized believing what people tell you. Vic had given fuller emphasis to indigenous exegesis than ethnographers had usually done hitherto—to listening to and reporting how the participants themselves articulated what the various aspects of a ritual meant, for example—but Edie has taken this much further. Vic had warned: 'On the other hand, those anthropologists who regard only indigenous interpretations as relevant, are being equally one-sided'.[150] Edith Turner is inclined to allow her 'field people' to have veto power over interpretation. For example, she noticed structuralist binaries in Iñupiat rituals, but dutifully abandoned this line of analysis after she tried it out on her informants and they did not find it very interesting.[151] (Evans-Pritchard would have retorted that the ordinary speakers of a language would not usually be excited by a discussion of its underlying grammar, but such insights might nevertheless be valid and of interest to scholars.) Even Clifford Geertz, in a retort that nettled Edie, observed that identification must have its limits: 'We cannot live other people's lives, and it is a piece of bad faith to try'.[152] Edie's *modus operandi* is for anthropologists to accept what they are told in the field as true. For example, Marian apparitions are real because they have been reported: 'If the villagers said they saw a visionary mother, they did. If the critics themselves once experienced something *they* couldn't explain, they might be able to understand the event and not pick on the poor'.[153] Vic might have accepted that argument as it was in a Catholic context, but Edie has made it universal: if the residents of Calcutta tell you that the goddess Kali has worked miracles, then she has.[154] Edie has frequently referred to herself as a guinea pig and counseled ethnographers to be guinea pigs and this too gets at the notion of the observer crossing over to

[148] Turner, *Heart*, pp. 6, 135.

[149] Edith Turner, 'Theology and the Anthropological Study of Spirit Events in an Iñupiat Village', in Walter Randolph Adams and Frank A. Salamone (eds.), *Anthropology and Theology: Gods, Icons, and God-talk* (Lanham: University Press of America, 2000), p. 141.

[150] Turner, *Forest*, p. 36.   [151] Turner, *Hands Feel It*, p. 197.

[152] Clifford Geertz, 'Making Experiences, Authoring Selves', in Victor W. Turner and Edward M. Bruner, *The Anthropology of Experience* (Urbana: University of Illinois Press, 1986), p. 373; Turner, 'Reality of Spirits', p. 11.

[153] Turner, *Ancient*, ch. 4, p. 14.   [154] Turner, *Among the Healers*, p. 59.

become fully a participant: now the experiment is being done on one-self. Such a radical engagement means that one's beliefs and practices will be permanently transformed. As Edith Turner has profoundly remarked: 'We are not writing societies; this time they seem to be bent on writing us'.[155]

* * *

Edie's Catholic identity needs to be placed in the context of her life-long rebellion against authorities. Authorities *qua* authorities she rejects and despises: her writings are punctuated with attacks on, for example, the police—just to take a case that bears no obvious rela-tionship to any of her other beliefs. To defy the powers that be is, for her, both a duty and a pleasure. Medical doctors are also denounced on occasion—and this antipathy clearly does fit with her defence of traditional healing practices. All this goes to say that, for Edith Turner, Church authorities—priests, the Vatican, traditional theo-logians, dogmas, the hierarchy—are often better spited than fol-lowed. Hers is a consulting-the-faithful kind of Catholicism; a folk Catholicism. She is anti-clerical in principle. That this is a response at the level of policy is underlined by the fact that she seems to like most every priest she actually gets to know. There is not a single account of a bad priest in her entire oeuvre, but rather her writings are leavened with named priests who she admires—both as close to home as her own parish pastor and others she meets on pilgrim-age in foreign countries. Indeed, her autobiography is dedicated to a priest who has achieved the rank of monsignor in the hier-archy. A priest in Ireland so impressed her that she did the most un-Edie-like thing imaginable and dramatically made a confession of submission to him: 'I, Edie, of my own free will and because I need to, grant you, Father Riordan, authority, because you know how to do the Mass. You are my link with God. I need you'.[156] One of the interesting things about Edith Turner's view of Catholicism for this study as a whole is how antithetical her instincts are to those held by her friend Mary Douglas. 'Hierarchy' is always a pejorative term for Edie. Sometimes these two anthropologists even hit upon the exact

---

[155] Edith Turner, 'There Are No Peripheries to Humanity: Northern Alaska Nuclear Dumping and the Iñupiat's Search for Redress', *Anthropology and Humanism*, 22, 1 (1997), p. 108.

[156] Turner, *Ancient*, ch. 4, p. 12.

same cases and adjudicate them in opposing ways. While Douglas singles out Thoreau as an unpleasant creature, Turner lauds him as a heroic one; while Douglas decided that the tragedy of Sartre was that he lacked structure, the Turners thought it was that he did not experience anti-structure.[157]

Edie beyond Vic primarily parts ways with the official teaching of the Roman Catholic Church when it appears to conflict with her generous affirmation of religious pluralism: 'That's my old enemy exclusivism'.[158] Many times she has declared her belief in the numerous different spiritual traditions she has encountered: 'all these religions are real, every one of them'.[159] Thus, in the banal binary our primary sources will somehow never let us escape, Edie concedes: 'I don't consider myself a "good Catholic" and have all kinds of contrary views'.[160] What many people mean by such a binary, however, quickly exposes it as lacking much utility. Edie, for example, is a strong believer in the Church's convictions regarding miracles. In fact, her attacks against the hierarchy, the Vatican, and the priests are often directed against what she perceives to be their tendency to downplay the supernatural. Her most common indictment of Church leaders is for being too 'rationalistic'.[161] Turner was dismayed by changes at Knock that had taken place at the shrine between her pilgrimages such as the book of miracles no longer being on display, and she denounced them as 'a policy of rationalism' being imposed on the ordinary faithful by 'the church hierarchy'.[162] For Edie, siding with the people over the priests means believing unabashedly in grassroots Catholic tales of signs and wonders. She naturally affirms the supernatural elements at the heart of official Catholic teaching as well. Turner believes, for example, in 'the miracle' of transubstantiation.[163] Most of all, she has certitude in the bodily resurrection of Jesus Christ. She has frequently denounced those professional theologians who reduce the miracles of the Gospels to metaphors and the resurrection to a 'mythic tale'.[164] She has observed that the apostle Thomas was actually able to feel the physical wounds of the crucifixion on Christ's body: 'And people say

[157] Turner, *Communitas*, p. 110; Turner, *Dramas*, p. 54.
[158] Turner, *Experiencing Ritual*, pp. 121–22.
[159] Mentore, 'Interview', p. xiv.   [160] Mentore, 'Interview', p. xiv.
[161] Turner, 'Theology and the Anthropological Study', p. 139.
[162] Turner, *Heart*, pp. 113–14.
[163] Turner, *Experiencing Ritual*, p. 99; Turner, *Heart*, p. 225.
[164] Turner, 'Soul and Communication between Souls', p. 80.

this is a myth. How could it be?'[165] Hear the word of the Lord: do not doubt but believe (John 20:27).

Edith Turner has unfailingly self-identified as a Roman Catholic. While she believes in all religions, she *is* a Catholic. To take one of numerous such declarations: 'To lay my position on the table: first I am a Catholic and go to communion'.[166] Moreover, this is integral to her anthropology. Notably, she wrote an article in 2011 for the Catholic journal *New Hibernia Review* which was tellingly subtitled: 'Reflections of a Believing Anthropologist'.[167] Indeed, Edie is a kind of über-practising Catholic. She attends church faithfully and receives communion. More than that, she sings in the choir and has done so for over a quarter of a century now. While her anti-clerical, rebellious streak no doubt sometimes grates against the sacrament of confession, there are numerous accounts in her writings of her participating in this spiritual practice. Endearingly, on one occasion she confessed that she might be hurting the Church by criticizing it: 'the priest told me to tell the truth as I saw it'.[168] Most of all, she is such an active member of her congregation that she is also involved in small groups. These are named in a variety of ways by Edie, and presumably most of them are different ways of describing the same thing. Still, she thanks 'the church and its small groups' (plural) which suggests she is involved in more than one.[169] Other references are to 'my Cursillo prayer group' and 'my Catholic ladies' circle'.[170] She also went on a life-transforming Catholic retreat which she calls 'the Weekend', and a spiritual direction course led by Monsignor Chester Michael also had a deep impact on her. Turner is so committed to being a practising Catholic that she continues to seek out corporate worship even in the field. She did this on her return to Africa despite the fact that she was trying to recover the traditional practices of the people there before they had been disrupted by Christian missions. Moreover, she 'continued to go to Mass' even though the priest was from a Nazi family: 'I wondered if I was right to do that'.[171] Bidding farewell to binaries, Edie's own self-description is the best: 'I am a kind of Catholic'.[172]

* * *

[165] Engelke, 'Interview', p. 852.
[166] Turner, 'Psychology, Metaphor, or Actuality?', p. 2.
[167] Turner, 'Our Lady of Knock'.   [168] Turner, *Ancient*, ch. 3, p. 32.
[169] Turner, *Among the Healers*, p. xvii.
[170] Turner, *Ancient*, p. [i]; Edith Turner to Timothy Larsen, email, 17 September 2012.
[171] Turner, *Heart*, p. 152.
[172] Turner, 'Soul and Communication between Souls', p. 94.

More fundamentally, believing in all religions and in what informants tell one in widely different cultural and geographical locations seems to create a problem for intellectual integration. To take just one obvious question: what happens to someone when they die? Edith Turner seems to believe in their becoming afflicting spirits when she is with the Ndembu in Zambia, in their going to purgatory when she is with Catholics in Ireland, and in their becoming reincarnated when she is with the Iñupiat in Alaska. At times this seems to reflect no more than anthropology's tilt towards relativism: 'As for me, familiar with so many of the multitudinous forms of power, spirit, and ambiance, I know it is useless to try classifying and categorizing and clearing up the ambiguities in all these, because each is right in its own context'.[173] Yet Edie's anti-postmodern declaration that these phenomenon are empirically real will not allow matters to lie there. These claims are in some sense universally true—true even in contexts outside their own. Thus she seems to believe her traditional African doctor when he tells her that Ihamba can also work in other parts of the world such as the United States, tells a story about her colleague falling ill in London which is offered as confirmation of this truth, and went on to perform the ritual back in America and thereby free a woman named Marcia Perkins from a spirit that was afflicting her in the heart of Virginia.[174]

Edith Turner's main response to this challenge is to claim that the very desire for such integrative thinking is the result of unduly privileging logic. She can even pronounce somewhat breezily: 'The fact of their difference is to be celebrated, not deplored, and because religion is beyond logical articulation their differences present no problem on the score of logic'.[175] Victor Turner also emphasized that some realities are beyond logic. Nevertheless, following Evans-Pritchard, he would observe that the Ndembu were highly rational: 'In all this, he is as logical as Linnaeus himself... The diviner, as I have said, behaves in an astute and rational way, given his axiomatic beliefs in spirits, mystical forces, and witches'.[176] Moreover, Vic was careful to put a limit on what

---

[173] Turner, *Heart*, p. 259. For a meditation on the perils of trying to classify Edie herself, see Matthew Engelke, 'Books Can Be Deceiving: Edith Turner and the Problem of Categories in Anthropology', *Anthropology and Humanism*, 26 (2001), pp. 124–33.

[174] Edith Turner, 'Taking Seriously the Nature of Religious Healing in America', in Linda L. Barnes and Susan S. Sered (eds.), *Religion and Healing in America* (New York: Oxford University Press, 2005), p. 399.

[175] Turner, 'Psychology, Metaphor, or Actuality?', p. 2.

[176] Turner, *Revelation*, pp. 218, 229.

was being implied by using phrases such as 'nonrational (though not *ir*rational)' or 'saving truths that transcend but do not deny rationality'.[177] Edie has been much more willing simply to set logic aside as too limiting. She is a champion of experience over coherence; she is for an anthropology that is not only 'nonlogical' but also 'nonunitary'.[178] She believes that defining, classifying, and systematizing prompt realities and truths to melt away under our burning gaze of analysis. Edie refuses to submit to the 'direct cause and effect model created by Western logic'.[179] Indeed, she has even gone so far as openly to defy the 'law of noncontradiction'—which she also views as a Western imposition.[180] (In keeping with her lifelong rebelliousness, any 'law' is *ipso facto* just one more authority to be resisted.) Indeed, it is striking how often Edie frames an argument with which she disagrees, not as an idea to be refuted, but rather as an authority to be defied. If she disagrees with a theorist, she can tend to think of this not in terms of an exchange of contrasting views but rather as if their very formulation of their ideas is somehow an illegitimate and outrageous demand for submission: 'Was Durkheim some kind of fascist?'[181] Occasionally, Edie has made a direct attempt to confront the issue being posed here:

> And I continue with the thorny question: 'What of the great diversity of ideas about them [spirits] throughout the world? How is a student of the anthropology of consciousness who participates during fieldwork expected to regard all the conflicting spirit systems in different cultures? Is there not a fatal lack of logic inherent in this diversity?' And the reply: 'Is this kind of subject matter logical anyway?' We also need to ask, 'Have we the right to force it into logical frameworks?'[182]

The second question, by evoking the issue of having 'the right', once again reframes a question of individual intellectual coherence so as to make it about the presumptuous imposition of power. The first question comes very close to advising one to try not to think about it. Edith Turner is certainly right to remind people not to assume that Western standards of rationality are the only valid ones. She is also right to challenge us not to allow a procrustean logic to cut reality down to fit a tidy scheme. She has been a valiant advocate for the realm of the

---

[177] Turner, *Dramas*, p. 47; Turner, *Blazing*, p. 70.
[178] Edith Turner, 'Editorial', *Anthropology and Humanism*, 18, 1 (1993), p. 2.
[179] Mentore, 'Interview', p. xi.   [180] Turner, *Experiencing Ritual*, p. 93.
[181] Turner, 'Advances in the Study of Spirit Experience', p. 39.
[182] Turner, 'Reality of Spirits', p. 11.

spirit. Nevertheless, if human beings are incurably spiritual they are also incurably rational, and this inherent and enduring part of what it means to be human cannot just be pushed away as unwelcome or inconvenient either: one longs for an anthropology in which *homo spiritualis* and *homo rationalis* are both given their full due.

Most of the time, however, Edie elides such philosophical questions by taking on the role of the storyteller. This is befitting her lifelong literary interests. Such a mode of discourse has been a leading one in her writings. In *The Spirit and the Drum*, Turner warns in the preface that she is doing 'something different' from how anthropologists usually write their books: 'This means writing a narrative, a story'.[183] Likewise the introduction of *Communitas* alerts the reader: 'Communitas can only be conveyed properly through stories'.[184] Her ethnographies from Alaska and Ireland have been overwhelmingly in the form of narrative. *Among the Healers* is perhaps most thoroughly in this genre, and thus it is aptly subtitled, 'Stories of Spiritual and Ritual Healing around the World'. *Heart of Lightness* is, of course, her own story. Tellingly, several sections of it are lifted from her academic writings: for Edie, ethnography and autobiography are often one and the same. Moreover, given the theme of this study, it is worth emphasizing that although her memoir is subtitled 'The Life Story of an Anthropologist', it is actually a spiritual autobiography, 'the story of a spiritual journey',[185] and thus rather than shelve it in one's personal library with other scholars' accounts of their careers one could just as appropriately place it alongside works such as Augustine's *Confessions*, Bunyan's *Grace Abounding to the Chief of Sinners*, and Merton's *The Seven Storey Mountain*.

Edith Turner commends narrative over and over again as a form of truth-telling that does not kill off realities by dissecting them, nor does it reduce them to logic or a unified worldview: 'The reader may still be trying to make a single philosophical system out of these stories. But the stories are too down-to-earth to be transmuted into something abstract. They are too particular'.[186] While the Roman Catholic Church has traditionally championed a unified philosophical system, Edie's emphasis on story is nevertheless drawing upon a theme at the heart of the Christian faith. She was thrilled when Father Zee, an Irish priest, told her: 'Jesus did it all with story. There is no theory anywhere

---

[183] Turner, *Spirit and the Drum*, p. ix.　　[184] Turner, *Communitas*, p. 1.
[185] Turner, *Heart*, p. 1.　　[186] Turner, *Among the Healers*, p. 165.

in the gospels'.[187] Christians bear witness; they tell testimonies. Turner has described her work as simply pointing things out: 'I say "Look!" '[188] She is John the Baptist, crying out: 'Behold!' Likewise the First Epistle of John promises that what is being proclaimed is: 'That which was from the beginning which we have heard, which we have seen with our eyes, which we have looked upon, and our hands have handled' (1 John 1:1). So Edie tells her spiritual testimonies of what she has seen with her own eyes; what her hands have felt.

When Edith Turner does offer speculations in the direction of a more systematic way of thinking, these often indicate that the category of shamanism has become a unifying one for her. Christians from the early church to the present are relabelled in this way. St Patrick was a shaman. Blake was a shaman. Edie implies that Vic himself had shamanistic traits.[189] Even St Paul was a shaman, as is Monsignor Chester Michael.[190] As 'animism' became the generic category for Tylor, so shamanism serves this function for Edith Turner; and just as Tylor tended to see even Catholicism as just 'Christian animism', so Turner often thinks of expressions of Christianity as really 'Christian shamanism'. Moreover, just as Tylor thought he had discovered the origin of religion, so does Turner. She has come to view working with spirits as 'at the origin of ritual and religion' or as 'the primal root of religion'.[191] And again: 'It is very likely that all the religions are based on something shamanic. Shamanism has to do with direct encounters with spirits'.[192] It is the 'ur-theology'; 'an underlying universal'.[193]

The effect of this emphasis is that—in her writings at least—God has become more like *Nzambi*, the high god of the Ndembu, 'a distant creator figure, rarely in touch with humanity'.[194] In fact, bringing her perilously close to violating her own principles of deferring to native exegesis and not being reductionistic, Edie is repeatedly tempted to downplay or reinterpret the place of God in a narrative. In her work in Alaska, for example, when informants tell her that they

---

[187] Turner, *Ancient*, ch. 5, p. 4.   [188] Turner, *Communitas*, p. 222.

[189] Turner, *Heart*, p. 186.

[190] Turner, *Among the Healers*, pp. 126, 128; Turner, *Heart*, p. 236.

[191] Turner, 'Anthropology of Experience', pp. 193, 195.

[192] Turner, *Heart*, pp. 142–43.

[193] Turner, 'Theology and the Anthropological Study', p. 147; Turner, *Among the Healers*, p. xxi.

[194] Edith Turner, 'Philip Kabwita, Ghost Doctor: The Ndembu in 1985', *TDR: The Drama Review*, 30, 4 (Winter 1986), p. 17.

heal by the power of God she translates this as by 'some spiritual force beyond the human', and when they credit Jesus she explains that he is really (whether they think of it in these terms or not) their 'spirit healer', the equivalent of an assisting ancestor spirit.[195] When Iñupiat Christians held a prayer meeting in an Episcopal church and their petition was answered, Edie did not feel bound by her informants' desire to give glory to God: 'My own interpretation...was that this was the old and excellent shamanism'.[196] Likewise, when she wrote reports on the methods of alternative healers who came to her home, Turner faithfully acknowledges that prayer is a component, but it is not apparently a feature that interests her as she does not even bother to record to whom they addressed their prayer or what they said in it.[197] Charismatic Catholics, Edie informs readers (again, in contrast to their own exegesis), are practising 'the good old magic'.[198] She even wonders if Our Lady of Lourdes was 'a very important nature spirit, whose message has not yet been understood'.[199] At times, Turner can sound almost patronizing: 'If people want to call it God they can'.[200] Or again: 'It is God to Monsignor Chester Michael'.[201] Such distancing language suggests that her own primary category is different. *Among the Healers* gives credit as follows: 'Finally, I owe the existence of the book to the great-spirit-energy-power-communitas of the universe. Thank you'.[202] *Nzambi*, is that you? Such instincts certainly tie into Edie's tendency towards pantheism: 'that God *is* the works of his creation'.[203] Turner's current book project is provisionally entitled, 'Nature's Gift of Spirituality'.[204] Edie would no doubt not want this line of argument to proceed any further, however, for it is in danger of making her sound like she is denying something, and she is, above all, an affirmer not a denier; an includer not an excluder; an adder not a subtractor.

* * *

[195] Turner, 'Psychology, Metaphor, or Actuality?', pp. 4–5.

[196] Turner, 'There Are No Peripheries', p. 107.

[197] See, for example, Turner, 'Taking Seriously the Nature of Religious Healing in America', p. 397.

[198] Turner, *Among the Healers*, p. 70.

[199] Turner, Preface, in Turner and Turner, *Image* (2011), p. xviii.

[200] Turner, *Ancient*, conclusion, p. 4.

[201] Turner, 'Soul and Communication between Souls', p. 93.

[202] Turner, *Among the Healers*, p. xviii.   [203] Turner, *Ancient*, ch. 3. p. 6.

[204] Edith Turner to Timothy Larsen, email, 17 September 2012.

Thus Edith Turner is the undoing of Edward Tylor; the inverse of Tylor; in Tylorian categories, a revival of a survival. Tylor's dismissal of religion was built up by exposing as part of its fallacious origins the absurd misconception held by 'savages' that even objects have souls. Edie's response, however, is not to deny that this is the view of 'primitive' peoples, nor to challenge the assumption that such beliefs being held in traditional contexts somehow undermines the credibility of a world religion such as Christianity, but rather to commend it as a profound insight.[205] Likewise, Evans-Pritchard expended much energy opposing Lévy-Bruhl's assertion that the thinking of primitive peoples was 'prelogical'. Vic followed this lead, affirming of the Ndembu that 'far from being "prelogical," they are obsessively logical'.[206] Edie, however, hears in this term freedom rather than a slur, and happily acknowledges her debt to Lévy-Bruhl and her agreement with the designation prelogical.[207] The project of both Tylor and Frazer was to show the pagan beneath the Christian and, curiously, the Turners often did the exact same thing. They even used Mexico, the same location where it all began for Tylor: for the Turners as well, Aztec goddess worship provided the glowing embers that fired the cult of Our Lady of Guadalupe.[208] While for Tylor this pagan origin served to discredit Christianity, for Edie it serves to authenticate it—to demonstrate that it is part of the great, enveloping and enduring shamanistic reality which gives life to all genuine spirituality. Curiously, Tylor and the Turners also both homed in on the same remote and obscure place, St Patrick's Purgatory, to uncover what religion is really about (although the Turners rejected as Protestant propaganda Tylor's assumption that people believed it provided a literal access to a physical purgatory).[209] Vic had explained 'that Ndembu religion must be characterized as animistic or monistic rather than theistic'.[210] Edie has no quarrel with this assessment; her only addition to it was that she had come to learn that Ndembu religion is also real and true. Admittedly, she was unable to comprehend this insight when she was first among them in the mid-twentieth century: 'How could I know then that the Africans were right? These were pagans, animists. In 1953 no one in

---

[205] See, for example, Turner, 'Theology and the Anthropological Study', p. 150; Turner, *Heart*, p. 128.

[206] Turner, *Forest*, p. 300.   [207] Turner, *Hands*, p. xxiv.

[208] Turner, *Dramas*, p. 152–53.

[209] Turner and Turner, *Image* (1978), p. 126.   [210] Turner, *Drums*, p. 14.

the West believed in African animism, no one'.[211] Tylor was surprised enough that modern Britons and Americans could believe in spiritualism; he would no doubt have been flabbergasted to learn that a respected anthropologist in the twenty-first century would confess her faith in African animism. And pointing out that she is also a practising Catholic who affirms the supernatural claims of the Church and revels in the miraculous stories of the faithful would not have been the way to reassure him either.

[211] Turner, *Heart*, p. 78.

Afterword: The Ever-Recurring Drama

In the thick of researching this book, I had a stunning revelation. To be more specific, it was while I was reading my way through the works of Mary Douglas. In a gestalt moment, I suddenly realized that the book I was writing was structured as a ring composition. I was particularly bemused by this discovery because I had only known what a ring composition was for just a few weeks, while the outline of this book had been proposed and approved years earlier. Yet there it was. The spirit of Dame Mary Douglas the seer came upon me and I saw an elegant pattern crystallize before my very eyes.

In a ring composition, the meaning of a book is not announced at the beginning, nor arrived at when one reaches the end. Rather, it is found at the centre. In the case of this study, the one on E. E. Evans-Pritchard is the central chapter. Evans-Pritchard—his life, work, and thought—is at the heart of the argument of this book as well. He is the turning point. E-P is the scholar who so resolutely rejected the anthropological critiques of Christianity held by Tylor and Frazer; he is the Oxford don who became a sign of hope that one could be both a Christian and a pre-eminent anthropologist. Douglas and the Turners would read this sign and draw comfort and strength from it, as would others such as Godfrey Lienhardt and David Brokensha. Evans-Pritchard was totally confident that the anti-religious views of leading theorists could be demonstrated to be wrongheaded, even risibly unscientific and erroneous; yet, on the other hand, he was remarkably circumspect about the possibility of proving Christian beliefs to the satisfaction of sceptics. This careful balancing act often makes those chronologically on either side of him seem like they overplayed their hands a bit, whether it is E. B. Tylor too glibly dismissing the realm of the spirit, or Edith Turner too breezily asserting that it can be established empirically. Find a centre more to your own liking if you wish, but one could do worse than E-P's unabashed, yet not brash faith.

As Douglas demonstrated with the book of Numbers, in a ring composition the surrounding material on each side of the centre is arranged in parallel rungs. So my other chapters align with one another, with the outer ones and inner ones matching. Tylor corresponds to the Turners, as was shown at the end of the last chapter. E. B. Tylor was the Christian who lost his faith through studying anthropology; the Turners were the agnostics who found their Christian faith through studying anthropology. The Frazer chapter likewise corresponds to the chapter on Douglas. Both Sir James Frazer and Dame Mary Douglas advanced theses through a bold use of the comparative method. Both wrote in a lively manner that allowed their works to reach a wider audience. Frazer, however, sought to use general anthropological theories to undermine the case for Christianity, while Douglas advanced broader anthropological categories in order to make the claims of the Church more compelling. Frazer, Douglas. Tick, tock. We see him straining to find a malevolent subtext even for what one encounters as apparently wholesome and innocent, and her grasping for a benign interpretation even for what initially strikes one as rather sinister or unpleasant.

A ring is also a fitting metaphor as it helps to counteract a tendency to think in terms of a linear progression—one of the habits of Tylor and Frazer that later generations sought to unlearn. Maybe I have fallen under Douglas's spell here as well and have also come to assume that there is nothing new under the sun. Of course, this book can be read as a linear progression. There is mischievous value, if nothing else, in upending tired assumptions in this way. The complacent, secularist myth of linear progression is neatly encapsulated in Jean La Fontaine's dictum: 'Once you stop religious thought, you start thinking anthropologically'.[1] Therefore, it can be bracing for those who think of the study of anthropology as a victory march away from religious errors and towards secular truths to confront the possibility that the history of their discipline can be read plausibly in the exact opposite manner.

[1] Sheila Hale, 'Closely Observed Brains', *Harper's Bazaar and Queen*, January 1977, p. 71.

In this alternative to the stereotypical account some anthropologists tell themselves, the story of their discipline is actually a progression away from rationalistic errors and toward veritable faith. Anthropologists have an unusually strong tendency to kill their fathers. What emerges therefore in this somewhat playful revisionist tale is a scene in which the old, unbelieving, rationalistic fathers are defied by their faithful sons and daughters. *There is no God but Society*, came the new creed for the determinedly modern twentieth century. Yet in the second half of that century and into the new millennium one continues to hear leading anthropologists confessing in a clear voice of quiet conviction: *I believe in God, the Father Almighty, creator of heaven and earth. And in Jesus Christ, His only Son, our Lord, who was conceived by the Holy Spirit, born of the Virgin Mary, suffered under Pontius Pilate, was crucified, died, and was buried. He descended to hell. On the third day he rose again from the dead.*

J. G. Frazer, in an effort to deflate the story of this Jesus who suffered under Pontius Pilate, placed it in the context of 'the ever-recurring drama of the divine resurrection and death'.[2] Frazer's covert and contorting animus is on display in the strange construction of this phrase: as everyone knows, death comes first, then the resurrection. The slain God will not remain entombed. To the extent that history can guide us, anthropologists are certainly apt to be wrong whenever they start to imagine that the findings of their discipline are incompatible with belief in the existence of God, and even specifically with orthodox Christian doctrine. This study offers abundant evidence that some eminent anthropologists who have been most respected for their ethnography and their theory have been able to combine their professional knowledge and insights with a robust Christian identity and set of theological convictions. One would have to throw the lessons of history to the wind to assume that it will be any different in the decades ahead. As Victor Turner put it:

> We are born into the faith of our fathers, we distance ourselves from it, and then, in a movement of return, we re-enter it in sophisticated naiveté, civilized earnestness. Religion, like Watergate, is a scandal that will not go away. We have to live it through; it cannot be dispelled by a magical incantation or reduced to a non-sense by positivist or linguistic philosophy...[3]

[2] J. G. Frazer, *The Golden Bough: A Study in Magic and Religion*, 2nd ed., 3 vols (London: Macmillan and Co., 1900), III, p. 197.

[3] Victor Turner, *Revelation and Divination in Ndembu Ritual* (Ithaca: Cornell University Press, 1975), p. 32.

One hears in that quotation echoes of Paul Ricoeur's 'second naiveté'. As Frazer himself observed: 'The killing of the god, that is, of his human incarnation, is therefore merely a necessary step to his revival or resurrection in a better form'.[4]

Still, it would be no less ridiculous to over-learn such a lesson and imagine some kind of linear trajectory in which the discipline of anthropology is becoming ever more dominated by people of faith. If history still be our guide for future expectations, then anthropology will always also be an area of study that attracts religious sceptics and that rattles some erstwhile believers into a crisis of faith. While I was doing research for this book at All Souls College, Oxford, I discussed my project with another Visiting Fellow. She became immediately animated by my theme and announced excitedly that her own father had been a missionary who had lost his faith and shifted from a theological to an anthropological way of thinking.[5] Such lives will presumably always be with us. Thus anthropology—befitting its very nature, which lends itself to asking the most basic questions about the contours and meaning of human experience—will always be a site of both deconversions and conversions, gain and loss, doubt and faith. Any narrative which latches on to only one half of this equation is likely to be disproven by events as they continue to unfold.

Thus, the metaphor of the ring: rather than a linear progression we have recurring concerns. One is struck by all the issues that will not go away. Even what looks like it has been discredited sometimes finds a way to crop up in a new form. In his Gifford lectures, Tylor worked industriously to destroy the category of natural revelation, yet the best part of a century later Victor Turner still found it serviceable. Indeed, the Gifford lectures are themselves a common cord, as Tylor, Frazer, and Douglas all gave them. (And how one would like to read what Evans-Pritchard and the Turners would have said if chosen for this prestigious task!) Tylor and Frazer's focus on the origins of religion was seemingly quashed forever by functionalism, yet Edith Turner could not resist reintroducing speculations in this regard in the twenty-first century. Likewise, although Evans-Pritchard represents a retreat from the comparative method practised so flamboyantly by

---

[4] Frazer, *Golden Bough*, II, p. 65.

[5] He has published an account of this journey: Elmer S. Miller, *Nurturing Doubt: From Mennonite Missionary to Anthropologist in the Argentine Chaco* (Urbana: University of Illinois Press, 1995).

Frazer, Douglas found her way back to it. Closer to this volume's primary theme of religious belief and practice, the same issues appear over and over again as the decades roll by. These include: whether or not spirits are real, and whether or not this question has been begged or can be sidestepped; the relationship between magic and religion; the credibility of miracles; the relationship between Christianity and pagan or folk religious practices and beliefs; and the question of whether or not an account has been marred by reductionism.

All the anthropologists in this study wanted to have some wider anthropological category which would shed light on the specific case of Christianity. For Tylor, it was animism; for Frazer, it was human sacrifice; for Evans-Pritchard, it was mysticism; for Douglas, it was hierarchy; for the Turners, it was *communitas*. Moreover, the work of all these scholars, even when it is thought of as largely refuted, lives on in the discipline. Tylor's category of animism, for example, is still widely employed, as is Frazer's distinction between sympathetic and contagious magic. The murdered fathers are never really done away with but continue to haunt us as afflicting and aiding ancestor spirits.

Perhaps one of the more counterintuitive findings of this study is how much theology not only has been but continues to be a conversation partner for anthropology. If asked to hazard a guess, one could assume that the influence of the discipline of theology had steadily diminished as the study of anthropology matured, and would have well nigh disappeared some decades ago. Yet, if anything, the later anthropologists in this volume cite theologians more frequently and evoke doctrinal formulas and categories more freely than the earlier ones did. Douglas and the Turners were even apt to publish in theological journals. If one thinks of the leading scholars in the second half of the twentieth century from other disciplines—say psychology or economics, just to stay within the social sciences—and then were to ask, 'Who were their favourite theologians?', one would presumably be met with blank stares. Yet it is surprisingly easy to find an answer to this question for anthropologists such as Evans-Pritchard and Victor Turner simply by reading their academic monographs. It is a tribute to anthropology's continued willingness to ask life's great questions that it has not so narrowed its enquires as to exclude theological voices.

Most of all, the question of the truthfulness of the Christian faith was existentially alive to all these anthropologists (and others who we have met along the way such as William Robertson Smith,

Andrew Lang, Godfrey Lienhardt, and Edmund Leach). This, too, is a remarkable constant. This is not a story of this question having been answered decisively in one way or the other and thereafter receding into the background. Rather it is a story of the question of the credibility of the claims of Christianity being earnestly asked over and over again by some leading anthropologists in each new generation. Tylor cared deeply about what implications a knowledge of African animism might have for the plausibility of Catholic doctrine, and Edith Turner, at the time this is being written, is still resolutely wrestling with that same question.

And, strangest of all, anthropologists have never stopped being drawn to the slain God. Frazer, of course, made this motif the central theme of *The Golden Bough*, but anthropologists have thought of him largely as an embarrassment since his death. Yet the concept of the slain God was not packed away for good when the old Edwardian armchair was put in permanent storage. Christian interpretation has traditionally seen the blood sacrifice of the ancient Hebrews as finding its fulfilment in the atoning death of Jesus of Nazareth, and Evans-Pritchard presented Nuer religion as akin to Old Testament faith; as a sacrificial religion which was spiritually profound in a way reminiscent of the divine revelation that comes to Christians through the Hebrew prophets, priests, and teachers of the law. While among the Lele, Douglas found the pangolin as explicated by its cult to be 'uncannily...like Christ'.[6] It, too, depicts a voluntary victim that makes atonement for the people. Victor Turner's detailed comparison of *Chihamba* with the empty tomb narratives of the Gospels brought this preoccupation even closer to the level of sustained attention that it had during Frazer's day. Edith Turner has continued this trajectory by, for example, observing parallels between Christological teaching and Iñupiat beliefs about how the whale allows itself to be pierced and killed for the life of the people.[7] I suspect that the best way to explain this preoccupation is not to assume that the ethnographic evidence is so emphatic on this point that anthropologists are unable to ignore it. More likely, it is a tribute to the way that Christian thought continues to invite and repel anthropologists, to intrigue and to haunt them, even in the second half of the twentieth century and into the new millennium. Reflecting the post-colonial turn towards reflexivity, Edith Turner has

---

[6] Mary Douglas, *Purity and Danger: An Analysis of Concepts of Pollution and Taboo* (New York: Frederick A. Praeger, 1966), p. 169.

[7] Edith Turner, *Heart of Lightness: The Life Story of an Anthropologist* (Oxford: Berghahn, 2005), pp. 191–92.

observed: 'We are not writing societies; this time they seem to be bent on writing us'.[8] The salient point is thus no longer merely that so-called 'primitive' peoples are drawn to the theme of the slain God. What is no less telling is that anthropologists themselves, generation after generation, continue to be caught up in the ever-recurring drama of the divine death and resurrection.

---

[8] Edith Turner, 'There Are No Peripheries to Humanity: Northern Alaska Nuclear Dumping and the Iñupiat's Search for Redress', *Anthropology and Humanism*, 22, 1 (1997), p. 108.

Works Cited

Personal Communication

Personal interviews and/or written communication with the following: Tom Arcaro, Wendy Doniger, Philip Douglas, Ambrose Evans-Pritchard, Janet Farnsworth, Fergus Kerr, Timothy Radcliffe, Bruce Ross-Smith, André Singer, and Edith Turner

Manuscripts

Association of Social Anthropologists, London School of Economics Library, London

The College of Wooster Special Collections, The College of Wooster, Wooster, Ohio

Cora Blanche Soule Papers, Presbyterian Historical Archives, Philadelphia

Evans-Pritchard Papers, Tylor Library, Institute of Social and Cultural Anthropology, University of Oxford

Frazer Papers, Trinity College, Cambridge

Gifford Lectures 1989–1990: Series A, Mary Douglas, National Library of Scotland, Edinburgh

Greenslade Special Collections and Archives, Kenyon College, Gambier, Ohio

Mary Douglas Papers, Northwestern University, Evanston, Illinois

Nuer Field Notes Collection, Indiana University Library Digital Program

Devonshire House Monthly Meeting records, Friends House Library, London

Digest of Marriages of the Society of Friends, Friends House Library, London

Tablet Publishing Company Records, Burns Library, Boston College

Tylor Papers, Manuscript Collections, Pitt Rivers Museum, Oxford

Tylor Papers, Natural History Museum, London

Victor Turner Papers, Private Collection of Edith Turner

Published Sources

Ackerman, Robert, *J. G. Frazer: His Life and Work*, Cambridge: Cambridge University Press, 1987.

Ackerman, Robert, *The Myth and Ritual School: J. G. Frazer and the Cambridge Ritualists*, New York: Garland Publishing, 1991.

Ackerman, Robert, *Selected Letters of Sir J. G. Frazer*, Oxford: Oxford University Press, 2005.

Adler, Jeremy and Richard Fardon (eds.), *Taboo, Truth and Religion: Franz Baermann Steiner Selected Writings Volume 1*, Oxford: Berghahn Books, 1999.

The Annual Monitor for 1866, London: A. W. Bennett, 1865.

Alexander, Bobby C., *Victor Turner Revisited: Ritual as Social Change* (American Academy of Religion Series), Atlanta: Scholars Press, 1991.

Al-Shahi, Ahmed, 'Evans-Pritchard, Anthropology and Catholicism at Oxford: Godfrey Lienhardt's view', *Journal of the Anthropological Society of Oxford*, 30, 1 (1999) 67–72.

Barnes, J. A., 'Edward Evan Evans-Pritchard', *Proceedings of the British Academy*, 73 (1987) 447–90.

Barth, Fredrick, 'Britain and the Commonwealth', in Fredrick Barth (ed.), *One Discipline, Four Ways: British, German, French, And American Anthropology*, Chicago: University of Chicago Press, 2005, 3–57.

Beard, Mary, 'Frazer, Leach, and Virgil: The Popularity (and Unpopularity) of *The Golden Bough*', *Comparative Studies in Society and History*, 34, 2, April (1992): 203–24.

Beattie, J. H. M. and R. G. Lienhardt (eds.), *Studies in Social Anthropology: Essays in Memory of E. E. Evans-Pritchard by his former Oxford colleagues*, Oxford: Clarendon Press, 1975.

Beidelman, T. O., *A Bibliography of the Writings of E. E. Evans-Pritchard*, London: Tavistock, 1974.

Beidelman, T. O., 'E. E. Evans-Pritchard', in Christopher Winters (ed.), *International Dictionary of Anthropologists*, New York: Garland, 1991, 185–87.

Beidelman, T. O., 'Sir Edward Evan Evans-Pritchard (1902–1973): An Appreciation', *Anthropos*, 69 (1974) 553–67.

Bourdillon, M. F. C. and Meyer Fortes (eds.), *Sacrifice*, London: Academic Press for the Royal Anthropological Institute of Great Britain and Ireland, 1980.

Bradshaw, Paul and John Melloh (eds.), *Foundations in Ritual Studies: A reader for students of Christian Worship*, Grand Rapids: Baker Academic, 2007.

Brash, Bradsley W. and Charles J. Wright (eds.), *Didsbury College Centenary, 1842–1942*, London: Epworth Press, 1942.

Brokensha, David, *Brokie's Way: An Anthropologist's Story*, Cape Town: Amani Press, 2007.

Brown, Alison, Jeremy Coote, and Chris Gosden, 'Tylor's Tongue: Material Culture, Evidence, and Social Networks', *Journal of the Anthropological Society of Oxford*, 31, 3 (2000) 257–76.

Burton, John W., *An Introduction to Evans-Pritchard*, Studia Instituti Anthropos 45, Freibourg: Freibourg University Press, 1992.

Campion, Sarah, 'Autumn of an Anthropologist', *New Statesman*, 13 January 1951, 34–36.

A Catechism of Christian Doctrine, as Approved by the Archbishops and Bishops of England and Wales, and directed by them to be used in all their dioceses, Ditchling, Sussex: St. Dominic's Press, 1931.

Chesterton, G. K., *The Wisdom of Father Brown,* London: Cassell and Company, 1914.

Couchoud, Paul Louis, *The Enigma of Jesus,* Winifred Whale (trans.), London: Watts & Co., 1924.

Cunnison, Ian and Wendy James (eds.), *Essays in Sudan Ethnography presented to Sir Edward Evans-Pritchard,* London: C. Hurst & Company, 1972.

'Dame Mary Douglas', *Telegraph,* 22 May 2007 [www.telegraph.co.uk].

Darwin, Charles, *The Descent of Man,* London: John Murray, 1901.

Davis, John, 'Edward Evan Evans-Pritchard: A Great Englishman Nonetheless', in William Roger Louis (ed.), *Penultimate Adventures with Britannia,* London: I.B. Tauris, 2008, 169–84.

'Death of Lady Tylor', *Wellington Weekly News,* 1 June 1921, 8.

Douglas, Mary and Aaron Wildavsky, *Risk and Culture: An Essay on the Selection of Technological and Environmental Dangers,* Berkeley: University of California Press, 1982.

Douglas, Mary and Baron Isherwood, *The World of Goods,* New York: Basic Books, 1979.

Douglas, Mary, 'Being Fair to Hierarchists', *University of Pennsylvania Law Review,* 151, 4 April (2003) 1349–70.

Douglas, Mary, 'Can a scientist be objective about her faith?', interviewed by Deborah Jones, *Priests & People,* October (1999) 383–85.

Douglas, Mary, 'The cloud god and the shadow self', *Social Anthropology,* 3, 2 (1995) 83–94.

Douglas, Mary, 'The Contempt of Ritual', Part 1, *New Blackfriars,* 49, June (1968) 475–82.

Douglas, Mary, 'The Contempt of Ritual' Part 2, *New Blackfriars,* 49, July (1968) 528–35.

Douglas, Mary, 'Critique and Commentary', in Jacob Neusner (ed.), *The Idea of Purity in Ancient Judaism,* Leiden: E. J. Brill, 1973, 137–42.

Douglas, Mary, *Cultural Bias,* Royal Anthropological Institute Paper 34, London: Royal Anthropological Institute of Great Britain and Ireland, 1978.

Douglas, Mary, *Cultures and Crises: Understanding Risk and Resolution,* London: Sage, 2013.

Douglas, Mary, 'Demonology in William Robertson Smith's Theory of Religious Belief', in William Johnstone (ed.), *William Robertson Smith: Essays in Reassessment, Journal for the Study of the Old Testament* Supplement Series 189, Sheffield: Sheffield Academic Press, 1995, 274–92.

Douglas, Mary, 'The Devil Vanishes', *Tablet,* 28 April 1990, 513–14.

Douglas, Mary (ed.), *Perspectives on Drink from Anthropology*, Cambridge: Cambridge University Press, 1991.

Douglas, Mary, *Witchcraft, Confessions and Accusations*, London: Tavistock Publications, 1970.

Douglas, Mary, 'The Effects of Modernization on Religious Change', in Mary Douglas and Steven Tipton (eds.), *Religion and America: Spiritual Life in a Secular Age*, Boston: Beacon Press, 1983, 25–43.

Douglas, Mary, *Evans-Pritchard*, Brighton: Harvester Press, 1980.

Douglas, Mary, 'Evans-Pritchard' (letter to the editor), *New Society*, 24 July 1980, 187.

Douglas, Mary, 'A Feeling for Hierarchy', in James L. Heft SM (ed.), *Believing Scholars: Ten Catholic Intellectuals*, New York: Fordham University Press, 2005, 94–120.

Douglas, Mary, 'Full turn of the secular wheel' (review of Peter L. Berger, *A Rumour of Angels*), *New Society*, 15 April 1970, 610.

Douglas, Mary, 'The Gender of the Beloved', *Heythrop Journal*, 36 (1995) 397–408.

Douglas, Mary, 'The Glorious Book of Numbers', *Jewish Studies Quarterly*, 1, 3 (1994) 193–216.

Douglas, Mary, *How Institutions Think*, Syracuse: Syracuse University Press, 1986.

Douglas, Mary, *Implicit Meanings: Essays in Anthropology*, London: Routledge & Kegan Paul, 1975.

Douglas, Mary, *Implicit Meanings: Essays in Anthropology*, new ed., London: Routledge, 1999.

Douglas, Mary, *In the Wilderness: The Doctrine of Defilement in the Book of Numbers*, Journal for the Study of the Old Testament Supplement Series 158, Sheffield: Sheffield Academic Press, 1993.

Douglas, Mary, 'Introduction' (Review Colloquium on *In the Wilderness*), *Religion*, 26 (1996) 69–71.

Douglas, Mary, *Jacob's Tears: The Priestly Work of Reconciliation*, Oxford: Oxford University Press, 2004.

Douglas, Mary, 'The Lele of the Congo', in Adrian Hastings (ed.), *The Church and the Nations: A study of minority Catholicism in England, India, Norway, America, Lebanon, Australia, Wales, Japan, the Netherlands, Vietnam, Brazil, Egypt, Southern Africa and among the Lele of the Congo*, London: Sheed and Ward, 1959, 73–89.

Douglas, Mary, *The Lele of the Kasai*, London: Oxford University Press for the International African Institute, 1963.

Douglas, Mary, *Leviticus as Literature*, Oxford: Oxford University Press, 1999.

Douglas, Mary, 'Mary Douglas interviewed by Alan Macfarlane' (26 February 2006), Cambridge University Video & Audio Collections, Quick Time Video, 88:08. [www.sms.cam.ac.uk/media/1115926].

Douglas, Mary, 'The Meaning of Myth: with special reference to "La Geste d'Asdiwal"', in Edmund Leach (ed.), *The Structural Study of Myth and Totemism*, London: Tavistock Publications, 1967, 49–69.

Douglas, Mary, 'The Myth of Primitive Religion', *Commonweal*, 9 October 1970, 41–44.

Douglas, Mary, *Natural Symbols: Explorations in Cosmology*, New York: Pantheon Books, 1970.

Douglas, Mary, *Natural Symbols: Explorations in Cosmology*, new ed., London: Routledge, 1996.

Douglas, Mary, 'Obituary: Godfrey Lienhardt', *Anthropology Today*, 10, 1 February (1994) 15–17.

Douglas, Mary, 'Obituary: Victor Turner', *RAIN*, 61 (1984) 11.

Douglas, Mary, *Purity and Danger: An Analysis of Concepts of Pollution and Taboo*, New York: Frederick A. Praegar, 1966.

Douglas, Mary, *Purity and Danger: An Analysis of Concepts of Pollution and Taboo*, new edition, London: Routledge Classics, 2002.

Douglas, Mary, Review of Victor W. Turner and Edward M. Bruner (eds.), *The Anthropology of Experience, American Anthropologist*, new series 92, 1 March (1990) 252–54.

Douglas, Mary, Review of William Watson, *Tribal Cohesion in a Money Economy, Man*, 59 (1959) 168.

Douglas, Mary, *Risk and Blame: Essays in Cultural Theory*, London: Routledge, 1992.

Douglas, Mary, 'Sacraments and Society: An Anthropologist Asks, What Women Could be Doing in the Church', *New Blackfriars*, 77, 900, January (1996) 28–39.

Douglas, Mary, 'Smothering the Differences—Mary Douglas in a savage mind about Lévi-Strauss', *Listener*, 3 September 1970, 313–14.

Douglas, Mary, 'Social Preconditions of Enthusiasm and Heterodoxy', in Robert F. Spencer (ed.), *Forms of Symbolic Action: Proceedings of the 1969 Annual Spring Meeting of the American Ethnological Society*, Seattle: University of Washington Press, 1969, 69–79.

Douglas, Mary, 'The Stranger in the Bible', *Archives européennes de sociologie*, 35, 2 (1994) 283–98.

Douglas, Mary, 'Taboo and Sin', in John Middleton (ed.), *Encyclopedia of Africa south of the Sahara*, New York: Charles Scribner's Sons, 1997, 205–208.

Douglas, Mary, *Thinking in Circles: An Essay on Ring Composition*, New Haven: Yale University Press, 2007.

Douglas, Mary, *Thought Styles: Critical Essays on Good Taste*, London: Sage, 1996.

Douglas, Mary, *A Very Personal Method: Anthropological Writings Drawn from Life*, London: Sage, 2013.

Douglas, Mary, 'Why I Have to Learn Hebrew: The Doctrine of Sanctification', in Thomas Ryba, George D. Bond, and Herman Tull (eds.), *The Comity and Grace of Method: Essays in Honor of Edmund F. Perry*, Evanston, Ill: Northwestern University Press, 2004, 147–65.

Downie, R. Angus, *Frazer and The Golden Bough*, London: Victor Gollancz, 1970.

Downie, R. Angus, *James George Frazer: The Portrait of a Scholar*, London: Watts & Co., 1940.

Draper, John William, *History of the Conflict between Religion and Science*, New York: D. Appleton, 1874.

Engelke, Matthew, 'An Interview with Edith Turner', *Current Anthropology*, 41, 5 December (2000) 843–52.

Engelke, Matthew, 'Books Can Be Deceiving: Edith Turner and the Problem of Categories in Anthropology', *Anthropology and Humanism*, 26 (2001) 124–33.

Engelke, Matthew, "The Endless Conversation": Fieldwork, Writing, and the Marriage of Victor and Edith Turner', in Richard Handler (ed.), *Significant Others: Interpersonal and Professional Commitments in Anthropology* (History of Anthropology 10), Madison: University of Wisconsin Press, 2004, 6–50.

Engelke, Matthew, 'The Problem of Belief: Evans-Pritchard and Victor Turner on "the inner life"', *Anthropology Today*, 18, 6 December (2002) 3–8.

Ernst, Cornelius, 'The Relevance of Primitive Religion', *New Blackfriars*, 38, 452, November (1957) 524–28.

Evans-Pritchard, E. E, 'Anthropology and the Social Sciences', in J. E. Dugdale (ed.), *The Social Sciences: Their Relations in Theory and in Teaching*, London: Le Play House Press, 1937, 62–73.

Evans-Pritchard, E. E., *The Divine Kingship of the Shilluk of the Nilotic Sudan*, Cambridge: Cambridge University Press, 1948.

Evans-Pritchard, E. E., 'Does Anthropology Undermine Faith?', *The Listener*, 8 May 1947, 714–15.

Evans-Pritchard, E. E., 'Fragment of an Autobiography', *New Blackfriars*, 54: 632, January (1973) 35–37.

Evans-Pritchard, E. E., 'Genesis of a Social Anthropologist: An Autobiographical Note', *New Diffusionist*, 3, 10 January (1973) 17–23.

Evans-Pritchard, E. E., *A History of Anthropology Thought*, André Singer (ed.), London: Faber & Faber, 1981.

Evans-Pritchard, E. E., 'The Intellectual (English) Interpretation of Magic', *Journal of the Anthropological Society of Oxford*, 1 (1970) 123–42, reprint, *Bulletin of the Faculty of Arts* (Cairo), 1, 2 (1933).

Evans-Pritchard, E. E., *Kinship and Marriage among the Nuer*, Oxford: Clarendon Press, 1951.

Evans-Pritchard, E. E., 'Just-So Stories' (review of Theodor Reik, *Myth and Guilt*), *The Tablet*, 8 March 1958, 229–30.

Evans-Pritchard, E. E., *The Nuer: A Description of the Modes of Livelihood and Political Institutions of a Nilotic People*, Oxford: Clarendon Press, 1940.

Evans-Pritchard, E. E., *Nuer Religion*, Oxford: Clarendon Press, 1956.

Evans-Pritchard, E. E., 'Obituaries: Jack Herbert Driberg: 1888–1946', *Man*, 47, January (1947) 11–13.

Evans-Pritchard, E. E., 'Operations on the Akobo and Gila Rivers 1940–1941', *Army Quarterly*, 103 (1973) 470–79.

Evans-Pritchard, E. E., 'The Perils of Translation', *New Blackfriars*, December (1969) 813–15.

Evans-Pritchard, E. E., *The Position of Women in Primitive Societies and other Essays in Social Anthropology*, London: Faber and Faber, 1965.

Evans-Pritchard, E. E., Raymond First, E. R. Leach, J. G. Peristiany, John Layard, Max Gluckman, Meyer Fortes, and Godfrey Lienhardt, *The Institutions of Primitive Society: A Series of Broadcast Talks*, Oxford: Basil Blackwell, 1954.

Evans-Pritchard, E. E., 'Recollections and Reflections', *New Diffusionist*, 2 (1971) 37–39.

Evans-Pritchard, E. E., Review of John S. Mbiti, *African Religions and Philosophy*, *Journal of Religion in Africa*, 2, 2 (1969) 214–16.

Evans-Pritchard, E. E., Review of Brian Hugh MacDermot, *Cult of the Sacred Spear: The Story of the Nuer Tribe in Ethiopia*, *Bible Lands*, 18, 8, Autumn (1972) 247–48.

Evans-Pritchard, E. E., *The Sanusi of Cyrenaica*, Oxford: Clarendon Press, 1949.

Evans-Pritchard, E. E., *Social Anthropology and Other Essays*, New York: The Free Press, 1962.

Evans-Pritchard, E. E., 'Social Anthropology at Oxford', *Journal of the Anthropological Society of Oxford*, 1, 3 (1970) 103–09.

Evans-Pritchard, E. E., 'Social Anthropology: Past and Present' (The Marett lecture, 1950), *Man*, 198, September (1950) 118–24.

Evans-Pritchard, E. E., 'Some Features of Nuer Religion (Presidential Address)', *Journal of the Royal Anthropological Institute of Great Britain and Ireland*, 81 (1951) 1–13.

Evans-Pritchard, E. E., 'Some Reflections on Mysticism', *Dyn*, 1 (1970) 101–15.

Evans-Pritchard, E. E., 'Some Reminiscences and Reflections on Fieldwork', *Journal of the Anthropological Society of Oxford*, 4, 1 (1973) 1–12.

Evans-Pritchard, E. E., *Theories of Primitive Religion*, Oxford: Clarendon Press, 1965.

Evans-Pritchard, E. E., *Witchcraft, Oracles and Magic among the Azande*, Oxford: Clarendon Press, 1937.

Evans-Pritchard, E. E., 'Zande Theology', *Sudan Notes and Records*, XIX (1936) 5–46.

Evans-Pritchard, E. E., *The Zande Trickster*, Oxford: Clarendon Press, 1967.

Evans-Pritchard, Ioma, *Bong and Wong*, Prairie City, Ill: Decker Press, 1950.

Evens, T. M. S, and Don Handelman (eds.), *The Manchester School: Practice and Ethnographic Praxis in Anthropology*, Oxford: Berghahn Books, 2008.

Fardon, Richard, 'Dame (Margaret) Mary Douglas [*née* Tew] (1921–2007)', *Oxford Dictionary of National Biography* [www.oxforddnb.com].

Fardon, Richard, 'Margaret Mary Douglas 1921–2007', *Proceedings of the British Academy*, 166 (2010) 135–58.

Fardon, Richard, *Mary Douglas: An Intellectual Biography*, London: Routledge, 1999.

Fardon, Richard, 'Obituary: Dame Mary Douglas', *Guardian*, 18 May 2007 [www.guardian.co.uk].

Fardon, Richard, ' "Religion and the Anthropologists" revisited: Reflections on Franz Baermann Steiner, E. E. Evans-Pritchard, and the "Oxford School" at their Century's End', in Jeremy Adler, Richard Fardon, and Carol Tully (eds.), *From Prague Poet to Oxford Anthropologist: Franz Baermann Steiner Celebrated*, München: Iudicium, 2003, 21–42.

Fardon, Richard, 'Turner, Victor Witter (1920–1983)', *Oxford Dictionary of National Biography* [www.oxforddnb.com], accessed 10 March 2009.

Filby, P. W., 'Life with the Frazers', *Cambridge Review*, 30 January 1984, 26–30.

Forde, Daryll (ed.), *African Worlds: Studies in the Cosmological Ideas and Social Values of African Peoples*, London: Oxford University Press for the International African Institute, 1970.

Fortes, M. and E. E. Evans-Pritchard (eds.), *African Political Systems*, Oxford: Oxford University Press, 1940.

Frankenberg, Ronald, 'Foreword', in Edith Turner, *Heart of Lightness: The Life Story of an Anthropologist*, Oxford: Berghahn, 2005, xi–xxvi.

Fraser, Robert (ed.), *Sir James Frazer and the Literary Imagination*, London: Macmillan, 1990.

Frazer, James George, *Balder the Beautiful: The Fire-Festivals of Europe and the Doctrine of the External Soul*, part VII of *The Golden Bough: A Study in Comparative Religion*, third edition, London: Macmillan and Co., 1951.

Frazer, James George, *Creation and Evolution in Primitive Cosmogonies, and other pieces*, London: Macmillan, 1935.

Frazer, James George, *The Devil's Advocate, a Plea for Superstition*, second edition, revised and expanded, London: Macmillan, 1927.

Frazer, James George, *The Dying God*, part III of *The Golden Bough: A Study in Comparative Religion*, third edition, London: Macmillan, 1951.

Frazer, James George, *Folk-Lore in the Old Testament: Studies in Comparative Religion, Legend and Law*, 3 vols., London: Macmillan, 1918.

Frazer, James George, *The Golden Bough: A Study in Comparative Religion*, 2 vols., London: Macmillan and Co., 1890.

Frazer, James George, *The Golden Bough: A Study in Comparative Religion*, 2nd ed., 3 vols., London: Macmillan and Co., 1900.

Frazer, James George, *Letters of William Cowper*, 2 vols., Freeport, NY: Books for Libraries Press, 1969.

Frazer, James George, *Man, God and Immortality: Thoughts on Human Progress*, New York: Macmillan, 1927.

Frazer, James George, *Passages of the Bible chosen for their literary beauty and interest*, London: Adam and Charles Black, 1895.

Frazer, James George, *Psyche's Task: A Discourse Concerning the Influence of Superstition on the Growth of Institutions*, London: Macmillan, 1909.

Frazer, James George, *The Scapegoat*, part IV of *The Golden Bough: A Study in Comparative Religion*, 3rd ed., London: Macmillan, 1951.

Frazer, James George, *Spirits of the Corn and of the Wild*, part V of *The Golden Bough: A Study in Comparative Religion*, third edition, London: Macmillan, 1951.

Frazer, James George, *Taboo and the Perils of the Soul*, part II of *The Golden Bough: A Study in Comparative Religion*, 3rd ed., London: Macmillan, 1951.

Frazer, James George, *Questions on the Customs, Beliefs, and Languages of Savages*, third impression, Cambridge: Cambridge University Press, 1916.

Geertz, Clifford, 'Making Experiences, Authoring Selves', in Victor W. Turner and Edward M. Bruner, *The Anthropology of Experience*, Urbana: University of Illinois Press, 1986, 373–80.

Geertz, Clifford, *Works and Lives: The Anthropologist as Author*, Stanford: Stanford University Press, 1988.

Gluckman, Max (ed.), *The Allocation of Responsibility*, Manchester: Manchester University Press, 1972.

Godwin-Austin, Henry Haversham, John Knox Laughton, Douglas W. Freshfield (eds.), *Hints to Travellers: Scientific and General*, London: Royal Geographical Society, 1883.

Goody, Jack, *The Expansive Movement: Anthropology in Britain and Africa, 1918–1970*, Cambridge: Cambridge University Press, 1995.

Gosse, Edmund, *Books on the Table*, New York: Charles Scribner's, 1921.

Gosse, Edmund, *Father and Son*, London: Penguin, 1983.

Grimshaw, Anna and Keith Hart, *Anthropology and the Crisis of the Intellectuals*, Cambridge: Prickly Pear Press, 1993.

Haddon, A. C. 'Sir E. B. Tylor, F.R.S.', *Nature*, 98, 2463, 11 January (1917) 373–74.

Hale, Sheila, 'Closely Observed Brains', *Harper's Bazaar and Queen*, January (1977) 70–73, 144.

Holdsworth, Chris, 'Sir Edward Burnett Tylor (1832–1917)', in *Oxford Dictionary of National Biography*, H. C. G. Matthew and Brian Harrison (eds.), Oxford: Oxford University Press, 2004, vol. 55, 773–75.

Horton, Robin and Ruth Finnegan (eds.), *Modes of Thought: Essays on Thinking in Western and Non-Western Societies*, London: Faber & Faber, 1973.

Howse, Christopher, 'The Pangolin and al'Qaeda', *Spectator*, 25 April 2007 [www.spectator.co.uk].

'The Hundred Most Influential Books Since the War', *Bulletin of the American Academy of Arts and Sciences*, 49, 8, May (1996) 12–13. Reprint, *Times Literary Supplement*, 6 October 1995.

Isenberg, Sheldon R. and Dennis E. Owen, 'Bodies, Natural and Contrived: The Work of Mary Douglas', *Religious Studies Review*, 3, 1, January (1977) 1–17.

Isichei, Elizabeth, *Victorian Quakers*, Oxford: Oxford University Press, 1970.

James, Wendy, ' "A Feeling for Form and Pattern, and a Touch of Genius": E-P's Vision and the Institute, 1946–1970', in Peter Rivière (ed.), *A History of Oxford Anthropology*, Oxford: Berghahn Books, 2007, 98–118.

Johnson, Douglas H., 'Evans-Pritchard, The Nuer, and the Sudan Political Service', *African Affairs*, 81, 323, April (1982) 231–46.

Kenny, Michael G., 'Trickster and Mystic: The Anthropological Persona of E. E. Evans-Pritchard', *Anthropology and Humanism Quarterly*, 12, 1 (1987) 9–15.

Kuklick, Henrika, 'The British Tradition' in Henrika Kuklick (ed.), *A New History of Anthropology*, Oxford: Blackwell, 2009, 52–78.

Kuklick, Henrika, *The Savage Within: The Social History of British Anthropology, 1885–1945*, Cambridge: Cambridge University Press, 1991.

Kuper, Adam, 'Alternative Histories of British Social Anthropology', *Social Anthropology*, 13, 1 (2005) 47–64.

Kuper, Adam, *Anthropologists and Anthropology: The British School 1922–1972*, New York: Pica Press, 1973.

Kuper, Adam, *Anthropology and Anthropologists: The Modern British School*, London: Routledge & Kegan Paul, 1983.

Kuper, Adam, *The Reinvention of Primitive Society: Transformations of a myth*, London: Routledge, 2005.

Lang, Andrew, *XXXII Ballades in Blue China*, London: Kegan Paul, Trench, & Co., 1888.

Lang, Andrew, *Magic and Religion*, London: Longmans, Green, and Co., 1901.

Lang, Andrew, *The Making of Religion*, London: Longmans, Green, 1898.

Langham, Ian, *The Building of British Social Anthropology: W. H. R. Rivers and his Cambridge disciples in the development of kinship studies, 1898–1931*, Dordrecht: D. Reidel, 1981.

Larsen, Timothy, *Contested Christianity: The Political and Social Contexts of Victorian Theology*, Waco: Baylor University Press, 2004.

Larsen, Timothy, *Crisis of Doubt: Honest Faith in Nineteenth-Century England*, Oxford: Oxford University Press, 2006.

Larsen, Timothy, *A People of One Book: The Bible and the Victorians*, Oxford: Oxford University Press, 2011.

'Late Sir Edward B. Tylor', *Wellington Weekly News*, 10 January 1907, 8.

Leach, Edmund R., 'Anthropology of Religion: British and French Schools', in Ninian Smart, John Clayton, Steven Katz, and Patrick Sherry (eds.), *Nineteenth-Century Religious Thought in the West*, Cambridge: Cambridge University Press, 1985, vol. III, 215–62.

Leach, Edmund R., 'Cairo Essays' (review of Mary Douglas, *Evans-Pritchard*), *London Review of Books*, 2, 23, 4 December 1980, 24–25.

Leach, Edmund R., 'Glimpses of the Unmentionable in the History of British Social Anthropology', *Annual Review of Anthropology*, 13 (1984) 1–23.

Leach, Edmund R., 'Mythical Inequalities', *New York Review of Books*, 28 January 1971 [www.nybooks.com].

Leopold, Joan, *Culture in Comparative and Evolutionary Perspective: E. B. Tylor and the Making of 'Primitive Culture'*, Berlin: Dietrich Reimer Verlag, 1980.

Lienhardt, Godfrey, *Divinity and Experience: The Religion of the Dinka*, Oxford: Clarendon Press, 1961.

Lienhardt, Godfrey, 'E-P: A Personal View', *Man*, new series, 9, 2 June (1974) 299–304.

Lienhardt, Godfrey, 'Sir Edward Evan Evans-Pritchard 1902–1973', in Robert Black and C. S. Nicholls (eds.), *The Dictionary of National Biography: 1971–1980*, Oxford: Oxford University Press, 1986, 297–98.

Lightman, Bernard, 'Interpreting Agnosticism as a Nonconformist Sect: T. H. Huxley's "New Reformation,"' in *Science and Dissent in England, 1688–1945*, Paul Wood (ed.), Aldershot: Ashgate, 2004, 197–214.

Logan, Peter Melville, *Victorian Fetishism: Intellectuals and Primitives*, Albany: State University of New York Press, 2009.

Lynch, John, 'England' in Adrian Hastings (ed.), *The Church and the Nations: A study of minority Catholicism in England, India, Norway, America, Lebanon, Australia, Wales, Japan, the Netherlands, Vietnam, Brazil, Egypt, Southern Africa and among the Lele of the Congo*, London: Sheed and Ward, 1959, 1–19.

Manning, Frank E, 'Victor Turner's Career and Publications', in Kathleen M. Ashley (ed.), *Victor Turner and the Construction of Cultural Criticism Between Literature and Anthropology*, Bloomington: Indiana University Press, 1990, 170–77.

Marett, R. R. and T. K. Penniman (eds.), *Spencer's Scientific Correspondence with Sir J. G. Frazer and Others*, Oxford: Clarendon Press, 1932.

Marett, R. R., *Tylor*, London: Chapman and Hall, 1936.

Martineau, Harriet (trans. and ed.), *The Positive Philosophy of Auguste Comte*, 3 vols., London: George Bell & Sons, 1896.

Martin, G. H., 'Thomas Hodgkin (1831–1913)', *Oxford Dictionary of National Biography*, vol. 27, 476–77.

Matthey, Piero, 'A Glimpse of Evans-Pritchard through his correspondence with Lowie and Kroeber', *Journal of the Anthropological Society of Oxford*, 27, 1 (1996) 21–45.

Maugham, Robin, *Nomad*, New York: Viking Press, 1948.

McLaren, Peter L., 'A Tribute to Victor Turner (1920–1983)', *Anthropologica*, n.s. 27 (1985) 17–22.

Mentore, George, 'Interview with Edith Turner', *AIBR (Journal of Iberoamerican Anthropology)*, 4, 3 (2009) i–xviii.

Miller, Elmer S., *Nurturing Doubt: From Mennonite Missionary to Anthropologist in the Argentine Chaco*, Urbana: University of Illinois Press, 1995.

Mills, David, *Difficult Folk? A Political History of Social Anthropology*, Oxford: Berghahn Books, 2008.

Moore, James R., *The Post Darwinian Controversies: A study of the Protestant struggle to come to terms with Darwin in Great Britain and America, 1800–1900*, Cambridge: Cambridge University Press, 1979.

Moore, Kenneth (ed.), *Waymarks: The Notre Dame Inaugural Lectures in Anthropology*, Notre Dame: University of Notre Dame Press, 1987.

Morinis, Alan (ed.), *Sacred Journeys: The Anthropology of Pilgrimage*, Westport, Conn: Greenwood Press, 1992.

Morton, Christopher, 'Double Alienation: Evans-Pritchard's Zande and Nuer Photographs in Comparative Perspective', in Richard Vokes (ed.), *Photography in Africa: Ethnographic Perspectives*, Woodbridge: James Currey, 2012, 33–55.

Morton, Christopher, 'Evans-Pritchard and Malinowski: the Roots of a Complex Relationship', *History of Anthropology Newsletter*, 34, 2 December (2007) 10–14.

Nichols, J. Randall, 'Worship as Anti-Structure: The Contribution of Victor Turner', *Theology Today*, 41, 4 January (1985) 401–09.

Nygren, Anders, *Agape and Eros*, Philip S. Watson (trans.), London: SPCK, 1953.

'Oxford Scientists: Professor E. E. Evans-Pritchard', *Zenith*, VII. 3 (1970) 20–21.

Pals, Daniel L., *Seven Theories of Religion*, New York: Oxford University Press, 1996.

Parkin, David, 'An Interview with Raymond Firth', *Current Anthropology*, 29, 2 April (1988) 327–41.

Pius XII, *Haurietis Aquas: On Devotion to the Sacred Heart*, 15 May 1956. [www.vatican.va]

Pocock, David F., 'Sir Edward Evans-Pritchard 1902–1973: An Appreciation', *Africa: Journal of the International African Institute*, 45, 3 (1975) 327–30.

Polanyi, Michael, *Personal Knowledge: Towards a Post-Critical Philosophy*, Chicago: University of Chicago Press, 1958.

Powell, Anthony, *Infants of the Spring*, London: Heinemann, 1976.

Regard, Frédéric, 'The Catholic Mule: E. B. Tylor's Chimeric Perception of Otherness', *Journal of Victorian Culture* 12, 2 (2007) 225–37.

Regard, Frédéric, 'Catholicism, Spiritual Progress, and Ethnology: E. B. Tylor's Secret War of Culture" *REAL* 20 (2004) 209–28.

Richard, Lucien OMI, 'Anthropology and Theology: The Emergence of Incarnational Faith According to Mary Douglas', *Église et Théologie*, 15 (1984) 131–54.

Richards, Paul, 'Obituary: Mary Tew Douglas 1921–2007', *American Anthropologist*, 110, 3 September (2008) 404–07.

Rivière, Peter (ed.), *A History of Oxford Anthropology*, Oxford: Berghahn Books, 2007.

St John, Graham (ed.), *Victor Turner and Contemporary Cultural Performance*, Oxford: Berghahn Books, 2008.

Sawyer, John F. A. (ed.), *Reading Leviticus: A Conversation with Mary Douglas, Journal for the Study of the Old Testament* Supplement Series 227, Sheffield: Sheffield Academic Press, 1996.

Sayers, Dorothy L., 'Introduction', in Dante, *The Divine Comedy: Hell*, London: Penguin, 1949 9–66.

Schechner, Richard, 'Victor Turner's Last Adventure' (Preface), in Victor Turner, *The Anthropology of Performance*, New York: PAJ Publications, 1987, 7–20.

Schechner, Richard and Willa Appel (eds.), *By Means of Performance: Intercultural studies of theatre and ritual*, Cambridge: Cambridge University Press, 1990.

Scott, David and Charles Hirschkind (eds.), *Powers of the Secular Modern: Talal Asad and His Interlocutors*, Stanford: Stanford University Press, 2006.

Singer, André and Brian V. Street (eds.), *Zande Themes: Essays presented to Sir Edward Evans-Pritchard*, Oxford: Basil Blackwell, 1972.

Singer, André, *Strange Beliefs: Sir Edward Evans-Pritchard* (Princeton: Films for the Humanities & Sciences, Inc, 1990) [film/video recording].

Singleton, Michael, 'Theology, "Zande Theology" and Secular Theology', in Singer, André and Brian V. Street (eds.), *Zande Themes: Essays presented to Sir Edward Evans-Pritchard*, Oxford: Basil Blackwell, 1972, 130–57.

Srinivas, M. N., 'Why I am a Hindu', *Illustrated Weekly of India*, 17 November 1974, 9–10.

Stenski, Ivan, 'The Spiritual Dimension', in Henrika Kuklick (ed.), *A New History of Anthropology*, Oxford: Blackwell, 2009, 113–27.

Stocking, George W. Jr., *After Tylor: British Social Anthropology, 1888–1951*, Madison: University of Wisconsin Press, 1995.

Stocking, George W. Jr., 'Animism in Theory and Practice: E. B. Tylor's Unpublished "Notes on *Spiritualism*", *Man*, new series, 6, 1 March (1971) 88–104.

Stocking, George W. Jr., 'Charting the Progress of Animism: E. B. Tylor on "The Common Religion of Mankind,"' *History of Anthropology Newsletter* 19 (1992) 3–10.

Stocking, George W. Jr., 'Edward Burnett Tylor and the Mission of Primitive Man', in *The Collected Works of Edward Burnett Tylor*, 8 vols., George W. Stocking, Jr. (ed.), London: Routledge, 1994, i–xxvi.

Stocking, George W. Jr., *Functionalism Historicized: Essays on British Social Anthropology*, Madison: University of Wisconsin Press, 1984.

Stocking, George W. Jr., *Victorian Anthropology*, New York: Free Press, 1987.

Tambiah, Stanley J., *Edmund Leach: An Anthropological Life*, Cambridge: Cambridge University Press, 2002.

Taylor, Charles, *A Secular Age*, Cambridge, Mass: Harvard University Press, 2007.

Tew, Mary [later Douglas], *Peoples of the Lake Nyasa Region, East Central Africa*, Part 1: Ethnographic Survey of Africa, London: Oxford University Press for the International African Institute, 1950.

Thomas, Northcote W. (ed.), *Anthropological Essays presented to Edward Burnett Tylor in honour of his 75th birthday Oct. 2 1907*, Oxford: Clarendon Press, 1907.

Turner, Edith, 'Advances in the Study of Spirit Experience: Drawing Together Many Threads', *Anthropology of Consciousness*, 17, 2 (2006), 33–61.

Turner, Edith, *Among the Healers: Stories of Spiritual and Ritual Healing from around the World*, Westport, Conn: Praeger, 2006.

Turner, Edith, 'The Anthropology of Experience: The Way to Teach Religion and Healing', in Linda L. Barnes and Inés Talamantez (eds.), *Teaching Religion and Healing*, New York: Oxford University Press, 2006, 193–205.

Turner, Edith, *Communitas: The Anthropology of Collective Joy*, Contemporary Anthropology of Religion series, New York: Palgrave Macmillan, 2012.

Turner, Edith, 'Drumming, Divination, and Healing: The Community at Work', in Michael Winkelman and Philip M. Peek (eds.), *Divination and Healing: Potent Vision*, Tucson: University of Arizona Press, 2004, 55–79.

Turner, Edith, *The Hands Feel It: Healing and Spirit Presence among a Northern Alaskan People*, DeKalb: Northern Illinois University Press, 1996.

Turner, Edith, *Heart of Lightness: The Life Story of an Anthropologist*, Oxford: Berghahn, 2005.

Turner, Edith, 'Our Lady of Knock: Reflections of a Believing Anthropology', *New Hibernia Review*, 15, 2, Summer (2011) 121–25.

Turner, Edith, 'Philip Kabwita, Ghost Doctor: The Ndembu in 1985', *TDR: The Drama Review*, 30, 4, Winter (1986) 12–33.

Turner, Edith, 'Prologue: From the Ndembu to Broadway', in Victor Turner, *On the Edge of the Bush: Anthropology as Experience*, edited by Edith L. B. Turner, Tucson: University of Arizona Press, 1985, 1–15.

Turner, Edith, 'Psychology, Metaphor, or Actuality? A Probe into Iñupiaq Eskimo Healing', *Anthropology of Consciousness*, 3 (1992) 1–8.

Turner, Edith, 'The Reality of Spirits: A Tabooed or Permitted Field of Study?', *Anthropology of Consciousness*, 4, 1 March (1993) 9–12.

Turner, Edith, 'The Soul and Communication between Souls', in Helmut Wautischer (ed.), *Ontology of Consciousness: Percipient Action*, Cambridge, Mass: MIT Press, 2008, 79–96.

Turner, Edith, *The Spirit and the Drum: A Memoir of Africa*, Tucson: University of Arizona Press, 1987.

Turner, Edith, 'Taking Seriously the Nature of Religious Healing in America', in Linda L. Barnes and Susan S. Sered (eds.), *Religion and Healing in America*, New York: Oxford University Press, 2005, 387–404.

Turner, Edith, 'Theology and the Anthropological Study of Spirit Events in an Iñupiat Village', in Walter Randolph Adams and Frank A. Salamone (eds.), *Anthropology and Theology: Gods, Icons, and God-talk*, Lanham: University Press of America, 2000, 137–61.

Turner, Edith, 'There Are No Peripheries to Humanity: Northern Alaska Nuclear Dumping and the Iñupiat's Search for Redress', *Anthropology and Humanism*, 22, 1 (1997) 95–109.

Turner, Edith, and Frederick Turner, 'Victor Turner as We Remember Him', *Anthropologica*, n.s., 27 (1985) 11–16.

Turner, Edith and Victor Turner, 'Money Economy among the Mwinilunga Ndembu: A study of some individual cash budgets', *Rhodes-Livingstone Journal*, xviii (1955) 19–37.

Turner, Edith, William Blodgett, Singleton Kahona, and Fideli Benwa, *Experiencing Ritual: A New Interpretation of African Healing*, Philadelphia: University of Pennsylvania Press, 1992.

Turner, James, *Without God, Without Creed: The Origins of Unbelief in America*, Baltimore: John Hopkins University Press, 1985.

Turner, Rory P. B. 'A Sense of Presence', *Anthropology and Humanism*, 26, 2 (2002) 188–89.

Turner, Victor, *The Anthropology of Performance*, New York: PAJ Publications, 1987.

Turner, Victor, *Blazing the Trail: Way Marks in the Exploration of Symbols*, Edith Turner (ed.), Tucson: University of Arizona Press, 1992.

Turner, Victor, *Chihamba, The White Spirit: A Ritual Drama of the Ndembu*, Rhodes-Livingstone Papers 33, Manchester: Manchester University Press, 1962.

Turner, Victor, *Dramas, Fields, and Metaphors: Symbolic Action in Human Society*, Ithaca: Cornell University Press, 1974.

Turner, Victor, *The Drums of Affliction: A Study of Religious Processes among the Ndembu of Zambia*, Oxford: Clarendon Press, 1968.

Turner, Victor, *The Forest of Symbols: Aspects of Ndembu Ritual*, Ithaca: Cornell University Press, 1967.

Turner, Victor, *From Ritual to Theatre: The Human Seriousness of Play*, New York: PAJ Publications, 1982.

Turner, Victor, 'Passages, Margins and Poverty: Religious Symbols of Communitas', *Worship*, 46, 7 (1972) 390–412.

Turner, Victor, 'Religion in Current Cultural Anthropology', in Mircea Eliade and David Tracy (eds.), *What Is Religion? An Inquiry for Christian Theology, Concilium* 136, New York: Seabury Press, 1980, 68-71.

Turner, Victor, *Revelation and Divination in Ndembu Ritual*, Ithaca: Cornell University Press, 1975.

Turner, Victor, *The Ritual Process: Structure and Anti-Structure*, Chicago: Aldine Publishing Company, 1969.

Turner, Victor, 'Ritual, Tribal and Catholic', *Worship*, 50, 6 (1976) 504–26.

Turner, Victor, *Schism and Continuity in an African Society: A Study of Ndembu Village Life*, Manchester: Manchester University Press for the Rhodes-Livingstone Institute, 1957.

Turner, Victor and Edith Turner, *Image and Pilgrimage in Christian Culture*, New York: Columbia University Press, 1978.

Tylor, Edward B., *Anahuac, Or Mexico and the Mexicans, Ancient and Modern*, Boston: Indy Publish, 2007 [originally 1861].

Tylor, Edward B., *Anthropology: An Introduction to the Study of Man and Civilization*, London: Macmillan and Co., 1881.

Tylor, Edward B., 'How the Problems of American Anthropology Present Themselves to the English Mind', *Science* IV, 98, 19 December (1884) 545–51.

Tylor, Edward B., *Primitive Culture: Researches into the development of mythology, philosophy, religion, language, art and custom*, 2 vols., New York: Henry Holt and Company, 1874.

Tylor, Edward B., *Researches into the Early History of Mankind and the Development of Civilization*, 3rd ed., London: John Murray, 1878.

Urry, James, *Before Social Anthropology: Essays on the history of British anthropology*, London: Routledge, 1993.

Vandervort, Eleanor, *A Leopard Tamed: The Story of an African Pastor, his People, and his Problems*, New York: Harper & Row, 1968.

Vickery, John B., *The Literary Impact of The Golden Bough*, Princeton: Princeton University Press, 1973.

Wallace, Alfred R., 'Physical Science and Philosophy', *Academy*, 3, 15 February (1872) 69–71.

Wachtel, Eleanor (ed.), *Original Minds*, Toronto: HarperCollins Canada, 2003.

Waugh, Evelyn, *Brideshead Revisited: The Sacred and Profane Memories of Captain Charles Ryder*, Boston: Little, Brown and Company, 1945.

Weld, A., 'Our Ancestors', *The Month*, XVII (1872) 78–106.

Werbner, Richard P, 'The Manchester School in South-Central Africa', *Annual Review of Anthropology*, 13 (1984) 157–85.

Wheeler-Barclay, Marjorie, *The Science of Religion in Britain, 1860–1915*, Charlottesville: University of Virginia Press, 2010.

White, Andrew Dickson, *A History of the Warfare of Science and Theology in Christendom*, New York: D. Appleton, 1896.

White, Antonia, *Frost in May*, London: Eyre & Spottiswoode, 1948.

Wildavsky, Aaron, *The Nursing Father: Moses as a Political Leader*, Tuscaloosa: University of Alabama Press, 1984.

Young, W. John, *The Quiet Wise Spirit: Edwin W. Smith (1876–1957) and Africa*, Peterborough: Epworth Press, 2002.

About the Author

Timothy Larsen is McManis Professor of Christian Thought, Wheaton College, Wheaton, Illinois. He is a Fellow of both the Royal Historical Society and the Royal Anthropological Institute. He has been a Visiting Fellow, Trinity College, Cambridge, and some of the research for this volume was undertaken while a Visiting Fellow, All Souls College, Oxford. His previous monographs published by Oxford University Press are *Crisis of Doubt: Honest Faith in Nineteenth-Century England* and *A People of One Book: The Bible and the Victorians.*

Index

Printed and bound by CPI Group (UK) Ltd, Croydon, CR0 4YY